Laughter and Tears

Laughter and Tears

A Family's Journey
to Understanding the Autism Spectrum

Ann Hewetson

Jessica Kingsley Publishers
London and Philadelphia

First published in the United Kingdom in 2005
by Jessica Kingsley Publishers
116 Pentonville Road
London N1 9JB, UK
and
400 Market Street, Suite 400
Philadelphia, PA 19106, USA

www.jkp.com

Copyright © Ann Hewetson 2005

Library of Congress Cataloging in Publication Data

Hewetson, Ann.
Laughter and tears : a family's journey to understanding the autism spectrum / Ann Hewetson.
p. cm.
Includes bibliographical references and index.
ISBN-13: 978-1-84310-331-8
ISBN-10: 1-84310-331-1
1. Hewetson, Mark. 2. Hewetson, Ann. 3. Autistic children—Biography. 4. Parents of autistic children—Biography.
5. Autistic children—Family relationships. 6. Mothers and sons. 7. Autism. I. Title.
RJ506.A9H494 2005
618.92'85882'0092—dc22

2004030442

British Library Cataloguing in Publication Data

A CIP catalogue record for this book is available from the British Library

ISBN-13: 978 1 84310 331 8
ISBN-10: 1 84310 331 1

Printed and Bound in Great Britain by
Athenaeum Press, Gateshed, Tyne and Wear

*To Mark, who brought us much laughter and a few
tears and taught us that love is unconditional,
and to Barry, who has enriched all our lives beyond measure*

Disclaimer

All the information provided in this book is for information purposes only, and the author and publisher cannot be held liable for any errors or omissions or actions undertaken as a result of using it. Reference to any intervention, treatment or therapy does not constitute an endorsement of that intervention, treatment or therapy by the author or publisher, and they assume no responsibility for the use made of any information published in this book. At all times it is the individual's care giver, medical adviser or other qualified professional who should decide on intervention options or therapies.

Contents

CHAPTER 1

Blowing in the Wind

I'm woken up again. As I struggle through the mists of sleep, rising, slipping back, clawing my way upwards to the noise – to the now familiar rhythm of the metal wheels of the cot grinding on the bare linoleum of the floor, I focus instantly. Slipping noiselessly out of bed, I move silently down the corridor to peer in at the door. Little Mark, just ten months old, up on all fours with palms and knees firmly pushed down on the cot blanket, rocks rhythmically back and forth, moving to some internal clock, responding involuntarily to the commands of some innate brain waves. I watch, holding my breath, as he works out this cycle and flops motionless on his tummy – silent again.

This is the second time tonight that I have come to keep this silent vigil. Will he rock again before dawn? I stand a moment longer – watching – waiting. No sound – he sleeps peacefully. It is eerie – this silent rocking, eyes closed. Afraid to approach lest I awaken or frighten him, I slip away. Fear gnaws at me.

Cold, I make my way back to bed. No, I tell myself firmly there is nothing wrong. Babies can have different sleeping patterns – that's all. Things always seem worse in the night.

A month later I am back again in the same spot still keeping my strange nightly vigil. Stronger now, and more in command of his muscles, Mark rocks more vigorously but still in the same pattern – moved it would seem by an invisible hand. Could there really be something wrong? I try to push the fear away but it is back – gnawing again.

Why does he rock? What causes that unconscious disturbance of movement even in the midst of sleep? How long will it continue? Questions float around in my mind but the answers are light years away – hidden in the future.

Twelve months old in a busy shopping mall in the centre of the city Mark, held securely in his father's arms, reacts strangely to his surroundings. He goes bar tight, all muscles clenched rigid, stretched taut from head to toe, unbending, as if he would snap. Yet all the while, tremors of tension ripple and tremble through his skin although he does not utter a sound. This Saturday afternoon, all around us relaxed babies smile, or cuddle – moulded perfectly to their fathers' arms – or sleep soundly – bending to the cocoon of a buggy's warmth. Their surroundings are the same as those that appear so intolerable to Mark. Only he remains rigid, unable to yield even to the arms that hold him so securely.

Above his head our eyes meet in unspoken agreement. Yes – we will take him home. Perhaps in his own familiar surroundings he will recover.

Why did he react so strangely? Could it be the sight of so many people? *Or perhaps his senses became overloaded.* We console ourselves by remembering that he had never been a cuddly baby. When picked up he never adjusts himself to the arms that surround him. But the fear which had never been put into words is back again – gnawing.

The screams begin.

Dropping the phone I run to the cot where a few moments earlier I had left him, chortling happily, sitting surrounded by soft, fluffy toys which he enjoys throwing over the bars and having them brought back. The sound is frightening. Picking him up I check everything and find nothing. But the screams continue. Pausing only to get more breath Mark screams again and again. The sound reverberates around the room. We walk around the house, out into the garden – anywhere, looking for distraction everywhere, in all our usual haunts – with the sparrows splashing and frolicking at the fountain – with Oscar, the grey striped tabby cat licking his paws and stretching blissfully in the heat – with the sunlight dappling through the movement of the leaves as the tall poplar trees sigh in the breeze. Mark loves sunbeams, always putting out his small hands to catch them. But today he is blind to everything.

His screams frighten away the tabby cat and the birds. Curious, they retreat to a safe distance to watch and perhaps to listen – the row of sparrows, heads cocked, looking down from the phone lines – the cat inaccessible under the hedge. We are left alone with the poplars. Even the sun has gone in – a frightening omen. I shiver.

Watching Mark I see there are no tears. Detachedly I come to the realization that I have never seen him shed tears, never seen his lower lip tremble when he was frightened or upset. No teardrops had ever caused those bright blue eyes to cloud or swim; no drops of saline had ever splashed down that beautiful, perfect face.

We go indoors to sit at the piano stool in the hope that music, which had always delighted Mark, will work its magic again. In time the screaming lessens and eventually, tempted by food, he stops as suddenly as he began. The silence lies around us – a crescendo of silence surreal and more deafening in its impact than the screaming.

The following day the screams begin again; screams that over the next two years will periodically arise – beginning suddenly for no apparent reason, to continue for hours and stop as dramatically as they began.

A battery of medical tests reveals nothing. Mark is passed as a perfectly healthy baby. It is suggested that as first-time parents we are over-anxious and too detached. Were we more relaxed and more interactive we would manage him better. Our present attitude is not considered helpful to his development.

It is time for the last of his immunization visits.

This morning the clinic is busy. I sit in the waiting room chatting happily to the group of mothers – all of us comparing notes and exchanging anecdotes. Eager to use the opportunity to learn from more experienced minds, I listen mainly, as the line moves along, my eyes roving around the floor where babies and toddlers of all ages mingle. It is a sea of moving activity, of little people making their way in the world of their peers. Some snatch, acquisitive, acquiring. Others, suddenly deprived of possession, wail to assert their rights. Some, bashful, make forays into the moving scene but, discouraged by a sudden push, retreat quickly to the safety of a mother's knee. Watching carefully for a while one ventures out again, this time to triumph, as he grabs a coveted toy and retreats once more to safety.

A small, solitary figure sits in the centre of the floor in proud possession of the clinic's most spectacular toy – determined to enjoy it alone. With grunts and gestures he wards off the opposition. Occasionally he turns towards his mother, *pointing* and gurgling – *sharing*. She smiles back, encouraging.

Subconsciously, I register – "I have never seen Mark *point* to anything or anybody, I have never seen him *share*."

Why had I not noticed this before?

Why? – Because I had no wish to notice. If I did I would have to face the fear that gnawed daily at me. Now those elusive words which have hovered on the fringes of my consciousness for so long without recognition cannot be avoided. In this present scene they crystallize sharply into one word – *aloneness*.

I look at Mark. He sits close by on the floor in the exact spot where I placed him some thirty minutes ago. He rocks quietly back and forth, oblivious to his surroundings and even, it appears, to my presence. I had tried so often to pin down what made him so different from other babies – that one key factor that overlay all other considerations. Today I have the answer if not the cause. It is this *profound aura of aloneness* that he exudes.

As I watch, a golden-haired, doll-like figure, all in pink, her flaxen hair topped with a silver bow, stumbles over Mark. She clutches at him to steady herself. Peering into his face she smiles. He continues to rock, seemingly unaware of her presence or of that dazzling smile. Puzzled she pats his face to see if he is real. Getting no reaction she crawls away leaving him, in the midst of a crowd and yet so awesomely alone.

My thinking is questioning.

"He is not blind, it cannot be that. We know he can see. He loves to catch the sunbeams. He laughs at the cat's face. He crawls across the grass to follow the brilliant red carnation when I trail it before him. When I stop I see his delight as he catches it, staring in wonder at the petals."

The scenes flit past me like slides in a projector – Mark lost in absorption sitting on the beach sifting the grains of sand watching intently as they flow to earth.

"No! This child is not blind, but why does he act as if he were?"

My name is called. The doctor will see me now. Lifting Mark up I make my way to the door. In the clinic I ask for a referral to the eye specialist. I will face my fear because I am learning that it is preferable to face fear rather than to live with the immobilizing helplessness of gnawing anxiety.

Another day, another clinic, another waiting room, but this time Mark does not rock on the floor. His screams penetrate the solid wall of the hundred-year-old building. We are allowed to jump the queue and ushered into the doctor's office. But it is not possible to test Mark today. The delicate, minute, procedures involved in an eye examination are beyond the scope of the existing conditions even though the specialist rises impressively to the task. The appointment is rescheduled for a time when he is likely to be more receptive; they will fit us in at short notice. Fraught, we prepare to leave but not without a result as the doctor, having watched Mark carefully while listening to our case history, observes that he is fairly sure that our son's visual acuity lies within the normal range. Walking with us to the door he remarks,

"I have six myself – it gets easier; the first is always the hardest."

Shaking hands we feel reassured.

We fall prey to ritual and routine. Becoming obsessed with maintaining sameness, Mark, now able to assert himself, begins to resist all change. On the morning stroll to the village shops we routinely turn left at the garden gate. This day I turn right to drop a letter in the post box. Instantly Mark struggles, stiffening and arching his back, trying to break out of the straps of the buggy. He kicks – the screams blowing into a full-scale tantrum. I abandon the post and turn left, intent on making a quick visit to the nearest shop for emergency supplies. With the change in direction the scream stops in mid-air and he subsides comfortably back into the buggy, at ease again. We continue at our usual leisurely pace.

Could he have been disturbed by the unfamiliar route? And yet he gives the impression of being oblivious to his surroundings, eyes unfocused and fixed on infinity. He does not look at his environment or at the people in it; yet could it be that he scans it, recording the minutest details, filing them away for future reference? Can you have vision without obvious viewing? Can you see the ambience of your surroundings while gazing at the far horizon?

The following day I turn right again, the unposted letter in my hand. The screams begin. Instantly I change direction, turning left. The screaming stops. Familiarity must bring security to his troubled world. Never again will I turn right at the garden gate. In time he will be able to walk to the gate and then he may choose his own route. Meanwhile we succumb to the tyranny of sameness and the stultifying monotony of ritual and routine.

At seventeen months he hauls himself up by the wooden arms of my chair and takes his first lone steps. Unaided, steady and in control, he walks the length of the room. Although an active toddler, his preferred mode of transport had been that of crawling or sliding. With this long-awaited milestone now reached it seems a time to take stock. Taking pen and paper we divide the sheet into assets and deficits.

On the credit side we write:

- excellent physical health, strong sturdy build

- loves food, no fads – in fact will eat anything

- has great stamina, can keep going for hours, never seeming to tire

- walked alone today for the first time

- bright-eyed, beautiful baby – strangers captivated, stop in the street to admire him

- professional medical assessments reveal nothing.

On the debit side we write:

- this striking aloneness, he does not interact – not even with us

- he does not point or share

- this bizarre night rocking

- persistent daily screaming

- massive over-reaction to new situations and places

- obsessed with sameness

- had some words but lost them – since then no attempt to communicate.

We stop there. Where would we begin? Where could we begin? How do you interact with someone who shows no wish to interact with you?

Looking down that list the key factor crystallizes. *It is the lack of ability to communicate at any level.* Mark never, in the seventeen months of his life, had made eye contact or even face contact with us. We have had no recognition from him – no signal that he is aware of us as human creatures other than as a pair of hands to feed, clothe, bathe, change and carry him. We have to do something – anything – everything, to break into that cocoon of isolating aloneness that our son has surrounded himself with.

But how to crack open that formidable shell and get to the embryo within?

What can we use as our nutcracker?

Does Mark react in any significant way to his surroundings? Does he give any indication that he is aware of what goes on around him? Pausing to think we find our answer blowing in the wind through the open window.

It is the sound of a barking dog from the kennels a mile away.

Mark can imitate to perfection the particular bark of every dog in that kennel and he seems to enjoy doing so. He responds well to playing the game of "What does the donkey say? What does the horsie say?" His favourite is "What does the doggie say?" when he will utter such a cacophony of dog sounds that we are left in no doubt as to his ability to understand the question. The channel of sound appears to be his strongest conduit into the outside world. Therefore, we will smelt our hammer and chisel in the furnace of sound. Surrounding him with speech sounds, we will endeavour to make him aware of us as people and not just disembodied voices coming to him from out of the ether.

The next step would be to regain his own words – his own lost vocabulary. At around eleven months Mark had about a dozen words which he had used appropriately – words such as "mama", "dada", "baba", "brew" (the cat), "bye-bye", "edes" (the cat's eyes), "arb" (arm), "wuff" (the neighbour's dog), and four or five others. A few months later the words had disappeared as if in regression.

Having set ourselves the challenge we face it with confidence, but if our system is to work Mark also will have to accept the challenge and a challenge requires motivation. He is oblivious to praise and approval and shies away from cuddles and kisses. He is now beginning to resist all contact, struggling actively when picked up or held. Is there anything he wants badly enough to be prepared to work for? Anything that would entice him to rupture the membranes of that embryonic amnion of his aloneness?

We pause while memory automatically flips through the slides indelibly imprinted in the mind. It rejects – pauses at a frame, whirrs forward, finally stopping to select one. The frame has just one word on it – *food*.

Mark's reaction to food is one of ecstasy and the greatest delight of his young life is being taken out for a meal. Then he can be guaranteed to behave perfectly. Within the ambience of a restaurant and close to the ceremony of food he inevitably rises superbly to the occasion, often drawing envious glances from other parents struggling to cope with difficult behaviours.

To celebrate his first birthday some months ago, our extended family lunched together. Mark, dressed in a blue silk suit and white woollen booties, sat aloft in a high chair enjoying a commanding view of the restaurant and the busy waiters to-ing and fro-ing between the tables. Absorbed in the scene, his excitement was palpable and infectious – chubby, bronzed arms and legs twitching, wrists flicking from side to side, silver-blond hair bobbing, he reacted ecstatically to the odours of the passing food and when his meal was placed before him he ate with gusto and relish.

On reaching the coffee stage, an older gentleman, dining nearby with his wife, approached our table and, handing me his card, introduced himself to our circle. He was the headmaster of a boys' junior school from another country and wished to be introduced to Mark who had apparently contributed greatly to their enjoyment of the meal. He complimented us on him saying, "Mark is such a beautiful little boy. He would be a wonderful advertisement for baby food. You should look into it. He is an absolute natural for the camera – the perfect, photographic child. If you are interested I can give you an introduction to a suitable agency who would be delighted to give him a test."

So we will use food as our enticer. Involving as it does the senses of sight, taste and smell it will extend his use of his senses and give him other ways of interacting with his world. It will be a challenge of trial and error. As to the practicality of it – how will we do it? Can we think of anything else in the world that interests him apart from sound and food? We remember his preoccupation with the minutiae of his environment (always it is the minuscule not the global that attracts him) with flowers, with sunlight and shade. Excitement stirring we realize we might have an answer – we will attract him with *size, shape and colour*.

It seems almost too easy. We will use letters – multicoloured letters in different sizes and shapes – and we will use them to label food. With a sense almost of anticipation we plan. We will offer small amounts of his favourite foods accompanied by named coloured cards and each time we will say the name of the food again and again. As he eats we will let him handle the card.

It will be a tenuous beginning but, satisfied now to have a plan and a set goal, we put away our sheet of assets and deficits. We have worked long into the night. With the dawn I draw back the curtains, aware that some time during that night I passed through fear to acceptance of the challenge that lies ahead. With that passing has come a curious relief and a kind of courage.

Watching the pale yellow streaks spread across the lightening darkness of the early morning sky I see the shadows livening and the leaves of the poplar trees tremble before the birth of day. It is borne in on me how fragile is the beginning of every dawn.

CHAPTER 2

A Conflict in Space

Today Mark is two years old – a day of celebration. His cousins gather around to help him blow out the two blue candles on the white icing of the cake. We clap hands. He joins in the clapping – his first attempt at communication. It is a small but significant gesture to prove he is with us. Throughout the last six months he has continued to plough his solitary furrow and we have not been able to find the chink in his armour. Loving the food game he eats with delight all the proffered 'goodies' but has not attempted any new words, nor has he regained his original lost ones. We do not seem to be getting through to him and appear to be as invisible to him as ever. At times we feel him slipping away from us more and more.

There are now written words everywhere in the house. Every object has its coloured card – table – chair – fridge – door. Mark, while he ignores the object, is drawn almost with a magnetic force to the coloured labels. He traces the letters, patting them with his fingers, investing each with a life force of its own. Almost automatically we repeat the words and even the letters. It has become a habit, a part of the daily routine. In the early morning he sits in his cot, surrounded by wooden alphabet bricks – each letter a different colour, its shape engraved in the wood. Delicately, he fingers the shape of each letter before throwing the brick over the bars and awaiting its return.

Stronger and more adventurous, he becomes an active climber, scaling the bars of the cot. In the interest of safety the bars are raised higher because we notice he does not appear to have an appreciation of different levels of depth. He will scramble up on a chair and then try to walk out onto the air, not seeming to see the drop beneath him. If left out of sight for even a second he will head straight for the stairs and climb. Fortunately, my reflexes are quick. Watching him, it is obvious to me that he has no idea that he is higher than the floor level. The first time I caught him he was three steps up and ready to walk out onto the air. Thereafter we barred off the stairs – temporarily shutting down the upper part of the house.

It is troubling, this fissure in his ability to perceive depth.

"How can you give a child who is without an innate concept of depth an appreciation of the phenomenon of depth?"

Perhaps by giving him concrete experience of depth itself.

We introduce water play into his schedule. Four-year-old Darren and his twin brothers always come to spend Friday with us. The twins are six months older than Mark. Perhaps when he sees his peers enjoying the fun of water play he will be tempted to join in and imitate. An inflatable swimming pool is set up in the garden and the three small visitors splash happily in the warm August sunshine. Mark, remaining aloof, sits in the nearby sand-pit, sifting the grains of sand.

The children call –

"Come, Mark come, it's warm", but Mark, seeming to be unaware of what goes on around him, does not succumb to peer pressure and we learn once again that he does *not* learn by imitation. Content inside his aura he sees no necessity to conform and we have no bonus or incentive with which to tempt him. We will wait for another day.

A few weeks later, propped up on a chair in front of me, he stands at the kitchen sink enveloped in a plastic apron. The sink, half-filled with water, contains plastic jugs and cups. I pick up a jug and pour water into a cup, then into another, spilling it out again. He watches. I keep up the routine, all the time singing to keep him focused on me – holding his attention. It works – he does not struggle to get down. I move a little to one side. In one dashing attempt he is over the rim of the sink and sitting in the water. Astounded, I laugh. He looks towards my face – not *at* it, but towards the direction from which the sound comes. He laughs back. I resist the impulse to hug him – it would break the magic of that fragile bond developing between us. Instead, passing my hand over his silver blond head, I give it the merest touch. He does not resist.

Now I have a means of communication – the voice of laughter. I will remember to laugh more often.

The following day he pushes the same chair towards the sink and catching my hand pulls me towards it. Singing, I produce the plastic apron, half-filling the sink. He scrambles up on to the chair over the rim and into the water. Sitting down he catches my hand again and wielding it like an automatic grab, uses it to pick up the jugs and cups – placing them in the water. Continuing to sing, I begin the pouring routine.

As I write my journal tonight I give thanks for the miracle of communication at two levels – a moment of shared laughter and the communication of contact – that soft hand pulling mine with such purpose. I think back over the last ten months of painstaking work and write "How could I ever have doubted?" We celebrate.

Taking stock we feel it is time to alter our programme in view of the recent changes in his development. He has become hyperactive, is always on the move as if in the grip of propulsion, and consequently is a danger to himself.

We see further conflict to trouble us. This time the conflict is in linear space. Although he is steady on his feet he does not appear to understand the spatial elements of his world, seeming to have little concept of the limits of it. Could it be that his internal space parameters, the yardsticks by which he measures the space around him, are out of alignment with reality? We see examples of this.

He tries to walk off the end of the twelve-inch high wall on the patio.

On our first visit to the park we approach the small pond in the centre. The other children move to the side to skirt around it. Mark walks into it.

I take Darren and the twins to the beach. Taking my eye off Mark for a minute to get out the swimsuits, I turn back to find him stranded, up to his armpits in the sea, fully clothed complete with shoes. He has walked into the sea as if he could not fathom where the land ended and the sea began. A few feet away from him the twins, waiting patiently for their swimsuits, laugh happily at him. Darren scolds him – "Come out Mark. That's bold."

On a day trip to a local holiday camp I drive two friends and their three children the forty miles to get there. In the course of the afternoon I dash into the shop to buy some chocolate for the homeward journey, leaving Mark in the care of my friends with strict instructions – "Don't take your eyes off him."

Three minutes later I am back out.

Mark is missing.

One of us stands guard over the remaining children. The other two run in circles looking for Mark. We find him, three buildings away at the edge of the swimming pool, ready to step in at the deep end with one foot in mid-air. Just as he lifts the other foot the watchful young lifeguard swoops down on him, dragging him back from the edge.

It becomes obvious that Mark has no awareness of distance, depth or danger.

Thinking objectively about Mark's relationship with his environment one cannot but get the impression that somehow he has been born into a world the concrete concepts of which do not make much sense to him. Perhaps what he needs is a different medium in which to operate. What medium other than that of air is there available to us? Only one – the medium of water.

We join the local swimming-pool club. Perhaps here Mark will be able to work through his faulty concepts of distance and depth and begin to align them with the parameters of reality. Complete with arm wings and an inflatable ring Mark takes to the water like the proverbial duck, but without the instinctive caution of a true aquatic. He loves it but has no inbuilt appreciation of its dangers or even its parameters – deep end, shallow end, pool side or water – all appear indistinguishable. Always we carry him – in our arms, on our backs or on our shoulders. He laughs in delight as he bounces up and down. Perhaps one day he will be able to paddle free but for now the price of safety must be constant vigilance. For Mark has found his true medium. He is happier in the water than he ever is on land.

The days run into weeks and, conscious of the fact that we are in a race against time, I ponder more and more about ways of getting Mark to engage with the spatial elements of his environment. I decide to begin in a small way with the pieces of a wooden jigsaw puzzle – twelve pieces in all with a picture on one side and a blank face on the other. Sitting beside him as he rocks on the floor, I begin to whistle a marching tune. Captured by shape and sound he watches my fingers put the pieces together. When finished, I say –

"Look at the kittens Mark, all purring happily in their basket."

Ignoring both myself and the kittens he reaches out for the pieces, breaks them apart, and turning them upside-down puts them nimbly together in the right order – all done without appearing even to look at the pieces.

Getting up he walks away leaving me soundless, staring in disbelief at the blank face of the upside-down jigsaw. He had put the pieces together on the basis of shape alone faster than I had done on the basis of the picture. Borrowing a different jigsaw from Darren's mother, one more appropriate to an older age group, I try again. This time I will not make the picture. I will put the pieces on the floor in a jumbled pile. Vigorously humming the national anthem I wait for him to come over. Within minutes he has them sorted, turned upside-down, and put together. I look down at another pictureless completed jigsaw puzzle.

Some days later, thinking of the red, child-sized, plastic car and the blue tricycle standing unused and idle in the old summer house, I rack my brains for some inspiration. He has never ventured willingly on to the seat of either and if lifted on has screamed until taken off again. Surprising, because he loves travelling. Sitting happily in his high seat at the back of the car, eyes focused on the road ahead, he gives the impression that he could go on for ever. The more major the road, the more excited he becomes, limbs twirling and twisting as the car eats up the miles. Visualizing the scene I get the germ of an idea.

Would it work? It's worth a try.

I double back into the house, emerging again with some sticks of chalk. Mark, fresh from his afternoon nap, is with me. I walk out onto the concrete pathway running around the house and down the centre I draw a thick white line. I make it a double line in some areas. At the sides I draw yellow lines for the hard shoulder, some broken, some unbroken. Here and there I draw white arrows going left and right. Along the way I include some transverse white lines and write "stop" or "slow". My handiwork finished, I pause to admire it and give the chalk to Mark. He lets it drop but stares at the lines. I bring up the car and, placing it in the left-hand lane, attach a long string so that he can pull it along. No reaction from Mark. It does not work. We go in for tea leaving the car on the pathway.

Some days later as I put the washing on the clothes line, he comes over. Catching my hand he draws me to the car. I lift him in, remove the string and put his feet on the pedals. Slowly he pushes them back and forth, back and forth. The car moves down the left hand-lane and turns right at the arrow.

Considering again his use of his five senses we have established that at the auditory level he is capable of reacting to the full spectrum of sound – from the lowest to the highest frequency, although at times he will appear to act deaf. At the visual level it is still the minute details of the environment that appear to make the most impact.

Why does he constantly ignore the vast and the global to concentrate instead on the minute and the minuscule? In a swimming pool, unless kept occupied, he will spend his time watching and touching the small, round, overflow outlets along the side of the pool. All around us under the manipulation of his nimble fingers keys disappear from locks and handles from doors. An unpainted spot on the wall looms large. He will scream until it is painted over.

It is as if small objects are magnified out of all proportion to their surroundings so they assume gigantic proportions and threaten. The windscreen wipers and exhaust pipes of the car become targets; he tries to remove them and to sniff the exhaust fumes. He is happy when the wipers are in motion; then he fixates – swishing his hands from side to side in accompaniment. But when they are stationary he will try to pull them out. The small round funnels of chimneys are other objects of note – reaching upwards he will try to grasp them. It would appear that what is seen is seen only in terms of its individual components rather than as the sum of its component parts. It is as if his world lacked cohesion and proportionality. It points to fragmented vision – the splintered face of a cracked world – a jigsaw where the pieces are not joined.

It is our first visit to the zoo this year. We stand by the railings of the elephant enclosure on a quiet afternoon to watch Jill, the young elephant, being hand-fed by her keeper. Mark enthralled, is riveted, his body trembling, his small hands twirling from side to side in excitement, his eyes fastened on eight-year-old Jill deftly swinging her after-dinner treat of sliced bread from the tip of her trunk to her mouth, coiling and uncoiling her ridged, grey, proboscis again and again, swinging it up and down, the bread appearing and disappearing between her ivory tusks. Looking across the enclosure and noting his excitement, the keeper invites him to feed Jill.

In some trepidation we lead him across, but we need not have feared. He stands happily beside the elephant, leaning against her foot, his eyes fixated on the trunk, as she gently takes the six to eight slices of bread each time from his small hands, coiling the tip of her trunk around them and swinging them to her mouth. Back and forth swings the trunk while Mark's arms delve into the wrappings again and again until the six large loaves are gone and the party is over. We are both fully aware that he does not see the elephant – only that grey, ridged, proboscis and the slices of bread exist for him. They have a life of their own.

Watching anxiously, my senses all keyed up and alert for danger – concentrating intently on Mark's arm and the elephant's trunk – poised, hovering, to intervene – I become aware that I too do not see the elephant. For me at this moment there is nothing in my vision but the movement of Mark's arm and the trunk. The two moving objects stand out with a startling, disjointed clarity suspended in their own animation. They move on and on – pirouetting – like two figures performing their synchronized ballet against the backdrop of a darkened stage. I get a frightening glimpse into how Mark sees the world.

Relaxing my concentration I become conscious of the keeper lifting Mark up to pat Jill's side and my world slips back into its normal place. Jill is led away. I pick Mark up to carry him back across the enclosure. Behind us Jill lays back her ears and raising her trunk high in the air trumpets her thanks. We jump with the blast but from Mark there is no reaction.

Where then do we go from here? Over the last year we have looked into the research on child development but most of what we have read has dealt with the development of the normal child who is assumed to enter the world with an innate appreciation of the concepts of time, space and causality – these three categories of sense that appear to be dysfunctional in Mark. We have found virtually no material on the development of a child like him. We will have to extend and revise our own programme.

But first we must make a return visit to the eye specialist to clarify whether any of these defects could be related to Mark's ability to see.

At the clinic we sit opposite the consultant, giving a progress report – listing our concerns. Behind us Mark storms around the room. Concerned, I twist and turn, afraid some equipment might get damaged. The consultant smiles –

"It's all right, he is doing no damage. I'll watch him."

He turns on the illuminated panel of the letters of the alphabet beginning with the largest letters and graduating to the smallest. His attention diverted, Mark stops in his tracks.

"Mark, will you read some letters for me?"

The doctor's approach is casual. Before he has time to name even one letter this unfamiliar voice reads, clearly and with perfect diction, every letter from A to Z on the Snellen chart. On the last note of the Z the voice dies away.

Nothing breaks the silence of the room. In the outside office a phone rings. I feel my nose stinging – the tissues at the back of my eyes prickle sharply. Struggling to suppress the sensation, I hear vaguely the monologue in my head finding its voice –

"He can read – he could read all the time."

Clearing his throat the doctor kneels down in front of Mark.

"Now, Mark, look at me. Good boy, a little drop into this eye – now the other. Just look at the light."

Fixated by the light Mark responds perfectly to the commands of "Look up", "Look down", "Follow my finger", "Now the left eye."

The same procedure and in minutes the examination is over. Mark is pronounced as having healthy eyes and perfect 20/20 vision.

Somehow, I negotiate our thanks, the outer office and the stairway, to emerge into the darkened hall below. Picking Mark up I carry him across the threshold to the sunlight beyond. Like the poplar leaves I find myself trembling before the advent of dawn.

In the weeks that follow Mark begins cautiously to use some single words. All are words he had learned from the labels. Going over to the fridge, he says "fridge"; touching the wall, he calls out "wall". The words are pronounced clearly and with faultless diction. They are obviously learned words and not spontaneous baby words. But they are words and as the months slip by we hear more and more of them. Having established that the perception fault does not lie with his vision but with some other part of the nervous system, we are free to go ahead with our plans. Explaining our son's difficulties we arrange with the swimming coach at the pool to give him some special attention for a short time each day. Mark responds well to his coach and, watching him closely, I feel he is happy with the arrangement.

Meanwhile, every innovative method that will give him an appreciation of space is put into practice. But each day we leave periods for his recovery time when he can be by himself and rock – often in the dark. It appears that his tolerance of sensory stimuli is limited. He becomes overwhelmed easily. Then he has to opt out to recover and has devised his own recovery machine.

We will have to think about ways of alleviating this susceptibility to sensory input.

Summer has come – a warm, dry summer this year – the grass turns brown. To spend as much time as possible out of doors we section off a ten-metre square of grass in a shaded area for Mark, fencing it off securely with wooden poles and wire netting. We put in a small gate. Safe inside this area we feel he can play in the sand-pit, make mud pies, pour water from bottles and cups and scatter his toys. Watching him through the kitchen window, I realize that in reality he will do none of these things. If left alone even for a few minutes he wanders the perimeter of his large playpen looking for a way out. Today I plan to take him with Darren and the twins to the beach and am busy in the kitchen preparing food while keeping a wary eye on Mark through the open doorway – delighted to find that today he is digging in the sand-pit.

Ready to go, I come out to collect him. Stunned, I look. The area is empty. Mark is gone. How has he got out? The fence seems intact. Where is he? He was there a few minutes ago. One glance tells me he is not in the back garden. A wave of panic hits me – the road? – but the side gate is closed – locked. He couldn't get around to the front that way.

I know he didn't come through the kitchen. I would have seen him.

I race back through the house and out the front door. His red short pants and bright blue top are nowhere to be seen. I pound down the front steps through the shrubbery, past the garage, my feet hammering out the refrain in my brain –

"Let him go left at the gate, left at the gate – not straight across the road – not right where there's no footpath – left at the gate – left at the gate."

Flying down the long straight driveway I can see the road straight ahead. He's not on it.

I cannot see left or right.

Reaching the gate I look right. He's not there. Two flying steps take me to the jutting out wall on the left. As I turn I see the red and blue figure running ahead on the footpath – running – running. I catch up with him as he is about to cross the T-junction of the open road-way.

How had he got out? He had managed to dig a small space under the fence in the area of the sand-pit. After that he had squeezed through a little gap in the hedge between it and the locked side gate.

We had built securely but had reckoned without Mark's x-ray vision – without his ability to maximize the minutiae of his environment – to see the parts and not the whole. While we had been looking at the full picture Mark had seen only the parts and the gaps between them. Knowing now that it will no longer be of use, we dismantle the playpen.

It's a week later. I collapse with severe abdominal pain and am rushed to hospital for an emergency appendix operation. Although well cared for in my absence Mark manages to impale himself on a sharp toy and injures his palate. Late at night it is decided to admit him to the children's ward of the same hospital. Arriving in a wheelchair at the ward, I find a screaming, out-of-control, tearless Mark pacing his cot and biting the hands of every member of staff who comes within distance, while around him the small occupant of each cot sits wide awake, staring through the bars in silent astonishment. As I pass a tousled head, two bright eyes stare up at me and a five-year-old voice asks –

"Is he yours missus? I ain't never seen one like him before – he's woke us all up."

Approaching Mark's cot I begin to sing, softly at first then getting louder. The screams taper off. He stops his pacing, turns towards the direction of the singing and there is silence in the ward.

As the sound dies away I think –

"Why does he always act as if he were blind?"

In night-sister's office a conference is held. Mark's mouth injury has to be examined and treated; the only way this can be achieved is to give him a sedative injection. I give my permission and when he is asleep the examination shows that the injury is not serious but will require a further few days of observation. They will keep him for tonight in the children's ward but the staff make it clear that if he behaves like this again they cannot keep him.

The following morning I am back in the wheelchair to collect Mark and take him to my room where a cot has been set up for him. As our small cavalcade travels the underground passages connecting the two sections of the hospital, Mark, exhausted from the events of the previous night, sits buddha-like on the folded arms of the burly hospital porter – calm and at ease in the care of a father of eight. The night-sister's last words stay with me – sombre and sobering –

"Mark is quiet now and he should stay here. If that child leaves the ward I will not accept him back again."

I am thankful that he settles down in the cot in my room and, for the first time in his young life, begins to take an interest in the people around him; not in them as people but in their hair. Staff, visitors and ourselves – all who come near him have to submit to hair sniffing and stroking. This tactile experience appears to have a calming effect on him. Having strenuously rejected all physical contact up until now, why is he suddenly seeking it out? Perhaps because it is a limited contact and entirely on his own terms. He is doing the touching and is not being touched.

But over the days, on watching him and reflecting, I come to a very different conclusion and find a simpler, more practical explanation. I think he is using hair texture and smell, in addition to colour, to recognize and distin-

guish between the large number of people now entering his life on a daily
basis – the people he is most familiar with having to submit to the most
lengthy sessions. Whatever the reason, for now we will submit gracefully to
this practice. It is good to see him reaching out and making contact. Perhaps
he is already designing his own tactile acclimatization machine.

Because the nursing staff in my section of the hospital have refused to
have any input into Mark's care, putting forward their opinion that he should
have remained in the children's ward, we engage a young art student, Moira,
to come daily to the hospital to care for him in my room and afterwards at
home for the first few weeks of our return. Under her tutelage his store of
single words increases; he can now use about thirty words on the house
labelling system appropriately. Moira's long, blonde, silken hair is the enticer
– for every advancement he is rewarded with a time slot for rubbing.

She introduces him to colour – enthralled, he watches her mix. She
paints and hands him a brush – no, he will not partake, but he will identify.
She paints a rainbow and hangs it in the sunlight. She asks for "indigo?", he
identifies it; for "orange?", his finger is on it; for "violet?" his finger moves.
Mark is pointing.

She moves on to shape. Again he is captivated; in green, in blue, in
yellow, the shapes pile up on the page – she asks for "triangle?", for "square?",
for "circle?"; his finger moves, always accurate.

She colours them in. She asks for "yellow square?", "blue triangle?",
"green circle?"; he points to each and he repeats, "yellow square", "blue
triangle", "green circle". She moves to "octagon" and the game goes on.

Mark is pointing and joining words.

Moira returns to college. I sit on the soft grey chair in the hall, a picture
book in my hand. From the top pocket of my pinafore a bar of chocolate
sticks out. Mark runs up and down the hall engaged in his current ritual of
turning the light switches, now within his reach, on and off. He has being
doing this for almost an hour without stopping, seemingly oblivious to my
presence.

Taking the chocolate from my pocket I rustle the paper. He listens.
Having got his attention I begin to read aloud to him. He comes over and we
share a square of chocolate. Continuing to read I show him the book. He is
not interested – running back to the lights. Enough for today.

A week later I begin the daily reading session with a different coloured
pinafore, a different bar of chocolate and the same book. He stays longer,
long enough to share half the bar and for me to read him a page. The lights

come on again. Tomorrow I will be obtuse and not open the chocolate bar. I will just read aloud. About to close the book, at my side I hear "choc". I point to my top pocket. He will have to climb up on my knee to get it. He hesitates – going back to the light switches. Closing the book I begin to get up. He is back. Sitting down again I keep very still. Scrambling up on my knee he grasps my hand using it as a claw-grab to get the chocolate out of the pocket. Opening the bar I offer him a square. We munch – I read. He flops on my knee – listening.

The bar is finished.

I read on.

He listens.

CHAPTER 3

Searching for Causes

Within weeks we are back in hospital. Without any obvious fall Mark begins to limp. There are no tears, no signs of distress, just a reluctance to put his left foot on the ground. Now just past his third birthday, it is still not possible to elicit any information from him about himself and we are slowly being forced to the conclusion that he does not feel pain. On falling or taking a knock he never cries. He just picks himself up and keeps on going showing no reaction. It is as if he has no faculty for self-perception – as if he finds no sense in sensation. Either he is not aware of it because he cannot feel it or, having felt it, he cannot decipher it or find where it is coming from.

Another bizarre aspect of this lack of awareness centres around his attitude to his limbs. He constantly gives the impression that he is not aware of his limbs or does not recognize that they belong to him.

In the circumstances our family doctor can but refer him for x-ray to check out a number of possible causes as to why he would limp. In the x-ray department Mark, struggling wildly, screams – fighting every attempt to get him past the door. The kind staff offer help and understanding – to no avail. A paediatrician is called, a spoonful of syrupy tranquilliser offered, and we wait in a nearby room for it to take effect.

Mark races around the room climbing on tables and chairs. I take him down, try to hold him, but he is off again. This time the window-sills are his target. I sing. I chant. I whistle – all to no avail. An elderly gentleman, the only other occupant of the room, joins in the game. An expert on animal sounds he gives a magnificent rendition of "Old MacDonald's Farm". Mark, who would have loved it, could have loved it, should have loved it – today is deaf to it – continuing his rampage. Pausing for breath the elderly gentleman whispers –

"I think they must have given him the syrup from the wrong bottle."

Close to hysterical laughter, I manage a weak smile.

Twenty minutes and the staff are back to take him for x-ray. Startled they survey the wreck of the room – upturned chairs, scattered magazines. Resignedly, I strap Mark into his buggy and take him home.

He still limps, although less obviously now. We are referred on to a specialist in bone disease. He examines Mark's knee and ankle bones carefully, exerting pressure on the joints watching closely for any reaction. There is none.

"Nothing to worry about there; if there were he would certainly feel it."

He discusses possible hip injury, looking for early evidence of Perthes' disease.

"We will need a hip x-ray. I'll send him to a different hospital this time."

A week later we face an angry anaesthetist in a little anteroom off the x-ray department. It has again proved impossible to get Mark past the door of x-ray. Frightened, he is more out of control than ever. The vital necessity of early diagnosis of Perthes' disease, so that treatment can be started as soon as possible, is pointed out. In view of it I give my permission, allowing my objections to an anaesthetic to be overruled. We wait in the anteroom.

The door opens and a whitecoated professional whirls in informing me that she has been called away from more important work and that it is against all her medical principles to give an anaesthetic to such a young child merely for the purpose of an x-ray. She considers me the worst mother she has ever encountered in her career.

"A mother who cannot even control her own child – I have three young children myself so I am not without experience."

Stoically I remain silent. My natural reticence standing me in good stead, I will not be reduced to tears here.

Reluctantly Mark is given the anaesthetic and then is lifted gently onto the table by a uniformed attendant. His x-ray is taken. In the recovery room I sit beside the bed watching him breathe evenly, waiting for him to wake up. Saddened at the train of events I wonder aloud –

"Are there other children out there like this blond, beautiful, blue-eyed baby of ours?"

We return to the hospital for the result. There is no evidence of Perthes' disease or any other disease or injury. It is suggested that perhaps I am over-protective and should seek treatment for anxiety.

Gradually, over time, Mark's limp fades and disappears.

Principles of Piaget

We continue our research into child development. Perhaps by following the developmental pattern of the normal child we will, by comparison, find clues as to why Mark is so different. We review the work of Dr Jean Piaget, the Swiss psychologist who spent a number of decades observing the behaviour of children and who published many papers on the subject. He devised one of the most influential theories as to how intellectual development occurs in the normal child in a series of set stages, putting forward in the process the idea that each stage of cognitive development arises from the previous one in an orderly fashion and that this process begins at birth and ends in the teenage years. The core of his theory revolves around how children come to know and understand the world by actively engaging with it, and the manner in which this influences their intellectual development. Even at the infant stage, he held, the infant himself plays an active part in getting to know his world.

We have our first clue.

Since birth Mark has shown an active unwillingness to engage with his world. Even now, beginning his fourth year, unless kept actively engaged with his environment from outside, either his activity becomes aimless or he returns to the limiting arena of rituals and routines. That spark of lively interest in everything going on around him that one sees in the average child has never been present in him. His approach has always been to withdraw rather than to engage. The vital consequences of this become clearer in the light of Piaget's further observations. He suggests that the brain has to have the capacity to absorb the world of the concrete – the physical structure – before it can assimilate the world of the abstract – that of ideas and feelings. The clues now lead nearer to what might be the possible cause of Mark's condition, because Piaget suggests that thought organization arises out of adaptation to the environment and that one of the basic requirements for this adaptation to the environment is a concept of time and space.[1]

The possible implications of this for Mark are enormous.

We have always agreed that if a problem is to be solved it has to be stripped down layer by layer, folded back cover by cover, until the basic core is exposed. This then is the place to begin. Is there anything more basic to living in the world into which you have come than the ability to see it clearly as it is and not through the distorting spectacles of false parameters and fragmented vision? If your boundaries of time and space appear and disappear like some elusive will o' the wisp straying across marshland in a mist, how can you interact with its nebulousness? How can you adapt to the structure of a fog – now lifting to give tantalizing glimpses of the solid reality beneath it and now, as you stretch out to reach for that reality, becoming denser to blot it out again, or else drifting in patches to snatch it from your hand? How can you orientate yourself in that kind of ever-changing world for long enough to adapt to it? And if you cannot stabilize your physical environment, how then can you put down roots and grow in it?

Having already realized that Mark's concept of space was erroneous we set out to correct this error by keeping him actively engaged with the spatial elements of his environment. This programme is working well. Now, over a year into it, he moves around his world with greater sureness and control. He no longer tries to walk off the end of the patio wall, nor does he step out on to the air above ground level. In the swimming pool he rarely now has to be buffered against the wall tiles lest he knock himself. He has become more accurate in gauging his distance, although we still call out "stop."

A concept of time – how does one even define it for a small child? Having defined it, how does one develop an innate concept of the passage of time in another person? Mark's response to every situation is one of totality, as if he had a vision of neither hindsight nor foresight, as if he could not grasp the fact that the future will in time become the present and will then slide into the past never to come again.

"It will only take a minute"; "We'll be home soon"; "We'll get it tomorrow" are meaningless to someone who lives in the ever-present now. It is too early yet to gauge the full extent of his innate concept of time but we will be vigilant in watching for clues.

A busy morning – I am pressed for time. The grey chair in the hall sits empty. Beside it, on the carpet, Mark, busily occupied with his current ritual, is down on all fours lining up his set of train tracks in two parallel lines, adding them to the trail of bricks, building blocks and vehicles already covering the floor of his room and now moving out into the hallway. I watch as he lines up the carriages ahead of the tracks. Although he loves to travel on the railway he has never run a carriage on the rails of his toy set, showing no capacity for pretend or imitation play. He has never built with his bricks, sailed his boats in the bath, run in circles with his toy aeroplane simulating flight, reversed or advanced his Dinky toys on the table top or wound up his clockwork carriages to run on their tracks. Despite hours of demonstration from his peers he shows no willingness or indeed interest in playing with toys other than to line them up in parallel lines. They will now lie gathering dust on the floor because any attempt to remove them will be met with such screaming tantrums (when Mark will lie on the floor and drum both his head and his heels) that they will have to be put back again. Once they are replaced the screams are turned off and peace is restored. At this point in his life screaming is Mark's only way of communicating his wishes.

Only when he is out of the house can we remove them to clean – always making sure they go back in the right order – brick for brick, car for car. Even the minutest change – a car moved a centimetre to the right or left – will be noticed, and put right instantly the moment he returns. Mark's progress is defined by ritual. He delineates each new phase of his development by discarding an old ritual and adopting a new one. Until the next ritual, then, the parallel lines will remain on the floor and we will step over them and try to ignore them.

It is strange and ominous, this total absence of make-believe/ pretend play in a child who keeps himself constantly occupied with objects. Even though he ignores people Mark has an affinitive attachment to objects. He is rarely seen without one in his hand. Yet he appears to be devoid of the capacity for the imaginative use of objects. He can engage in object imitation play; we are aware of that. In the car, when he cannot entice the driver to turn on the windscreen wipers, he will swish his hands from side to side in imitation. This would indicate a degree of concrete imagination but not the kind of abstract imagination involved in running in circles with a toy aeroplane simulating flight and the roar of an engine.

Piaget has documented that, some time between the end of the first and the end of the second year of life, the average infant begins to engage in pretend play.[2]

How important is pretend play and what does it reflect?

Reality play and pretend play are considered to be part of the foundation for the mental processes by which knowledge is acquired; in other words, to be part of the foundation for cognition. They reflect an awareness of the people in one's environment and, following on from that, an understanding of social interaction. At this point in his life Mark's awareness of other people varies from nil to minimal. He appears to have little concept of a person as a person and if this is a necessary factor in pretend play then it is not surprising that he has not developed this normal aspect of childhood behaviour.

Memory man

The morning gets busier. I decide to miss out on the reading session today – just this once, being fully absorbed, he will not notice. I forge ahead – clearing the back-log. Time passes. Only the grandfather clock is conscious of it. Beside me I hear "book" and look to see Mark holding our latest story-book. I am towed by the hand to the grey chair and pushed into it. Climbing on my knee he sits, opening the book at the page we had finished on yesterday. He quotes verbatim the last three pages and with his finger on the exact word we had finished on says –

"Want–ut–Have–ut."

Catching my free arm he wraps it around himself and snuggles. Somehow I find my voice and keep it steady.

I read on.

This is our first indication that Mark has an excellent rote memory, because he has not been reading the words from the book. He has been quoting from memory. In the euphoria that followed it took some time to realize that the most significant event of that day was that spontaneous phrase of –

"Want–ut–Have–ut."

Mark has manufactured a whole sentence with understanding and purpose and it is a very useful one. Every day now when we sit down to read, he will quote the full text of what we have read the previous day, often over a hundred words, always turning the pages appropriately and putting his finger on the last word. This forecasts the beginnings of reading because it is obvious that he has no difficulty in recognizing the words by the shape of the letters although the quoted text is not being read from the book but produced from memory.

At times over the last few years, when my repertoire of songs had become exhausted, I had recited prayers, nursery rhymes, poems – anything that sounded different, particularly on days when it was difficult to calm him or keep his attention focused on me. Now my prayers are being returned to me and I gave thanks the first day I heard Mark recite "The Lord's Prayer" in three different languages – Irish, English and Latin, followed by that much longer prayer "The Credo" in two languages – English and Latin. I had never learned "The Credo" in Irish!

But how much comprehension lies behind Mark's repetition of the spoken word? It is difficult to gauge. The impression given is – very little. It is obvious that he is capable of attaching meaning to single words but it is less certain that he can attach meaning to sentences. Other than that one sentence of four very important words, Mark, even though now well into his fourth year, has not spoken in sentences. Meanwhile this rote memory is a very important asset in the battle for communication and we will continue to use it. Although, on reflection, one wonders if a mind overburdened with large tracts of texts will be less accessible or more accessible to the ebb and flow of normal sentence exchange? A difficult question to answer. Always I would have to operate from the premise that any type of communication is better than none.

In spite of the fact that he is now very receptive to the sound of the human voice Mark still does not look at people, seeming neither to see them nor sense their presence, other than visitors to the house who, at the hall door, have to submit to having their hair sniffed and rubbed. We find standing beside him has become an occupational hazard. A strong, sturdy child, he moves with speed and one is likely to get a punch in the face when he unwittingly brings his head or his fist up fast. To dodge the blows we have learned to keep a respectful distance. Wrapped in his aura of aloneness he is so much more aware of machines than of people. Machines can make sound, light up, move, mix, cut, wield, extract, demolish, rotate powertools; lawnmowers, rotating brushcutters, vacuum cleaners and their ilk become his fascinations. He peoples his world with them. For him they appear to have a greater reality.

Tonight, out walking at dusk, he watches the headlights of the oncoming cars. With one quick twist of his wrist he breaks free from my hand running out onto the road straining to touch the lights. A fast sprint, a squeal of breaks – I catch him as the car stops. Rubbing the lights he is not aware of the ashen-faced driver shaking her fist and screaming at me.

Unwilling hands

It becomes quite obvious that at times Mark does not recognize that his hands belong to him. He has resorted to biting hands, both his own hands and those nearest to him. We feel the teeth marks. They point to frustration. Perhaps biting is his way of finding his own hands and distinguishing them from others. We concentrate on hand therapy.

Two basins of water – one cold, one warm – Mark, munching chocolate, enjoys swishing his hands from one to the other.

We sit at the table surrounded by fabrics and slabs. Smooth tiles, we trace the lines on them – fine sandpaper, we barely touch it.

We wrap things in warm wool, smooth out the silver chocolate wrappings, burrow into the soft down of feathers, make balls of wood shavings and roll them side by side with rubber balls.

The games are endless but motivation is lacking. Mark is apathetic about using his hands.

We make play-dough. Mixing flour with water we knead it, making animal shapes. Around us Darren and the twins knead, roll, twist, cut, shape and manipulate the dough. Alongside Mark just pats his portion as if he had little control and direction over his muscle movements.

It is curious – this inability, almost, to initiate constructive action. So often he appears to have no wind in his sails; nothing to propel his barque forward to safe havens or stormy seas. Riding motionless on the still sea of his own inertia one feels that if left to his own devices he will stay forever becalmed. And yet – and yet – one remembers those deft fingers that picked keys from our locks and now manipulate our light switches. He wanted to do it then and bent his will to it. What will it take now to break through this barrier and get him to turn on his *want-to-do-it* mechanism?

Memory delves again and comes up with the same answer – food is the only motivator we have. This time, however, it will take more than chocolate.

Hearing voices

Today it is cold outside but the kitchen is warm and the fan of the oven hums quietly. The aroma of fresh cinnamon bread cooling on the wire trays wafts around us. Mark wrinkles his nose in appreciation as he munches a slice, the oil running down his fingers. Dressed in his white chef's suit and white paper hat he is master of ceremonies helping to knead the dough for the next batch. Waiting for it to rise, together we set to work with wooden spoons to stir the mix for the cherry buns. I hand Mark the paper carton; he takes off the lid and pours in the cherries. I call out the menu for tomorrow –

"Gingerbread men and oatmeal and syrup cookies."

Stimulated by taste, smell and free will, the want-to-do-it mechanism has been turned on.

I call out –

"Come, Mark, we are ready now for baking."

I expect a stampede of feet down the corridor. For a minute there is silence – then I hear an echo – my words float back to me in a voice exactly like mine. Startled, I wonder if I am imagining things. I call out again –

"Come, Mark, we are ready now for baking."

Again I hear the echo. This time it comes nearer accompanied by the sound of running feet. Standing before me he says –

"Come, Mark, we are ready now for baking."

I laugh, ruffle his hair and call him my little Mister Echo.

I do not realize then that he is actually finding his own voice to communicate through my speech. This is his way of telling me that he also is ready for baking. Because he cannot produce the words spontaneously he is instead substituting my words which cover the same issue, and in this way he has established a means of communicating his wants. In the days that follow I never initiate the baking routine. Always I wait for him to come and say, "Come, Mark, we are ready now for baking," and he always comes and says it.

From this it appears to us that his acquisition of language will be by a circuitous route and thus will be very different from that of the average child. It is as if he does not have the innate, inherent ability to manufacture speech. It is not going to arise spontaneously. However, he has the intelligence to realize that there is a way around the problem. He can compensate by using the speech of others, thus using words that have already been introduced to him by ear in a given sequence. He does not appear to be able to manufacture words and sentences but *can* make use of the words and sentences spoken to him by others, and then adapt them for his own use. A few weeks later at the end of a particularly messy baking session, covered with flour, drips of milk and egg yolk, he catches my hand saying, "Now I'll put you into a nice fresh baking suit," meaning, of course, "Now will you put *me* into a nice fresh baking suit?"

CHAPTER 4

The Shadows Gather

At the harbour we stand in a group: mothers and children waiting for the yachts to come in and the last race of the day to finish. Overhead the gulls wheel and circle lazily – dropping lower – diving now with purpose as the incoming trawlers discard their undersized catch at the breakwater; flying out of the mêlée their raucous cries vie with each other in triumph. Far out to sea the white sails tack and, rounding the buoy, the yachts turn for home. Colourful, the bloated spinnakers collapse on deck and the taut mainsails are reined in even tighter. The wind has sprung up and the sails head into it, straining each stay to inch the boat forward. To the west the sun, molten and flaming, begins its descent below the hill. Closer inshore the moored yachts rock in the ruffled troughs of the lapping wavelets, halyards clanking against the mast. Facing us a solitary cormorant, raven black, stands motionless on a rock – wings held out to dry. Lined up along the pier the fish lorries shoulder their burden of iced boxes, reverse and depart.

The last trawler enters the harbour and ties up alongside. The children clamour to see it unloading and we make our way slowly onto the pier. Holding Mark's hand firmly, aware of the danger, I watch with all the intensity of a hovering hawk. I am on edge – alert to every possibility of a false move. How would Mark, who navigates his world by sound, cope with the differing levels of depth?

Surefooted and knowing, his three young companions, keeping well back from the edge of the pier, stand quietly – enthralled with watching the scene. The slippery boxes are swung from hand to hand overboard and up onto the lorry.

The trawler, relieved of its load, begins to ride higher on the water. Mark looks upwards intent on the cacophony of harsh, grating sounds from the massing gulls riding the updraft of the breeze. With the wind beneath their wings they cruise – to circle and rise again – awaiting that moment when they will plummet to earth for the catch. My fears fall away when I realize that he is fully engrossed and will be easily managed.

Shouldering its load the lorry is ready to depart. The driver reverses, turning slowly. Close to the edge the back wheels slip – spinning without a foothold. Instantly Mark's attention shifts earthwards to the sound of the hard-pressed engine as the driver revs the accelerator to gain momentum. But the load has shifted and the truck slides backwards into five fathoms of water. Jumping clear the driver rolls, to land beside us. The water closes over the lorry and the fish are returned to the sea.

Leaving his perch the cormorant flies towards the setting sun.

The screeching gulls scatter.

In the silence we hear only the clanking halyards and the lapping suction at the moorings. The first of the white-sailed yachts rounds the harbour wall and drops anchor. The race is over.

Beside me a small clear voice says –

"Lorry gone – driver here."

It is Mark's second sentence and it was to be the only spontaneous, strictly observational, comment he would make about the happenings around him in the first eight years of his life.

Later tonight, long after the yacht race trophies have been presented and the last of the speeches have died away, we talk about Mark. At four years and two months we have to come to terms with how far behind his peer group he really is. Watching his age-related companions react to the incident at the pier had hammered home that message. Their comprehension, their ability to relate the incident and to relate to it, their fears and worries and their ability to express them brought everything into sharp focus. It con- trasted starkly with Mark's single sentence of –

"Lorry gone – driver here."

There has been no further reaction from him since then.

We come to two decisions, one – to postpone his impending entrance to school for another year, the second – to seek professional help.

Assessment

Mark's assessment has finished and I sit tonight to record it in my journal. What is there to record? A hyperactive Mark rampaging through the offices of the clinic – trailing his mantle of aloneness. Two fraught parents in the spotlight – on trial – asked to render an account of their stewardship. And behind their desks the impassive faces of the professionals. Based as it was on circumstantial evidence and handed down in censure but not sagacity, the verdict could only ever be "guilty" – guilty of parental culpability. As the fault lay entirely with us no effort need be expended in seeking what innate dysfunctions Mark might have or what might be done about them.

Over time we will come to realize that, like so many other parents of that era, we were victims of the age in which we lived and of the distorted thinking of those years. But for now, as parents of an only child, we have no defence. Had we had other children – healthy, successful, outgoing – to point to, we could have challenged that verdict – marvelling at the dichotomy of parenting that could have produced on the one hand a normal child, and on the other a child like Mark. It is inevitable then tonight that we should ask ourselves this question –

"Could we have been responsible for, or have contributed to, Mark's condition?"

It is a question that will remain with us, and for now it casts a long shadow.

So we return to the research, taking turns to spend Saturday mornings in the university library. Apart from some hand-biting incidents Mark settles in well at the small Montessori pre-school playgroup we have chosen for him, although he remains on the fringes – still living in his own cocoon. Despite being more aware of what is going on around him he is still not a part of it. He begins to string words together, not into sentences but into jingles which he sings. He will summarize his day's events in words, giving the facts in order but without verbs or pronouns – "Play-school, painting, plasticine, rocking horse, pretty garden, flowers, wire fence."

Later he will extend it by adding verbs – "Go to play-school, do painting and plasticine, ride on rocking horse, go to pretty garden, see pretty flowers, climb on wire fence" – still in a singsong voice.

This forecasts what is to be his approach to language throughout his formative school years – that is, his speech is always concrete and functional but not observational. In addition, although his diction is perfect, his tone of voice is monotonic, with little inflection. From this period onwards he can always list the events of the day, the order of the homework, the results of the match, the names of all the other children in the class, the times of the trains – whatever – but he shows little facility for tossing or fielding the ball of conversation. His problem, then, lies in the area of two-way idea exchange and the fact that he appears to have little faculty for observational comment.

For now, however, it is time to introduce pronouns into his embryonic sentences. So we teach him, on a question and answer basis, to learn by rote the short phrases he will need to cope on a daily basis –

"What do you want?" – "I want a drink", "I want to go out" – whatever.

"Are you hungry?" – "I want my lunch", "I want orange juice" – whatever.

"Who are you?" "What's your name?" – "My name is Mark."

We extend it to cover all the contingencies he is likely to meet with. Taking into account his extraordinary rote memory, his faculty for mimicking sound and his uncanny ability to match question and answer on a purely concrete basis, it serves him well throughout his formative years.

Measurement

Mark's ability to perceive space improves. He can now swim the width of the pool and his coach pronounces him to be "water confident". At the pool he discovers the concept of measurement. Observing the marked-off metre-lines along the side, he homes in on linear distance and the "want-to-do-it" mechanism moves to overdrive – operating at full blast.

It is time to introduce metre sticks and measuring tapes. Now his willing hands are busy as deft fingers manipulate the tape. Becoming obsessed with scale, he seems intent on absorbing intellectually what he cannot process intuitively. Inside and out area is measured; from house to garden the work goes on – the wall whose end he tried so often to walk off – the base of the eucalyptus tree he loves to strip, sniffing the oil from the papery peelings of the bark – the bird table by the fountain – even the shadow cast by the setting sun – all come under his aegis. Motivation brings with it its own reward.

Graduating from great to small, now it is the turn of the callipers. Railway tracks, alphabet bricks, and trucks are retrieved from the dust and put between its jaws.

The parallel lines on the floor are no more.

Waiting in the wings, we bide our time, our agenda hidden. We will use this phase of development to direct his attention to depth and to the science of numbers.

"How deep is that wall you tried to walk off?"

"How high were the bars of the cot that night you vaulted over the top on to the mattress below and kept on going?"

"Let's measure the depth of the pond you had to be fished out of."

"How about drawing a line on the sand between sea and land?"

Then it will be time to read off the figures and write them down.

Time encapsulated

Space and time – time and space – are not these two categories of sense inexplicably intertwined? Do they not enshrine the basic laws that govern our universe? How can one live in this universe without an intrinsic evaluation of them? The average child coming into this world arrives equipped with a concept of time, space and causality. But Mark did not come so equipped.

It becomes obvious to us that for him the events of his life are kaleidoscoped and that, approaching five years of age, he is looking for some structure by which to order these events. We ponder about ways of giving him an intuitive evaluation of something as nebulous as time. We have noticed him standing in the hallway staring at the grandfather clock listening intently to the "tick-tock-tick-tock", swinging his hands to the rhythm of the pendulum.

Retrieving the ancient metronome from the attic we place it on the piano. He is drawn to it as if to a central field of force. Fixated, he watches it swing. We give him an old clock so that he can time the beats. Perhaps by surrounding him with time sounds we will provide him with some intellectual evaluation of what he lacks intrinsically. Perhaps time, like music and like space perception, can be learned. Often at night he will say – "Time for play-school now" – not seeming to notice the difference between night and day. Making a symbolic gesture, we hang daily and weekly calendars in the kitchen. At the day's end he removes the day, discarding it into the wastepaper basket. Tomorrow there will be a new dawn. At the end of each week the record of its seven days are detached from their base, crumpled and consigned to the bin – gone if not forgotten. We set to work making a time calendar – dividing it into day and night – colouring in suns, moons and stars.

It is Hallowe'en and we hold a small party for the children in the play-group. They dress up in carnival attire and have their faces painted. Mark will not submit to face painting but has his hands painted instead. In the kitchen apples hang from the ceiling ready for biting, arms held behind one's back; apples float in basins of water, coloured streamers attached, ready for bobbing; nuts lie on the board ready for cracking; candlelight shines out from behind the orange grimace of the scooped-out pumpkins and on the stove toffee apples sizzle. A witch's hat and tall broomstick decorate the cardboard figure in the corner.

Mark appears bewitched – not by his surroundings but by the painted faces of his companions. At party times normally he retreats to his hide-out in the corridor listening from a distance. Today he stays in the kitchen mingling with the other children – occasionally touching their faces. This afternoon there is no hand biting. Perhaps because his painted hands are so obvious to him he can now locate them visibly rather than having to rely on sensation alone. The hands around him are not painted but his own stand out like neon lights. There is an object lesson here as to how we might solve this now problematic issue of hand biting by making his hands more visible to him.

The last of the balloons have been released and the party is over. Outside it is dark. With the change to winter time all clocks were put back an hour the previous night. Going down the steps the children call out in surprise –

"It's dark! Why is it dark early tonight?"

I marvel at the sophisticated, effortless, innate grasp of the time concept of these five-year-olds and I think of how hard Mark will have to work to get to there – where they have always been.

Over the months that follow Mark decides to give us official recognition. This same Mark who still has never looked us in the eye or in the face – mostly his gaze is directed at our hair – and who would pass us by in the street without identifying us, other than on the basis of sound, has at last decided to acknowledge us. We have names, we have substance – we are no longer disembodied voices in the ether – we have come out of the ethereal shadows and *ipso facto* we exist. In Mark's eyes we are "Bubby" and "Dao."

It had taken almost six years to achieve this recognition!

When he wants something now he will catch our hand, tow us to the object and say "Bubby (Dao) will do it for you" – meaning of course "Bubby (Dao) will you do it for me?"

The phase of hand biting is over and the scars of the bitemarks begin to fade. Wearing a large-faced, colourful watch on each wrist he is no longer dependent solely on sensation to locate his hands. Wearing them day and night, listening intently to the ticking, he becomes acutely distressed at a missed beat or a stopped hand. If they are not synchronized to the second we can have a major crisis on our hands. Wisely we purchase some reserves; fortunately they are cheap. Meanwhile he is happy with his ticking machines, and we can now say – "We will leave in ten minutes" or "We will be home in half an hour" – and he will measure it off on the dial. It establishes boundaries – time boundaries – bringing a measure of order to what for him must be a world of chaos. With order comes security.

Adding a stop-watch to the mix he learns a further feature of time – its limitedness. Still navigating his world by sound, it is mainly the length of sounds that he measures –

"How long has the dog been barking?"

"How long did it take for the car to start?"

"How long is the air filled with the sound of the neighbour's chainsaw?"

He is learning that sound has limits set to it, so perhaps he will never again be quite so overwhelmed by it.

We have been preparing all week for the bonfire, collecting firewood and garden refuse. After dinner Mark catches his father's hand saying – "Bonfire – Dao will do it for you" – and leads him down the garden path. The blaze shoots high into the air and the sparks fly upwards. Holding Mark's hand I stand well back from the flames and the heat. A dark head appears above the garden wall, a voice says "Hello, can I come and join in?" and two feet land lightly on the ground beside us. Barry, three years older than Mark, has entered our world, to "adopt" us and become part of our family. Manfully, he takes on the role of older brother to Mark.

A lesson learned

We face mainstream school with some trepidation and misgiving. Mark has been enrolled in his father's old school, situated some miles from home – a large boys' school spanning kindergarten, junior and senior sections. We dither – should we? should we not? – weighing up the pros and cons. We decide to go ahead, consoling ourselves with – "We can always change if it does not work out; at least we will have tried and we will know."

With hindsight it was an unrealistic and unwise decision because the school conditions stretched far beyond anything that he was capable of coping with. The sheer size and scale of the buildings and grounds alone were daunting; it would be so easy to get lost. We should have known it – but – perhaps we lived in hope.

The noise alone – schools are among the noisiest places on this planet – would have defeated him and the bigger the establishment the louder the noise is. The close proximity of hundreds of other boys had the potential to swamp his fragile sense of identity. The challenge should have brought its own warnings, but somehow they went unheeded. But we learned the salutary lesson that for Mark small would always be best.

The kindergarten day-school section is a separate building with its own identity, although still part of the overall complex. We know that Mark is capable of shutting out sound when the level reaches a certain pitch; however, we have not taken into account the effects of the constant daily bombardment of sound.

But he finds his own answers – he escapes. For the first few weeks he withdraws into himself and goes into shutdown as a defence mechanism against what, for him, must be intolerable sensory overload. Thereafter he crawls out of the window of the classroom, escaping to the sun in the enclosed yard outside, separated from his peers but still under the watchful eye of a tolerant teacher.

The crisis comes on the day he goes missing and the entire senior school is turned out to look for him. Fortunately, he is in uniform. Eventually located, ready to board the correctly numbered bus to take him home, he has his tuck money ready in his hand. Mark, who has never in his young life travelled on a bus, has managed to cross some of the busiest roads in the city and to find the right bus stop – this same Mark who, navigating by sound, never appears to look at his environment and who gives the impression that he never sees what is going on around him. All the while he must have been scanning, storing, filing away the minute details to be effortlessly called to mind when the need arose.

Later, in the headmaster's study, there is general consensus that the school is not suitable for a child like Mark. Within a month of his first day he is home again. We look for a small school nearer home. Meanwhile he rejoins his original pre-school group, settling in happily.

One weekend

Saturday morning: the kitchen is busy. We prepare for picnicking and a day at the beach. Beside me Barry butters bread for the sandwiches. I spread on the fillings. Dao stacks gear into the car. Words float in from the garden. Mark moves around the shrubs chanting their Latin names – "grisilinia", "escallonia", "pyracantha", "cotoneaster". The litany goes on, accurate and precise – his latest ritual. Interestingly, it is to mark the beginning of moving from performing rituals to verbal rituals.

We are ready to leave. I call –

"Mark, we are ready now."

The stampede of feet, the echo and he is beside me. But there is one very significant change in the echo. The echo that comes back is not "Mark, we are ready now", but – "Mark is ready now."

It is our first indication that he is capable of manipulating learned phrases in order to produce more normal-sounding language.

Carrying the cylinder of gas, kettle, crockery and inflatable dinghy, Barry and Dao struggle across the dunes. Trailing behind, Mark and I share the load of food, swimming gear and camera. Reaching our favourite grass patch we brew up for a cup and a snack before our first swim.

As the sun goes down we trek back again to the outer dunes, pitching camp for the last meal of the day beside the highest dune. Laughing excitedly, Mark and Barry trudge to the top of the dune, bare feet digging into the soft sand, to roll, eyes closed, back down to the bottom – squealing with exuberance and delight.

Always, Mark has loved the motion of rough-and-tumble play – this same Mark who strenuously resists physical human contact, actively seeks out physical environmental contact. For him the climax of a day at the beach is the tossing in the waves and the roll down the "rumpadump". It surpasses even the food. Driving home we watch the sun sink into the west, its orange glow transforming the sky. Joining in harmony together we sing "My Little Grey Home in the West."

Sunday morning I awaken early, sensing something different on the edge of my consciousness. What is it? What is amiss? Then I remember – there was no sound from Mark's room last night and I did not go to keep my nightly vigil. Slipping out of bed I pass quickly down the corridor into his room. Slumped, crumpled against the headboard, pitched awkwardly on his back, Mark appears to be unconscious. I feel his forehead. He is burning up.

Softly I speak to him – his eyes flutter open – unfocused and uncomprehending. He does not seem able to move. Should I lift him?

Quietly I call – "Dao."

Alerted by the tone of my voice, within seconds he is beside me. Helpless, we look at Mark, afraid to move him lest we do damage. I speak rapidly into the phone. Dao sits beside him holding his limp, burning hand. At the door I watch the doctor take the front steps two at a time – his face grave. A gentle examination and we listen. Mark needs to be in the children's hospital. Wrapping him in a blanket the doctor lifts him to his car. I stumble behind, some clothes bundled into a bag. Sitting in the back, holding him, I rock him gently and pray. In the driving mirror I see Dao following behind.

The streets are almost empty this early Sunday morning.

Monday morning I slip fitfully in and out of the edges of sleep. I look at my watch – "Almost six – I'll take another look at Mark."

Slipping on my shoes I fumble for the light switch, lost in these strange surroundings. In the ward a nurse bends over the bed taking his temperature. She smiles.

"It's coming down. The consultant will be in about eight; you'll get the chance to speak with him then."

Looking at him asleep and seemingly comfortable between the white sheets I think of the nightmare that was yesterday, so relieved now that he is in professional care. Sitting by his bedside I wait. At seven, the attendant wheels Mark's bed to the lift and downstairs to x-ray and for a lumbar puncture. I walk with them to the door of x-ray, then return upstairs to the empty cubicle.

At eight I am called to sister's office to meet with the consultant. He confirms the details of my son's admission with me, filling in his age of six years and three months. I ask my questions.

"Yes – Mark is gravely ill."

"No – we do not yet have a positive diagnosis but we are leaning towards the strong possibility of Still's disease. We will need further tests to confirm it."

"Yes – it is rare and is an acute form of rheumatoid arthritis which affects children in their young years."

"No – the fluctuating fever is part of the illness."

"Yes – there can be serious complications involving other organs and there is a danger that the illness may become chronic."

"No – it is too early yet to say whether Mark will regain full mobility of his joints; unfortunately, he has the severe form but the fact that he is so very ill is a point in his favour. It has been picked up on instantly."

"No – the cause is not fully known but there is thought to be an inherited factor and this coupled with excessive pressure on the joints –"

I remember Mark's night-rocking and ask no more.

I return to the ward. Mark is back in his bed, awake. I sit holding his hand. Softly, I sing. His eyes close. He sleeps.

And so begin the days and nights of waiting and watching; waiting for confirmation of the diagnosis – waiting to see how he will respond to the powerful combination of penicillin, cortisone and analgesics; watching – watching for signs of recovery, the dropping temperature, the fading rash, the deflation of swollen joints; watching his courageous fight for survival and later for mobility as he inches his way back to movement.

CHAPTER 5

A Time to Learn

Findings

Six weeks into his treatment, Mark's fever has abated and he begins morning physiotherapy sessions at the pool. The hospital library is housed in the same building and, having obtained permission, I wait out these sessions here, searching among the journals. I read much on the pattern of normal child development, and much up-to-date material on organic diseases of childhood. This morning, working backwards along the shelves to material published in the past, I find something new in an old journal. Filed under pathology in a journal entitled *Nervous Child*, I read about eleven children. Each one is identical to Mark – the resemblance uncanny in its uniformity – each child seeming almost a clone.

Reading the classic lucidity of the clinical account I feel I am watching the same mosaic repeated in twelve different frames. Only the intensity of the colour varies. I read on, well able to anticipate what will come next. The paper, written by child psychiatrist Dr Leo Kanner, was, many years before, prepared for a symposium convened to consider the question of how children form the ability to relate emotionally to others – in other words to discuss if we are all "born alike" with regard to our ability to form this "affective contact". Also for discussion at the symposium was a consideration of what part parental attitudes and personalities might play in this development.

Feeling the shades of judgement close in around me once again I push them aside for the moment – my attention riveted now to Kanner's case histories. He considers the symptoms unique enough to form a syndrome. He lists them:

- extreme aloneness

- inability to relate to people in an ordinary way

- when being picked up the child fails to adjust his body to the person holding him

- the child may speak but cannot use language to convey meaning to others

- the presence of an excellent rote memory

- the tendency to lead people by the hand to get what the child wants

- the parrot-like repetition of word combinations already heard – Kanner calls this "echolaliac speech" or "echolalia"

- an obsessive desire to maintain sameness

- monotonous routines leading to lack of spontaneous activity

- the mixing up of personal pronouns using "You" instead of "I"

- a failure to look at faces

- a preoccupation with objects

- a terror of loud noises.

Finally, Kanner ends his list by referring again to that *profound aloneness* which dominates all other considerations.[3]

Raising my head I close the journal – symbolically pushing it away from me. Getting up to remove it further – I hide it back in the corner of the shelf where it must have lain since 1943. But there is no place to hide from what I have learned. One word has changed my world. Because of it life will never be the same again. Around me the library lies empty and silent. I am conscious only of the ticking of a clock. Wrapping my arms around me I hold myself together – listening as it ticks out the seconds – each beat sounding a knell. Far in the distance an ambulance siren dies away. Another patient arrives at the hospital. Coldness rises about me.

Would we have been better not knowing? Then we had hope. Now – one word – *autism* – the enormousness of that challenge – *autism* – an austere word, a comfortless word, forbidding and as uncompromising as the condition itself – *autism*. Of course we had heard of autism but the image the condition conjured up was one of a non-verbal, intellectually disabled, non-active child, living in solitary isolation, untouched by the world around him. Not that of a bright hyperactive toddler immersed in rituals and routines, with a reading ability and with a strong rote memory – cleverly using it to fund his own style of communication.

Kanner had stressed that his eleven young patients all had normal intelligence. So I begin to realize – having normal intelligence does not preclude autism!

I will search no more today. I have found too much. Looking at my watch I think, "Mark will be back in the ward, he'll be missing me."

Shutting the library door firmly behind me I wish I could shut out what I have learned – but it will forever now be a part of me.

Mark has been pronounced out of danger and I no longer have accommodation at the hospital. Driving home through the grey fog of the November night I think about how I will tell Dao. Around me the fog drifts heavily in patches, pierced only by the amber lights of oncoming cars. Cut by the light the gloom of it disperses momentarily, to close in again until the next headlight opens a pathway. My numbed senses find a familiar pattern in this passage of light and night – an echo of hope in those shafts that pierce the darkness. Because has not our work with Mark always been a sequence of dark patches and illuminating moments? Where we have found night, have we not also found light? Why should that stop now? We have found that light before. Then we will find it again. Why let a mere word defeat us? Even a word as awesome as *autism*.

As I approach the outskirts of the city the traffic moves faster. Here the pall of fog lifts. It begins to roll out to sea. Pulling into the driveway I notice Dao is home. Dinner will be ready. I park alongside his car.

Despite the lift in my thinking I lack the courage to face the library over the following days – afraid of what I might encounter. I know now where the beginning is; all I have to do is to proceed from there. Many days later I study Kanner's paper again. As well as being a famous child psychiatrist, Leo Kanner was also a skilled writer. His clarity of expression and the comprehensive detail of his case notes is impressive. Under his pen the children in his care come alive.

Donal T, at five, could recite by rote memory the Twenty-third Psalm and twenty-five questions and answers of the Presbyterian Catechism.

Seven-year-old Barbara K had an extraordinary ability to read and spell, but was obsessed with parts of objects and showed no indication of being able to connect affectively with people.

Paul G, for whom the people around him did not appear to exist, never looked at faces but treated hands as something to be used to get what he wanted and kept himself constantly occupied with objects.

All the children had possessed excellent rote memories and all had exuded that strange aura of aloneness. This aloneness registered more with Kanner than any other aspect of the condition. His wonder at it rises palpably from the pages. He called the condition "early infantile autism" in order to emphasize the fact that it occurred in infancy.

He was, however, sceptical with regard to the advisability of what he called the "stuffing" of such children – children who, while they had excellent rote memory, were not able to use language in any ordinary way. When "stuffed" with such material as psalms, verses, titles of musical scores, botanical names, a French lullaby, an encyclopaedia index page and the like, Kanner felt that it might have the effect of deflecting language to just a memory exercise. He rather thought that (1) it might have been an essential contributory factor to the condition of autism or (2) that it cut severely into the development of language as a two-way communication tool.

I remember my journal entry of two years before when I too had mulled over this same issue and had left it unresolved.

But for now, looking at Kanner's description of how the parents of these children approached their child's autism we, who thought we were unique, find ourselves looking into a mirror because in most cases their approach has been a mirror-image of our own. Why? Perhaps because autism is such a rigid, uncompromising condition that does not yield easily to change. One can only enter into its peculiarities and use them with benevolence to induce change. As we had done with Mark, these parents, so many years before, used the material presented to them by their child and worked with it to extend their child's involvement with the world around him. They had tapped into the strengths of autism, the rote memory and the ability to manipulate word combinations, and had fostered them to achieve communication. It would appear then that the worst approach to autism is to do nothing about it. Given the intransigence of autism, there may be no innate change. Change will have to be moulded from outside.

Some weeks later I study Kanner's work again, this time to see how he regarded these parents of autistic children. He studied them carefully, taking copious notes regarding grandparents and extended family members. Always he looked for evidence as to whether the parents themselves could have caused the condition. In seeking to evaluate this question he became ambivalent, pointing to a great deal of obsessiveness in the backgrounds of the families. He also pointed to a great lack of warmth in most of the parents and to the fact that three of the marriages were "dismal failures". He asked whether this fact could have contributed to the children's condition. And the answer? On balance he considered that because the children's aloneness was there from the very beginning of life it was difficult to attribute it exclusively to parental attitudes. In view of this he felt he must assume that the condition was innate and that the children were born with it.

In the year that followed I would read other papers discussing this same question – "What causes autism?"

Many of the authors of these papers subscribed to the psychogenic theory; that is, the view that autism is a condition of the mind rather than the body. The supporters of this theory assumed that at birth the child was normal but had developed autism as a result of inadequate nurturing, particularly inadequate mothering. The fault on the part of mothers was thought, among other considerations, to lie in the area of poor feeding habits – or giving their child too little tactile experience – or not making enough eye contact – or perhaps not speaking enough to the child. In addition such mothers were seen as abnormal personality types; they were thought to be cold, detached people, even perhaps people who lacked a sense of their own identity.

This view of autism appears to have gained considerable credibility and acceptance. In the light of this acceptance what, then, was the prevailing thinking about treating children with autism?

Again various theories were put forward, the main one being to treat the mothers with psychotherapy and if this were not successful then the child should be taken from home and placed with a foster mother.

Some years later I would meet with two mothers who would tell me that they had been refused services for their child until such time as they would either put their child into foster care or submit themselves for psychotherapy. Both had chosen to take the route of psychotherapy.

Within two years of reading Kanner's paper I find, among a bundle of old magazines bought at a jumble sale, a copy of TIME Magazine, dated 25 July, 1962. In it, in an article entitled "The child is father", I read about an interview given to TIME by Dr Leo Kanner almost twenty years after he had first diagnosed the condition. I quote from it the following extract:

Never Tell a Lie

It takes either a natural mother or a highly specialized expert to get close enough to a child to find out what is going on in his mind, normal or not. And Dr. Kanner is such an expert. His technique is disarmingly simple: be friendly and sympathetic; never lie to a child; never belittle his intelligence.

This approach has worked with the vast majority of the 20,000 child patients Dr. Kanner has seen in 31 years. But there is one type of child to whom even Dr. Kanner cannot get close. All too often this child is the offspring of highly organized professional parents, cold and rational – the type that Dr. Kanner describes as "just happening to defrost enough to produce a child". The youngster is unable, because of regression or a failure in emotional development, to establish normal relations with his parents or other people. He becomes withdrawn into himself. For this condition Dr. Kanner coined the term "infantile autism"... For it there is as yet no uniformly effective treatment.[4]

(Copyright © 1962 TIME Inc., reprinted by permission)

By this time, however, we are beginning to cast off those shackles of parent blame and assert our scientific thinking. Do we qualify?

- Highly organized professional parents – yes.

- Cold and rational, defrosted parents and all that it implies – no.

We have to ask the question – how could a condition as rigid, as conforming and above all as uniform as Kanner's first eleven cases of classic autism possibly have been caused by parental attitudes? It is time to open the shutters and let in the light of common sense. Autism of its very essence cannot possibly be a product of nurture. It has to be a product of nature. The answer has to lie within the genes.

Homecoming

Another early Sunday morning at the hospital and today, unaided, Mark walks the length of the ward flanked by Barry and Dao. Levering himself out of his wheelchair he moves haltingly, inching himself forward – each step an effort – down past the glass partitions of the twin-bedded cubicles, past sister's office with its commanding view of the ward, past the open door of the kitchen – the notched wooden floor-boards rough beneath his feet; he keeps moving to the swinging doors beyond, only courage and determination driving him on to the goal he has set for himself. At the doors Barry and Dao, stooping down, join their crossed hands to make a seat for him and carry him back to his chair. He puts an arm around each shoulder – exhausted but content.

Slowly he regains mobility. Each Sunday now that long walk down the ward becomes easier and seems shorter, until that final Sunday when all three of them – Barry and Dao matching their steps to Mark's – walk in unison to those swinging doors and pass through. *Mark is coming home.*

Tonight I open a new journal.

There is much to record, but where to begin?

Perhaps – starting with the end rather than the beginning – I will record what happened today – our final visit to the hospital consultant exactly one year after Mark's discharge. Mark was today pronounced free of the symptoms of Still's disease and, although the residue will remain in his system, it should not flair up again. It has burned out, the fires have died down, only the ashes remain. All medication can be gradually withdrawn and discontinued and as a result his increased body weight due to cortisone treatment will slowly return to normal.

Today also, at the instigation of the consultant (who had set up the appointment feeling that it might help our son) we saw the hospital psychiatrist. Mark, now well accustomed to hospital routine, co-operates fully with all tests. We remain outside waiting. An hour passes. Our turn comes. Opposite us a kindly father-confessor figure draws us out, listening with great interest to the details of the programme we have set up for Mark. He is impressed, telling us he is learning much from us and that our programme goes far beyond anything they could ever do to help Mark.

No, he will not give a diagnosis – he sees no advantage to labelling young children when there is nothing to be gained by it. Encouraging us to continue our work he comments – "I have only two pieces of advice to give you. Keep Mark happy and keep him on target. Come back and see me in a year or two – tell me more then."

Shaking hands, I find a mist in my eyes. I have stood stoically under censure and berating – kindness, so unexpected, is now what disarms me.

Understanding words

And what of Mark's progress during the past two years? Outwardly the Mark who returns to us from hospital is a changed child but inwardly the challenges remain – existing now in a less flamboyant form. Gone are the hyperactivity, the nightly rocking, the impulsive darting, the overwhelming drive to fulfil his obsessions (although the obsessions themselves remain) and the intense commitment to ritual, although he still clings closely to sameness and routine. Moving slowly, he has become more cautious, more aware of the pitfalls of the world around him and more receptive to sedentary pursuits. At eight years of age, his aloneness is still a tangible force. He merges better into the social scene but is still not a part of it. At a practical level his weight has increased enormously due to cortisone treatment, his entire wardrobe having to be replaced with clothes three or four sizes bigger. Always susceptible to rough-textured fabrics of any kind, Mark's skin has become more sensitive than ever. Manmade fibres cannot be tolerated so we confine our choices to soft brushed cotton and fine wool. Fortunately there is plenty of such material available and skilled hands to knit and sew.

This sedentary year of convalescence has given us the opportunity to turn his attention to board games. He is apathetic about all but two – namely Scrabble and Monopoly. Always loving strange sounds, he now comes to love strange words; chanting them he tests them on his tongue. On the Scrabble board, eager to make as many words as possible, he is disappointed when Barry tells him –

"That's not a real word. You can't make that with those letters. You must try again. Have another turn."

He is learning now by doing and not by rote memorizing. His cognitive faculties are being brought into play. In the process we discover a strange aspect to his association with words. He can use them to good effect to get what he wants, but appears to have little understanding of what the actual words themselves mean. He has not made the connection between meaning and word either in the repetition of our speech or in his learned formula.

We have read much over the last year.

Seeking to hold Mark's interest in stories I have found the perfect answer – adventure stories of the great outdoors combined with an emphasis on food and animals: the Enid Blyton series of Famous Five and Secret Seven stories, some thirty-six books in all. These will prove to be a vital factor for him in both the acquisition and comprehension of speech. Relying on his rote memory he focuses on the dialogue and is now using these learned phrases and sentences to fund his own conversation.

To answer questions he now has three options. He may use his original learned formula. He may repeat (echo) our speech. Or he may answer in "Famous Five" language. If asked, "Do you want some doughnuts Mark?" he may reply – "Do you want some doughnuts Mark?", thus *echoing our speech (echolalia)* to say yes, he does.

Or he may say, "I want doughnuts please", using his *learned formula* to say yes he does.

Or he may reply, "I jolly well do", using *"Famous Five"* language.

His answers are more slow and halting as it becomes obvious that he is choosing between three different options. On occasion he uses bits of all three and will give some bizarre answer such as –

"Do you want jolly well do doughnuts?"

This search for neurotypical speech is obviously frustrating for him but he is very determined about it and struggles hard to get it right. It would appear that he is trying to move away from echolaliac speech and learned formula.

To pause and digress for a moment and ponder further the question of the origins of echolalia in autism, we look at the two aspects of speech around which it appears to revolve. They are syntax and semantics.

- *Syntax* relates to sentence *structure* – putting words together in the right order, as governed by the rules of that language, with the purpose of making a sentence.

- *Semantics* deals with the development of *meaning* in a sentence. Words make up the semantic elements of language. The meaning is in the words. When we share words we share meanings.

A review of the literature on echolalia shows that about three-quarters of children who have autism go through a phase of echolalia on their way to developing functional language. It has been found that the greater the level of speech comprehension of the child, the less will he use echolalia. In other words, the more a child understands speech the less he will echo speech.

Echolalia then would appear to be a transient speech phase associated with poor comprehension.[5] Echolalia, of course, may also occur in the early speech of any young child.

It is also suggested that the actual acquisition of language in children with autism is different from that of the average child. In their early years, due to cognitive difficulties, they cannot develop spontaneous language. Consequently they rely heavily on their *associative memory*. They use this memory to redirect rote-learned tracts of speech which they will then manipulate for suitable situations, as we have seen Mark do.[6] This process is slow and halting to begin with, but over time its users become very adept at slotting in the right phrase, at the right time, to meet the right situation. This gives rise to a type of spontaneous speech, albeit lacking in intonation and inflection and which is often delivered in an imitation of the voice and style of the original source from which it was heard.

Because this speech is derived from blocks of speech already introduced by ear in a given sequence, it will automatically lack the facility of using personal pronouns correctly. We have seen examples of this in Mark's speech. In addition, because this language is being used by association the child will automatically substitute "you" or his name, say, "Mark", for the pronoun "me". In his mind he is "Mark" or "you" because he is constantly being addressed by these words. In turn the other person automatically becomes identified with the "I" or "me". In this way the personal pronouns are reversed.

Much has been written over the years about this reversal of pronouns in the speech of young children with autism and it has been attributed to the child's lack of a sense of identity, lack of the concept of self. But taken in this context of how children with autism acquire speech in blocks, and then manipulate and redirect it, the explanation would appear to be much simpler.

In view of the above, then, and looked at objectively, poor comprehension would appear to be the underlying deficit in Mark's acquisition of speech.

So we set out to improve Mark's word comprehension. On a tray I put ten items and place it beside the Scrabble board. Picking up the cup off the tray I spell it out and ask him to put the word on the board. Taking three letters he makes the word CUP. I pick up the saucer and do likewise. SAUCER appears on the board. Plate, jug, spoon, knife, fork, teapot, sugar, tea, follow. There are ten words on the board and the tray is empty. I ask him to match word with object. All ten are correct.

Some weeks later we turn our attention to abstract words. There are ten black and white pictures of faces on my tray. I put the first one beside him and spell "happy". Taking the five letters he puts HAPPY on the board. I hand him the next and spell "sad". SAD appears on the board. The third photograph depicts FUNNY. When there are ten words nicely spaced on the board. I pick up the pictures, jumble them, hand them back and ask him to match picture with word. All ten are incorrect.

I will leave facial expressions for the moment. They are obviously too complex. I will try drawing situations instead. I draw darkness, a pillow and a sleepy head with clothes up to the chin. I write "sleep". SLEEP comes up on the board. Next frame – the sun streams into the room, a figure sits up stretching, an alarm clock shrills, a cock crows – and I write "awake". AWAKE comes up on the board. At the end of ten such frames I run the "match each one" test. Result – four are correct and six incorrect.

We deserve a pot of tea and some toast. We will leave this "word blindness" for now. Grasping the concept of the abstract will take time and time is what we have to give.

We return to his favourite game – Monopoly. It has aroused his interest in money and has given him the concept of purchasing power. We discover a new trait in his character – he has a competitive spirit and does not like to lose. Usually Barry, Dao and I conspire to let him win.

We introduce card games and deal out hands. Setting up the green baize-topped card table beside his bed we play – Snap, Beggar-my-Neighbour, Pontoon. He joins in. He will cut the cards but never deal. He is not yet dextrous enough for the task. Card games teach him the principle of sequencing, order, and number. We find he has remarkable visual memory skills. Without even appearing to look at the cards he can remember the suits and numbers of the cards that have been played.

A sense of self

To what extent does Mark have a sense of his own identity? Does he really know who he is? Often we have wondered about this. He will not look in a mirror, becoming acutely distressed when confronted by one. On holiday, shortly before he became ill, he refused to walk down the main staircase of the hotel because of a large oval mirror hanging on the stairway. In an hotel without a lift we became backstairs travellers. Over the last few months we have again tried to introduce him to mirrors, only to receive the same reaction. We have abandoned the effort, trying old photographs from the family album instead. The move is successful. Ignoring black/white prints but enthralled by colour, he selects some to mount and frame – choosing to have them hung low down at eye level in his favourite part of the house, the front hallway and corridor. An artistic friend offered to help and joined in the effort by sketching an enlarged, coloured head-and-shoulder image of Mark. It captivates him and holds his attention.

We no longer worry that he will not know what he looks like. But although he will now have available to him pictures of his own likeness to refer to, he is not any nearer to having a sense of self – a true physical-body ego leading to an ego of the intellect. This will have to come from inside – not outside.

The passage of time

We continue to incorporate "time machines" into his day. An old-fashioned glass egg timer sits on the breakfast table.

"Do you want a four-minute egg or longer?"

Turning the timer upside down he watches the orange grains of sand run through the narrows to the glass below – recording the time on his watch. At baking sessions he turns on the oven timer, programming in "thirty-five minutes for bread". I add –

"Call me when the buzzer sounds."

At night-time he winds up the clocks setting the alarm for seven. On Sunday mornings Dao will hand him the brass key for the grandfather clock in the hall – watching him turn the spring slowly as he counts the turns for the next seven days.

Using comic strips we test him on sequencing events on the basis of time. We begin with *Beano* and *Dandy* – comics suitable for his age group, but find that his visual comprehension of the coloured pictures is not equal to the task, simply because the scenes depicted in the pictures involve social situations and interactions. So we return to the drawing board, making our own pictures and putting them into sequence.

We choose simple non-social events that are familiar to him, such as planting vegetable seeds in the spring or harvesting the fruit crop in the autumn. In the spring we depict the sowing of the seeds on trays indoors on the window-sills. Then we show the first shoots breaking through the soil. We draw a man outdoors digging to prepare the ground. We show the sun rising higher in the heavens as the seeds are planted out after frost. The frames move on – the increase in growth – the sun blazing down – the hose watering through the summer months – harvesting in the autumn – to the final frame as the vegetables are brought into the kitchen for cooking. He identifies each frame correctly for what it is, but does not grasp the drift of the sequence. By probing we discover one of the reasons and it is confirmed by some of his earlier comments – a bizarre feature of this time-perception deficit is that *he does not realize that time moves in one direction only* – and that that direction is forward.

One afternoon, sitting beside his bed at the hospital, I was startled to hear him say –

"When you get out of hospital and you're three again will I take you to the zoo again to feed Jill?"

How does one depict the one-way passage of time for another? For some months I tread softly around this obstacle, finally deciding to tap into his visual memory skills. Putting pen to paper I draw images but cannot find the right one. Beside me, he draws two parallel lines and puts some squares on them. Watching I pick it up – a travelling train. I wait. He shades in a flat countryside. Putting down his pencil he is finished. I notice there is no second track. The train will not be coming back. I hesitate – will I? – yes – I draw arrows across my paper. They are all going in one direction. Watching – he copies the arrows until they go off the page.

I write as I speak –

"Time, like the train, goes only one way and that is forward. In time there is no going back. You will never be three again."

He walks away appearing neither to have seen nor heard, but never again was he to talk about returning to the past.

CHAPTER 6

Is There No Sense
in Sensation?

I t is time to give more thought to sensation. How much sense does
sensation make to Mark? We list his difficulties with his senses.

Sound

Mark hears too much; from the sub-sound of a spider's web tearing, to the
rustle of the paper on the chocolate bar, to the roar of the jet flying overhead,
he is tuned into this full spectrum of sound and his hearing range stretches
even beyond it. In his earlier years he had an inbuilt defence mechanism
against heavy sound bombardment. He could tune out the sounds of the
world and switch them off, so giving the impression that he was deaf. But his
link with this outside world has now become so well established that he can
no longer tune it out. Consequently, we seek to protect him where possible
from the pain and debilitating effects of constant or intermittent sound
overload. But while we can exercise control over our own household appli-
ances, barking dogs, garden equipment, cars that will not start – whatever –
we are at the mercy of the sounds of our surroundings. Into these surroundings there has recently flown that noisiest of machines – the helicopter – and
its effect on Mark is devastating.

He appears to be acutely conscious of the vibration of the rotating blades coupled with the noise of the engine. When he hears one flying overhead he will clap his hands over his ears and run screaming for cover to the smallest, darkest cupboard in the house. Here he will sit balancing himself on a cushion with his feet off the ground to reduce the vibration, and will only emerge long after the chopper has become a speck in the distance. When we are out and about, if one flies into our orbit he will become immobilized on the pavement, jamming his fingers into his ears. At times like this the car can be a refuge because the rubber tyres will reduce the impact of the vibration and a car in motion will reduce it even further. But even this solution leaves us with a problem – how do you transport an immobilized, almost nine-year-old boy from the pavement to the car park? Everywhere we go we carry a wad of cotton wool to block his ears. It is of little help to him.

So we consider the feasibility of moving to the countryside. Weekends are spent house-hunting within a radius of fifty miles of the city and we mull over the sheer logistics of such a move. Eventually the priorities of transport to school and the workplace take precedence and we compromise with a small cottage in the heart of the country and yet close to the sea. It will be our refuge for weekends and holidays – particularly earning its place at times like Hallowe'en, New Year's Eve and other firework festivals when we have to leave home, to return in the small hours of the morning when the festivities are over and the last of the explosions have died away.

Meanwhile we try ear plugs to block out sound. They prove unsatisfactory. Mark becomes unhappy with them. They irritate him and prevent him from hearing speech.

He has returned to school this past year – a small establishment catering for about fifty children aged five to nine. He attends mornings only. Academically he copes well, but socially he remains on the fringes, in the group but not of it.

It is here in this school environment that we become most aware of the debilitating effects of prolonged sound exposure. He returns home after the four-hour morning session, his face ashen grey and a white luminous pallor down his nose and upper lip – the result of sensory overload. It is curious, this unhealthy facial pallor, arising as it does from the pain of too much sound. It will take a few hours of quiet at home to shed the overload before his facial colour returns to normal.

We consult an audiology clinic. They run their standards tests for hearing but can only tell us that Mark's hearing ability is within the normal range, emphasizing that their instruments are geared to testing children who hear too little. They have no facilities for testing those who hear too much, nor have they any treatment.

So we are left with the only route we can take – eliminate sounds we can control and escape from those we cannot. But how do you escape from the snail crawling inside your window who keeps you awake at night with the sounds of his slidings? Or from the nocturnal hedgehog scraping his spines on the concrete beneath your window, foraging for a midnight feast? Or the 3 a.m. badger digging nightly beneath the apple tree snuffling wild honey from the bees nest? These denizens of the night also belong in this world and must go their ways and fulfil their destinies.

We will escape when we can then, and be watchful and wary when we cannot. For now we leave his sense of hearing – this most problematic and insoluble of his perceptual faculties – to one side hoping that:

1. he will grow out of his hyperacusis (very acute hearing) or

2. he will become attuned to it and learn to exist with it or

3. that the scientific community will invest resources and research into this area and come up with some answers.

Vision

Mark sees too much; thankfully when it becomes too much for him he can close his eyes and shut out the light, or wrap up in a blanket and cover his head. Unlike too much hearing, he *can* escape from too much seeing – one wishes we had been born with earlids. But does he still view his world through the distorting spectacles of false parameters and fragmented vision?

His concept of linear space has become normalized, of that we are sure. With regard to fragmented vision we can only assume. It would appear to have improved because he is no longer preoccupied with the minutiae of his environment, seeming to take a more holistic view of the world. His perception of depth remains faulty and a troubling facet of it is its inconstancy. Recently, during a visit to an art gallery, he stood immobilized halfway down the curving, chalk-white, stone staircase – trapped between two floors. Going back up the stairs to rescue him I ask what I hope will be the right questions:

"Are your legs tired?"

"Your legs are not tired," he says.

"Are you afraid of the height?"

"You are not afraid of the height, there's no height."

He has given me my clue.

"Is the floor moving or the ceiling?"

"The floor and the ceiling are moving and you're squashed in the middle, you can't move."

I sit down, getting him to sit beside me.

"Now give me your hand and close your eyes – we'll slide down together."

We count as we slide – fifteen steps to the floor below. Around us astonished and disapproving gallery attendants and visitors alike look on. Never again will we climb that white, curving staircase.

He still looks through people as if they were made of glass and still scans his environment. Walking through this environment without appearing to look at it, he is yet conscious of everything in it. If an ornament is changed in place on a table or sideboard, on entering the room he will move directly there and change it back to where it was. This action will be carried out without his appearing to look at the object and with his gaze focused at infinity.

It is as if his surroundings become blueprinted on his subconscious mind the first time he sees them and that from then on he navigates his world by reference to this blueprint. If everything does not conform exactly to this photograph in his mind he becomes disturbed and has to put it right. This would account for his obsession with sameness, routine and ritual.

How can we move him on to viewing and photographing his environment with his adaptable conscious mind rather than relying on rigid subconscious memory?

Sensory receptors

Touch

Mark may feel too much or he may feel too little. His face is oversensitive to touch – feeling too much he will flinch at a light touch on the face. Conversely, his hands are undersensitive. However, tactility is the sense we have been most successful in altering. Mark is now more receptive to human touch, having grown from the one-and-a-half-year-old toddler who, when picked up, fought so hard to get free, to an affectionate eight-year-old who loves to cuddle up for a bed-time story. His reaction to pain also has become more normalized. At the time of his illness he appeared to break through the pain barrier. Perhaps the year on analgesics altered the action of the neurotransmitters at their receptor sites to render them more capable of registering pain. He is now able to feel pain and locate where it is coming from.

By contrast he has difficulty making sense of his internal sensations. The sensory receptors responsible for monitoring the sensations from his internal environment function poorly, giving no advance warning of either thirst or fatigue. We have learned never to leave the house without a large bottle of water in a handbag, a pocket, or the boot of the car – too often we have had to drive miles to the nearest store to purchase water or else beg some from a nearby house. Without warning Mark will suddenly come to a halt, unable to walk another step until he gets water. A notice on the back of the front door reads –

"Always drink a glass of water before you leave the house and take a bottle with you."

Temperature

Mark does not have a normal awareness of the heat/cold concept. As a toddler crawling around the kitchen it proved impossible to keep him away from the heating stove. Although it was hedged in by two fireguards, he could still get close enough to feel the heat of which he did not seem to be aware. In his second summer we solved the problem by changing our heating system to an outside oil-fired boiler.

He will sit sweltering in heavy clothes on the hottest day in summer and run in his bare feet and shirt sleeves around the garden in the frost. Does he not feel the sensation of heat or cold? Or is it that he does feel it, but is not able to decipher the sensation or relate it to the cause?

Whatever the reason, we set out to make him aware of the phenomenon by relating it to scale, again working on the principle that if one does not have an intrinsic evaluation of a concept then perhaps an intellectual evaluation of it can be acquired and substituted. Taking advantage of his newest fixation with measurement and scale we introduce thermometers, and basins of water all at different temperatures; as he measures he feels, calling out the figures which we record. We hope that over time this practice will stimulate these underactive skin receptors.

Faulty feedback

His sense of proprioception (the sense organs of which are located in his muscles and tendons), which should send a constant stream of information to the brain about the position of his limbs at any given moment, also fails him. As a result, as previously mentioned, at times he is not able to locate his arms and legs when he wants to, having no intuitive feel for where they are. When this happens he becomes dependent on his vision to locate them, and if he cannot see them he is lost. In order for Mark to see them successfully, both arms and legs must be clothed and he must always wear long trousers and long-sleeved shirts. He himself insists on this and prefers bright colours. Apparently, when his limbs are not covered, they are less visible to him or they may appear to be detached from his body and floating.

No-pressure suit

Environmental pressure is a sensation which Mark craves and actively seeks out. This would indicate underactivity in the pressure receptors in the skin or in the parts of the brain to which they send signals. He loves to wrap up tightly in a rug and roll around the carpet. At the beach he will bury his arms and legs in the wet sand, piling it up around him and will finish each day rolling down the "rumpadump."

Gravity is free-floating

Mark's vestibular system (located in the semicircular canals of the inner ear), which should send recurrent messages to the brain informing it of the position of the body in relation to gravity and the space around him, also malfunctions. As a result, when he was a toddler he walked off walls and vaulted over the bars of the cot, or walked into ponds seeming to have no awareness that they were there.

The work in the swimming pool has been of immense benefit in improving his sense of pressure and of gravity. More recently he has joined the children's yoga classes at the sports complex by the pool. The slow, controlled movement of body positions in yoga appeals to him and he derives immense satisfaction from both classes and home practice sessions. He particularly likes the asanas and inverted poses, and has perfected the shoulder stand. It is almost as if he were giving the impression that he is aware of what he lacks and when the opportunity and direction present themselves he will use them to help himself.

Some insights

Casting about for some answers to this dysfunction of sensory perception we find a book entitled *The Ultimate Stranger*. It was written by Dr Carl H. Delacato.[7] In it, the author described his work with a number of children with autism who had been referred to him for help in dealing with their problem behaviour.

He began by studying the children carefully and, drawing on his past experience over many years with children who had a range of disabilities such as blindness and deafness, came to the conclusion that these children with autism suffered from distorted sensory perception. This led him to conclude that their problem behaviours (rocking, screaming, handbiting, acting deaf and tuning out the world, hand twirling, spinning, head banging, self-injurious behaviour, slapping themselves and many more such behaviours) were an attempt by the children to cure their faulty sensory perception. He called these behaviours "sensoryisms".

He realized very early on that wise old adage that we had been so slow to learn, namely that *every behaviour tells a story*. Look at the story being acted out and then look behind it to find the root cause.

Delacato was sure that children with autism were not psychotic – rather it was that their sensory systems were damaged. Reading with intense interest, we are already beginning to look at Mark in a new light and with new hope.

He classified his young patients into three groups with regard to their five senses –

1.   those who were overstimulated

2.   their opposites who were understimulated

3.   a third category – those who were plagued by interference in the system. He called this interference "white noise" and pointed out that this white noise could occur in any of the five senses.

He came to realize that the most difficult behavioural problems were seen in those children who were oversensitive to sound and who had white noise interference in their sense of hearing. These white noise children could not cut out low background noises such as the humming coming from a fluorescent light and could in fact hear their own internal organs working, their food being digested and their blood circulating, particularly in the area around the ears.

This massive sensory interference, he considered, would greatly hamper their ability to deal with the world. Furthermore, they would be unable to concentrate on speech sufficiently well to acquire it. Writing of their screaming outbursts, their ashen grey faces and how they became agitated during times of barometric change (because this brought changes in their internal environment), he painted a vivid picture of how difficult life is for such children, and how challenged they must be. He recommended keeping them occupied constantly with speech, talking to them, and not letting them listen to their own sounds.

He did, however, make clear that these were very noisy children in their own right – they made a lot of noise themselves and that this fact had often confused parents. He considered their noisiness to be one of their sensoryisms. It was their attempt to drown out the noise around them and substitute their own noise for it. On plugging up their ears with wax he saw their behaviours change dramatically.

He moved on then to consider the hypervision and white noise vision child, and here again we see Mark come alive on the pages. These were the children who saw too much when viewing objects but who looked through people as if they did not exist. They acted as if they were very carefully watching something in the distance but it was something that was not there.

He remarked on their dilated pupils, recalling vividly to our minds the fact that for the first six years of his life Mark's eyes had been like large round orbs. Delacato travelled a path with these children now familiar to us when he wrote of their fixations with machines with moving parts, clocks with visual running parts – anything that would twirl and cause optical illusions. He highlighted their phenomenal memories, their astounding visual recall, their early reading ability, their dislike of mirrors.

His list grew longer and we could identify with everything on it. The resemblance was uncanny – culminating in the rhythmical body rocking and the compulsive watching of moving cars. He drew our attention to one illuminating facet of white noise vision of which we had been unaware, when he revealed that for children such as these, people *per se* may lack constancy and substance and may become vague and shadowy forms. If such a revelation could be substantiated for Mark it would give some explanation as to why for so many years we have appeared to be invisible to him and why at times we still feel that he does not recognize us and would pass us by if we did not speak first.

We learned much from Delacato's treatment of children who had mal-functioning of the sense organs of the skin. He wrote of Susan who, like Mark, could not feel her hands and who constantly bit them in an attempt to normalize the communication channel between hand and brain. He outlined the treatment that cured her of this biting. It took the form of stimulation of the skin of both hands and forearms using deep pressure, exposure to tem-perature change (iced water alternating with hot water), rough towelling and similar treatments, until such time as she was able to feel her hands normally and then of course she did not bite them because they hurt and felt painful.

This highlights for us a possible solution to a new type of problematic behaviour looming on our horizon. Mark, who still cannot tie his shoe-laces and who, although he has given up hand biting and is more comfortable with his hands, in frustration at not being able to tie the laces, is now slapping his hands and calling out "Hands won't do what they're told".

We will work out a course of such treatment.

Still considering the child who feels too little, Delacato held that children whose sensory receptors are underactive can be hurt and will not cry because they are not capable of feeling pain. By contrast, the overtactile child will feel too much because he is overstimulated, and will reject touch coming from outside. He mapped out a programme for dealing with this, the basis of which involved increasing the child's tolerance to touch. One of the hallmarks of such a child is that he or she feels warm to the touch and will perspire easily.

On reading I pause here, and lift my eyes from the book to remember how during Mark's illness I had been questioned so often and by so many doctors with regard to my son's excessive, night-time perspiration pattern, a pattern that we had grown used to over the years but which they had not encountered before. Now we have the reason if not the solution.

Delacato then referred to the mixed-states children who bring confusion into the picture because, like Mark, these children will experience some parts of the body as oversensitive – for example the face – while other parts such as the hand will be undersensitive. He gave guidelines on how to alleviate both conditions and outlined what are the hallmarks to look for.

Finally he discussed what is perhaps the most distressing aspect of mal-function in the tactile system in his reference to tactile white noise children – children who itch permanently, whose skin shivers, ripples and crawls for no apparent reason – children who are subject to tactile outbursts of slapping themselves or others and who then become calm for a period of time until the next outburst builds up again.

Delacato's work with children with autism gives us much to reflect upon. Its insights are sobering in their depiction of the pain and discomfort involved in living with faulty sensory perception. But they are also enlightening in their exposure of the root cause that lies behind many of the bizarre behaviours seen in autism – the way in which they make sense out of sensoryisms. Now that we have a greater understanding of Mark's behaviour, and even if the basic cause cannot be removed, coping strategies can be worked out and the situation managed more effectively. This book has crystallized for us just how much Mark is at the mercy of his malfunctioning senses and probably will always be so, to a greater or lesser extent. The key to successful management then is knowledge and forward planning. With knowledge comes insight and the ability to do something about it.

Our understanding of faulty sensory perception in autism has now been much enlightened and it is further illuminated by a paper entitled "Perceptual inconstancy in early infantile autism". This was written by Drs Ornitz and Ritvo.[8]

Following an in-depth discussion of the symptoms of autism, a consideration of their own cases and a review of the literature on autism to date, they ask whether it is possible to relate the symptoms of autism to an underlying pathological (disease) condition. They answer it by pointing out that all the symptoms can be viewed as arising from certain *developmental failures* that occur in the first year of the child's life. They list three failures:

1. a failure on the part of the infant to *distinguish* between himself and the outside world

2. an absence or delay of the ability to *imitate*

3. a failure in the infant's ability to *regulate* what he perceives in the world around him.

This results in his getting either too much or too little input from his environment. Following on from this, then, the feedback to the senses from the same environment, which should be stable, will be constantly changing. This in turn will lead to *inconstancy of perception*. To sum up, they consider that these failures can be explained by the assumption that autistic children "do not have the ability to maintain constancy of perception."

"Inconstancy of perception" – what is the reality behind the words and what does it translate into in terms of daily living? "Perception" is defined as the mental faculty whereby we recognize an object because we receive back from it certain sensations which are identical to those we had previously received from a similar object. "Inconstancy" – the word means changeable, variable, always altering.

Add the two together and they conjure up a nightmare world of instability. Small wonder then that for so long Mark has navigated his world by sound. Sound has obviously always been for him the most stable of his senses, whereas the sense of sight has always appeared more unstable. We retain our vivid memories of the child who walked onto air and into water.

We now have to come to grips with this third dimension to his distortion of perception – its inconstancy – the fact that the feedback from any given stimulus in his surroundings may be in a state of constant change, thus sending back different signals at different times from the same object. This would explain why, at times, we ourselves still do not appear visible to Mark. We have worked out coping strategies for too much stimulus and too little stimulus from each of his sensory modalities but have not recognized in him the phenomenon of *fluctuating feedback*. In other words, we have not thought in terms of inconstancy of perception, except possibly in the case of depth perception.

What, if anything, could be done about it?

Flashback

Finishing the sentence I close my journal to collect my thoughts. Seconds later I hear running feet thundering up the front steps and a young voice calling –

"Anyone there? Anyone there?"

Throwing open the front door I face a breathless Darren panting – "Come quick, come quick – Mark's been knocked down by a truck and he's nearly dead". Running fast down the steps I think – "How could it have happened? I told him to stay on the footpath and not to go beyond the bridge".

Rounding the corner I see the bridge. Closer, I see a limping Mark coming towards me supported by Barry. Beyond them a bicycle lies across the pathway, both wheels mangled. Black tyre marks show where the truck had rounded the bridge too fast, mounted the pathway and then, as the driver gained control, had veered off again to continue up the hill to the right. My eyes follow the tracks of the hit-and-run vehicle.

At the hospital Mark lies quietly on the x-ray table. His bruised left leg, which has taken the brunt of the impact, is being checked out for a possible break. Showing us the x-ray the radiologist assures us that, apart from bruising, Mark leg is not damaged. They have found no new injury. He is, however, curious about – "That old injury in Mark's left ankle where that large chip of bone, see there, has become detached – obviously it happened some years ago". He wonders why it was never checked out.

We tell him the story of Mark's inability to feel pain in his younger years and the consequent search for evidence of Perthes' disease.

I feel vindicated, thankful at last to have Mark's mysterious limp explained.

CHAPTER 7

Islets of Ability and Disability

July and August herald the holiday season and we transfer to our little grey cottage in the west to recuperate and regenerate. Here, away from the city environment, Mark unwinds and relaxes, losing much of his keyed-up tension. These are halcyon, timeless days of sun, sea and sand, of bright dawns, flaming sunsets and long indigo twilights: days of tramping over purple heather and by yellow gorse, of climbing the lower slopes of lofty mountain peaks towering into mysterious haze and picnicking in serene valleys clothed in softest green. Here against this backdrop of scenery and silence Mark's ashen grey pallor fades into nothingness and he sheds much of that coiled-spring-like tension – that feeling of being stretched almost to breaking point that seems necessary for him just to maintain his momentum in a hostile environment. In the absence of it we become aware of more fundamental problems simmering below the surface.

Stimulus

The first of these problems is that he cannot cope with taking more than one instruction at a time as if he is only capable of responding to one component of a stimulus at a time. If asked to "Pick up the book and place it on the table", he will pick up the book but it will never reach the table. If told to "Run back and get your swim-suit and bring the ball as well", he will get the swimsuit but never the ball. If encouraged to "Listen to the blackbird – see him over there on the yellow gorse", he will either hear the blackbird or see the yellow gorse, but does not seem capable of responding to both stimuli at the same time; as if he could not synchronize his senses of sight and hearing and use both together. At nine years of age and entering mainstream school in a few months' time, this lack of response will place him at a serious disadvantage when compared to his peer group.

In my teacher-training course I had studied something of the field of psychology in the area of children's ability to respond to surrounding stimuli and was aware that research had shown that from early infancy babies can respond to complex stimuli: that is, a stimulus with more than one component to it. It had also been found that, as they grow older, babies actually prefer complex stimuli to simple stimuli and that the average child of seven to eight years would have no difficulty in responding to an instruction containing three to four components: for example, "Change your shoes, pick up your school-bag off the floor, and put it in the press". By that age also they should be able to register and synchronize perfectly the senses of sight, hearing and touch.

Harking back to Mark's babyhood we remember his accurate imitation of dog-barking sounds, thus proving that he is capable of responding to a range of different pitches and frequencies within the sound bandwave. Hearing complex stimuli then do not present a problem to him. However, we have no such proof that he can respond to complex stimuli in sight. Hoping to get further information on this whole area of stimulus response I retrieve my psychology notes from the top shelf of the bookcase.

Delving through them I find a description of an enlightening piece of research, undertaken to find out if there were any differences in the way three diverse groups of children respond to a complex stimulus containing the elements of hearing, sight and touch. The three diverse groups were:

1. children without a disability

2. children with intellectual disabilities and

3. children with autism.

The results were conclusive showing that –

1. the non-disabled children responded on the basis of all three components

2. the children with intellectual disabilities responded on the basis of two

3. while the children with autism responded only on the basis of one out of the three components.

The group of researchers then set out to teach these children with autism how to respond to more than one stimulus at a time by giving them such instructions as: "Put the white spoon in the cup on the table", a stimulus containing four components. The experiment was successful. The children were then, over time, able to build on this foundation and move on to coping with more complex multicomponent stimuli.[9]

We have the answer.

It would be so easy to apply it were it not for our old enemies – crippling inertia, zero motivation and a great reluctance to interact at any level with the outside world. Food no longer works as a motivator. For a number of months Mark has regressed, falling back more and more into ritual and perseverated sameness; at times he will even sit and rock, his dilated pupils transforming his eyes into orb-like lamps. He has slipped away from us yet again to some unknown plateau where we cannot reach him. Sometimes we feel we may lose him for ever to this land of his retreat. The attraction of this inner world for him is obviously far greater than anything we can provide him with in the real one. Or perhaps the effort required to live in the real world at times just becomes too great.

This pattern of behaviour is becoming obvious in his life-cycle – a period of mental growth and progress will be followed by a period of withdrawal and stagnation. Perhaps he does need to withdraw in order to consolidate his gains, but he does not seem capable of breaking out of that stagnation by himself, and if left to his own devices will recede further and further into it. The motivation for change always has to come from outside and it has to be strong.

Mark, now in his tenth year, still has to be kept actively engaged with this world on a daily basis. This we have found to be the most wearisome aspect of the autistic condition – this constant one-way interaction – there can be no let-up. Mark can never be left mentally unattended because his embryonic amnion regenerates itself hourly and unless pruned away daily it has the potential to close over and harden – to re-form, again, that original, all-encompassing shell.

We are reminded day by day of how tenuous is his hold on the very environment in which he lives – of how fragile is his every dawn and of how easily it could be snuffed out. Slowly we come to a realization of the intransigence of the condition that is called autism and we wonder at what age, or if ever, Mark will become self-propelling.

Looking outwards

Writing in my journal tonight I ask the question – "So what now will we use to entice him to look again at this world around us?" Blankly I stare at the empty page. Nothing stirs in my imagination. I look at the sentence in silence – and from somewhere comes an echo – "this world around us". Clutching, as if at a straw, I grasp at it and quickly pen it before it escapes from me. "That's it – that's what we will use – the seashore, the rock pools, the butterflies, the birds…" My pen trails off – I need write no more.

Early next morning Barry and Dao are dispatched to the shops for supplies and by noon we appear on the shoreline with four new, coloured buckets and spades, as well as an assortment of coloured containers, shrimp nets and butterfly nets. The assault on the stimuli begins. Rewards are offered for "Whoever finds: the highest number of smooth, black, mussel shells; the most pearly, rough, oyster shells; the greatest number of creamy, spiral whelks and the biggest bucket of oval, brown cockles."

We gather around Dao as he explains the difference, handing each shell to Mark for us to see. I give the instructions – "Remember now, the black mussels go into the blue bucket, the pearl oysters into the white, the spiral whelks to the red and the brown cockles into the black". I put a label on each bucket.

We split into teams. Barry and Dao take the lower shore. Mark and I take the upper. By picnicking time there are hundreds of shells in the buckets, of which Mark has found just one – one oval, brown cockle shell.

Some days later we bring the buckets to the shore again, this time to collect pebbles – rough, smooth, green, white shiny quartz, old red sandstone, black limestone – whatever we can find. By tea-time there are just three stones in Mark's bucket.

A week later it rains, and looking at our fine collection of interesting shells and curious stones piled up in a corner of the patio, we decide to put them to good use. Dao mixes cement and lays the foundation for an extension to the covered patio. Barry and I spread the wet cement and talk about the patterns and mosaics we will make on it. Mark, taking no part in the work, remains in the house. I suggest, "When we're finished, Barry, how about making concentric circles of just mussels on this patch". He agrees, saying, "Yes, but we'll have to sort that pile again". Our trowels move fast, the cement smooths out, and we stand back to admire our finished handiwork. Behind me I hear – "You get all the smooth black mussel shells and put them in the blue bucket" and turn to find Mark holding the blue bucket which is full of just mussel shells.

"You'll get the oval brown cockle shells in the black bucket. You'll put all the shells and stones in parallel lines."

A few hours later the wet cement is covered with parallel lines of shells and stones neatly arranged in rows: two rows of identical shells followed by two rows of stones, if possible in the same or nearest colour. They run the length of the patio. Mark has decreed that there will be no concentric circles. Covered in wet cement he is back with us again and very much on target. It is the most dramatic turn-about we are ever to witness in him. Unwittingly, we have tapped into his fixation with shape and have broken some, for him, cardinal rule by suggesting circles. Always his concept of shape has been linear; circles, concentric or otherwise, will not be tolerated!

Encouraged and enthusiastic again we continue with our assault on the stimuli. At low tide, hanging over the rocks, we gaze down into the sunlit waters of the rock pools, Mark's now focused eyes taking in this cosmos of the littoral zone between the tide-marks. Below us the yellow-green shore crabs awkwardly sidewalk across the rock face, while their pink hermit brethren hide in whelk shells deep in the corners. Nearby the red anemones hang just under the surface, tentacles wafting, feeding in the clear crystal water. Above them their green, snakelocks cousins, reduced now to mere blobs, press against the dry rock and so avoid dehydration. They await the return of the tide when they too will expand to feed again.

A living sea urchin meanders across the pool rolling its round, purple skin rhythmically, balanced on a million, slender, tube feet. A ripple disturbs the tranquillity and the mood when the brown-speckled Blenny fish lunges from a dark corner to seize an unwary prey – darting back again to devour it in the shadows. Day by day, Mark becomes more enthralled with these denizens of the deep and this world of the survival of the fittest. By the end of the season he can name many of its inhabitants.

Isolated islets

Over the months that follow we notice a change in Mark's visual patterning. His compulsive fixation with shape continues but he is now focusing on larger and larger objects as if the cracks in his fragmented vision are beginning to knit together, making it possible for him to see a larger picture and thus take a more global view of his surroundings.

Bridges and lighthouses become his main preoccupation and we find ourselves enticed into photographing every bridge and lighthouse within radius of a hundred miles of home. Many of these autumn and winter weekends are spent standing in rushing water photographing Mark's beloved arches – arches of geometrically precise blocks of grey granite. He thrills visibly at the sight of these tunnels and, as always for him, small is more beautiful. It is to be the beginning of his love affair with bridges.

At Christmas time he gets a surprise present of a camera and he joins in the effort, taking his own pictures. The collections are pasted onto cardboard to hang on the walls of the den. Dao manages to secure a coloured chart of every lighthouse around our own and neighbouring coastlines, and produces with it a copy of *Reed's Nautical Almanac*.

Within weeks Mark can recite at will the exact specifications of every lighthouse around our coast – giving name, location, position, height, single flash/group flash, quick single flash/quick group flash, isophase one/isophase two, three, occult single flash/occult group flash, fixed flash red/green/white sectors, fixed flash, white/red sectors, fixed flash white/red/green sectors, red/green occasional – all of these variations being related to time, in seconds, from one to forty. This information has been gleaned unaided from the almanac and the chart. When asked for the data, relating to any one of the more than one hundred lighthouses involved, he will readily give all the above details from memory.

This is not just an exercise based on rote memory, nor is it the parroting of word combinations. Rather, it results from a firm grasp of the underlying principles on which the scheme is based. For example, he is aware that the coloured sectors are based on the degrees of the compass. Consequently, he visualizes the 360-degree radius of the compass in his mind and uses this to distinguish between the sectors. A number of lighthouse beams are visible from both home and the cottage and he will stand for hours at the window, stop-watch in hand, measuring the length of the flash and recording it.

We are now seeing what are obviously *islets of ability*. These are areas of extraordinary talent and intelligence that have always been associated with a percentage of people who have autism. In his original paper in 1943 Leo Kanner referred to this facet of autism when commenting on his child patients' astounding rote memories, excellent recall of events from previous years, and phenomenal recollection of "complex patterns and sequences". He referred to them as "islets of ability", adding that they were a forecast of good intelligence.[3]

It becomes obvious now that Mark is following in this pattern. He is combining his powerful capacity for visual imagery with his exceptional rote memory to record and reproduce at will what is in fact an extraordinarily complicated visual sequence, of rotation, number and colour, and all set against a background of specific varying time limits. If asked for the specifications of, for example, the Tuskar Rock lighthouse, his answer will be, "Latitude: 52 degrees 12 minutes north; longitude: 6 degrees 12 minutes west; height: 33 metres; rotating, group flash 2, 7.5 seconds; range 27 miles". For Roches Point lighthouse it will be, "Mainland, height 30 metres, occulting, white/red sectors, 20 seconds, range 20 miles."

One wonders if this feat of recall would have been within the capacity of the ordinary intelligent mind. What would it require to perfect the skills needed to achieve such a goal? Given the basic requirements of imagery and memory, it would require such intense interest as to amount to a fixation/obsession, a capacity for isolated single-minded concentration and an inordinate amount of time spent occupying the mind with a single replicateable set of facts. In other words, the ability to perseverate on the variations of a single repetitive theme.

Is this not autism in its purest, most basic form, and are not these qualities the very strengths of autism? There is talent here, could it but be put to constructive use. We become excited by this new development and see potential in it – perhaps the long-term potential for future employment. This excitement is, however, sobered by the realization that these islets of ability float in lacunae of disability.

Is it possible that they may have been propelled above the surface at the expense of other areas which remain submerged? Will a time come when we see a junction ahead and find ourselves faced with a choice either to foster this considerable talent or to sacrifice it to the development of an ordinary global mind? But perhaps the two could be tempered to run in harness. It will depend to what extent, if any, this excessive preoccupation with a single theme, at this age, will hinder the development of normal intelligence and cognitive growth. We can but watch and wait.

On reflection, of course, I realize that we will never have to choose. That choice will not be ours to make. The subject matter occupying these islets of ability is entirely personal and related only to Mark's will. It will never be influenced from outside. He may abandon these oases of extraordinary intelligence as readily as he sought them out. Then they may submerge again.

In the meantime it is for him a fulfilling hobby, albeit somewhat isolating; and he derives enormous enjoyment from it, always busy with his charts and almanac. Watching him at work one cannot but be struck forcibly by his calmness. Under the influence of this intense interest and absorption his anxieties and coiled-up tensions seem to have just fallen away. He has shut out the world – he is alone but he is relaxed. Mark is happy even if he is not "on target."

Strange shapes from out the sky

Perseveration continues – only the focus changes. Within a year his attention is shifting to other, larger objects – aircraft. He has not lost his interest in bridges or lighthouses; rather, he is now ready to add to this list another strange object that has impinged on his visual consciousness. On an evening visit to a remote airstrip we watch a solitary Cessna aircraft coming in to land against the backdrop of the fiery rays of a setting sun. Circling the sky, becoming larger and larger, the illuminated yellow monoplane finally drops to earth like some exotic, outsize bird. The experience is more than enough to press the red alert on the want-to-do-it button and we watch Mark, quivering with excitement, swing into action again.

The preoccupation with aircraft begins.

Mark's reaction to the aircraft recalls to mind the observations of Professor Oliver Sacks who, in his discussion concerning these extraordinary talents in individuals with autism, writes that it may be that there is a "neuromodule", that is, a highly specialized, hugely developed system somewhere in the brain, and that when the appropriate stimulus, e.g. something visual, impinges on this neuromodule at the appropriate moment, it will trigger a response and the system will swing into operation with full force.[10]

For Mark the Cessna is to trigger a preoccupation with aircraft that is set to become the dominant preoccupation of his life and, as the heroes of aviation become his heroes, it indicates for him a significant transition away from the inanimate to the animate. Lighthouses and bridges can stand alone but aircraft need pilots. Up until now the object *per se* has always been the focus of his fixation; now the object and the man, machine and pilot together, become the focus and he begins to develop a people concept. It is a significant move forward for a young ten-year-old for whom people have had but a vague, shadowy existence and who to date has mainly peopled his world with objects.

Now he becomes familiar with the great names of the aviation world – with Alcock and Brown and their non-stop Atlantic flight in the Vickers Vimy, with Charles Lindbergh who flew the same route solo in a monoplane, with Amy Johnson in her D H Moth on the long Croydon to Australia run, with Amelia Earhart, who disappeared on a round-the-world flight in her Lockheed Electra, and with the many others who have found their places in the annals of history.

But his real heroes become and remain the great flying aces of the two World Wars – among them that French prince of aces René Fonck and his German counterpart the Red Baron – Erich von Richthofen. Filed in rank they appear on the walls of the den to take their places among the curving arches of bridge tunnels and the striking, coloured columns of lighthouses.

Searching the shelves of the second-hand bookshop in the village, Mark himself finds and purchases, with a month's pocket money, two photographic manuals which include the descriptions and specifications of every aircraft flown in each of the two World Wars. This is the period of aviation he will become most knowledgeable about and within weeks of buying the manuals he has committed to memory the exact details of every aircraft listed in these books – including wing span, speed, bomb load, armament, engine design and horsepower, propeller design and mechanism, country of origin, flight type, ceiling and range. He never develops an interest in modern aviation; the shape and uniformity of modern aircraft having no appeal for him.

On these same bookshelves I later find what will become the jewel of his book collection – a series of books written by another flying ace of the first World War, Captain W.E. Johns – the Biggles books – some thirty books in all. These are the first storybooks he will read entirely by himself and they stimulate a lifelong interest in adventure stories. Also, because they contain wonderful passages of visual imagery, they provide him with a vehicle of words which he can use to describe his own not inconsiderable powers of visual imagery.

One day

Today we stand in line at the aeronautics museum awaiting Mark's turn to sit in the cockpit at the controls of a De Havilland Rapide aircraft – a special treat for today, his eleventh birthday. As he quivers with excitement and tension, his dilated pupils appear oblivious to their surroundings. His turn comes. He climbs in. He stares straight ahead with eyes unfocused. Sitting perfectly still he does nothing and appears to see nothing. The attendant calls "next please" and his turn is over.

Mentally I compare him with the previous occupant of the seat, a boy of about his own age who had twisted every available knob, lever and dial – some real, some imaginary – twisting with it his entire body in a perfect simulation of acrobatic flight, all accompanied by his own appropriate sound-score.

Disappointed for Mark we think that perhaps he has been overcome by sensory overload resulting from the noise and the crowd. We will try to organize a visit at a quieter time.

A week later Mark takes a number of large sheets of Bristol Board from the press in the den and sets to work on the floor. By now being well used to stepping over the work in progress I do not focus on it until it faces me propped up on three chairs in the corner. Going over to look, I see what appears to be a life-size representation of the interior of the cockpit of an aircraft. Could it be the De Havilland Rapide? Unbeknown to him I decide to check. I manage to acquire a photograph of the inside of the cockpit as Mark had seen it that day and can find no fault in his representation. It is accurate down to the last detail.

This representation remains in the corner of the den for the next three or four years and is subject to constant changes depicting take-off, landing and many different flying conditions – all of which necessitate corresponding changes in the dials. This is done by having at least six different sets of dial readings that can be stuck on and subsequently removed as the need arises.

On his birthday Mark's islets of ability were indeed on red alert.

We wait for the day when he will draw up a chair and sit at his own controls, simulating flight. It never happens. His interest lies only in recording what is perceived – in noting down what meets the eye. He has yet to bridge the gap between perceiving and so acquiring knowledge and applying the results of this perception. This, when it happens, will be a giant step forward. When he has achieved it he will then be in a position to move into the world of pretend play and so develop the mimicry of imaginative behaviour.

CHAPTER 8

An Uneven Playing Field

Decisions

Two years into his formal education it is time to assess Mark's school progress. At nine years of age he began mainstream junior school in a small private establishment a few miles from home and in the countryside. In a country and in an era where there was no special provision for education for a young person with autism, we had thought long and hard about the educational options open to us.

There were three.

The first was to continue to educate him ourselves at home. Because we had been following this option since he was eighteen months old we felt that to continue it would be too confining and would limit his potential. In addition, it would not prepare him for living in the real world. He needed to move forward then and break into the system before he reached his teenage years when the transition would become much more difficult.

We have come to realize that the older Mark grows the more obvious his differences are and the more he stands out from the crowd. Up to the age of about six he got by on the fringes of the group but by the time his peers moved into their seventh year they began to pull away rapidly, forging ahead, and he was left behind. His foundation for the rapid development of these important years had not yet been laid down, while theirs had developed in the first and second years of life and had been solidified since then by progress.

With hindsight we can pinpoint exactly when Mark's differences began to show up and when he began to lose developmental ground. It was not in the first year of life but in the second. Although his autism was there from birth it only began to become apparent (that is, apart from his nightly rocking) when he entered his second year of life. At the end of his second year his developmental delay was firmly established.

Even though we have managed with our programme to halt some of this developmental regression we have not been successful in halting it to a significant degree. Consequently, as he grows older, that initial delay has become more and more compounded, resulting now in a very uneven developmental profile. It shows up with significant gaps in it as well as great strengths: strengths far in advance of those of his peer group lying side by side with serious deficiencies.

Our second option is to enrol him in a school for young people with mixed diagnoses and degrees of disability – such as emotional disturbance, learning disabilities, sight and hearing impairments and other conditions. In view of Mark's own sensory impairments we know that this environment will not be suitable for him. His needs could never be met.

So we turn our attention to the third option of mainstream school and decide on this. We are fully aware that it is the most difficult choice for both Mark and ourselves. The challenges are formidable. And the chances of success? Only time will tell.

We choose the type of school that offers him the best chance of survival. This entails small class sizes of no more than fifteen children, a varied curriculum including non-academic subjects such as woodwork, music, art and hobbies and a strong emphasis on outdoor activities – gardening, swimming, gym and sports.

The decision made, a key question concentrates our minds – should we inform the school that Mark has autism?

We decided to follow the advice of the wise hospital consultant who had told us – "Never label your son. Let people see the person, not the disability. Never highlight it with a label. If you do, others will focus on the disability and Mark will become synonymous with it. Do not fetter him, rather let him be free to find his own place in the world." Looking back now over the last two years, with hindsight we ask – "Was this a wise decision?"

We can answer with clarity and conviction that, at that time and place – "Yes it was". There was nothing to be gained by labelling Mark. In fact, there was much to lose. Had we done so, in the climate of the time which favoured segregated education, it is more than probable that he would not have been admitted or indeed kept in the school.

These last two years have been daunting and difficult for both Mark and ourselves because we each have had to face into our own personal crisis as well as each other's – open heart surgery (Dao), cancer (me) and a massive struggle to cope in an alien environment (Mark). It has tested all our mettles and *Deo gratias* we have survived.

Strengths

The educational content of the curriculum at the school greatly expanded Mark's horizons. He copes now with four different languages – English, Irish, French and Latin. For a young pupil who

- speaks haltingly by manipulating learned phrases or else in "Famous Five" language

- still reverses his pronouns

- appears to have little abstract thought

- interprets speech entirely literally

how then does he cope with four different languages? The answer is *surprisingly well* – and the reason is because he uses his two great strengths – his phenomenal rote memory and his outstanding ability to mimic sound.

His native tongue, namely English, did not come spontaneously to Mark as it had done to other children. He has had to learn it as one would learn a foreign language with a phrase book – to fit words to a situation. You choose the appropriate words from the phrase book and fit them to a given situation. Mark's English phrase book is indelibly imprinted on his rote memory and he has now added to it a section for each of his three new languages.

When his class peers stutter and stammer over declining Latin and French verbs, Mark, who has always loved strange sounds, trips them blithely and faultlessly off his tongue. His pronunciation is near perfect because his tone is a replica of the source from which he heard the words – automatically the French master's tone and accent become Mark's tone and accent. He is fortunate that at this age and time much of the educational cur-

riculum is based on rote learning and memory skills. He has gained acceptance in English and history because of his good reading skills and his ability
to quote poetry and prose verbatim. However, having few spontaneous ideas
to contribute, he is not comfortable taking part in class discussion; nor has he
as yet acquired the capacity to keep pace with the ebb and flow of normal
conversation.

To my relief he has at last acquired the concept of answering "yes" and
"no" to a question and this has introduced much normality into his
day-to-day conversation. Now, if asked the question, "Do you want some
doughnuts, Mark?" he will simply say, "Yes please" or "No thanks" rather
than repeating the question to indicate that he does. Or he may answer in
"Famous Five" language with some phrase like, "Let's tuck in, I'm famished!"

Since his entrance to the school he relies more and more on the use of
"Famous Five" language. This has enabled him to fit in better because many
of his peers come from different English-speaking countries and tend to
speak in a similar vein. Consequently his FF language becomes quite
acceptable.

With regard to his acquiring an understanding of what is involved in
answering "yes" and "no" to a question, it is interesting to note that Leo
Kanner pointed out that the children whom he had diagnosed with autism
only came to a realization of the yes/no concept at about ten years of age.

He has gained popularity with some of his classmates who are intrigued
by his ability to quote long tracts of history texts/English prose/French/
Latin verbs – whatever. Before examinations they will gather around him to
tap into his memory, seeking to learn off by heart some of what Mark himself
will be able to reproduce at will on the examination paper. Always he has
been able to relate question to answer provided the question is concrete and
simple as all examination questions are for that age-group.

All of the above are his strengths and he has managed to survive in the
school because of them. A further strength has come to light in the last two
years. The music teacher at the school has discovered his hidden musical
talent. He has been found to have perfect pitch coupled with a remarkable
innate understanding of the concept of rhythm. He leads the recorder group
and has become an important member of the choir. This past year he came
second in the competition for the singing cup.

Perfect pitch refers to the ability to identify the pitch of an isolated tone.
It is also called absolute pitch. It is very rare, being estimated to occur in
about one-tenth of one per cent of the average population. The incidence of

it in the autism population is very much higher than this. It is an example of piecemeal information processing – that is, being able to process a stimulus in isolation without reference to its surroundings. Piecemeal processing is a characteristic of autism and it is the reason why autistic children do so well in the Block Design test (this test involves putting little building blocks together to copy an abstract pattern).

Absolute pitch is thought to be an innate ability – meaning we are born with it. There is a possibility that it may be genetic in origin. Those who do not have it can learn it, but only to a certain degree.[11]

Just recently Mark has been invited to become one of the leaders of the hobbies club, which specializes in making model aeroplanes. Because his manual skills are poor this honour was not bestowed due to his ability to make the models. Rather, it is because his peers have discovered his extraordinary knowledge of fighter aircraft and wish to use it to advantage.

Science classes this past year have been based mainly on nature walks, specimen collecting and preservation, and here again he has had the advantage of knowing the names of many of the creatures of the great outdoors as well as the botanical names of garden plants and trees. Continuing his fascination with measurement and scale he has developed an intense interest in the mysterious apparatus in the physics laboratory, where a talented science teacher with nerves of steel and a philosophy of "Now go and find out for yourself" allows his pupils to find their own answers to the many questions of science. This same science teacher, however, was not quite prepared for the fixated concentration of a new boy who wordlessly set himself the task of measuring, with the micrometre screw gauge, the width of every match in a large 360-unit box – writing down each answer as he did so! It was Mark's first encounter with this most fascinating of tools and he was captivated by both its size and shape.

But how does a youth for whom "People *per se* may lack constancy and substance and may become vague and shadowy forms" survive on the football field? The answer is, he has not. On his first day out an obviously bewildered Mark created such chaos and anarchy in the team that his peers permanently relegated him to the side-line as a spectator. He collided with every player in sight, and whenever he got near the ball he kicked it – generally in the wrong direction. On one occasion he even managed to score an own goal. Swarming around him in utter exasperation his shouting team-mates tried to explain, and when he ran off the field with the football under his arm in the middle of the match he was pursued by both teams!

The happiest man of the match was the sports master who, doubled up with paroxysms of laughter, said he had never enjoyed a practice game so much. Many of his peers thought Mark had deliberately set out to disrupt the game and had a sneaking respect for his "courage" but they were not going to risk a repeat performance!

However, three years later Mark will redeem himself when he captains the team leading them to victory in the first match of the inter-schools rounders competition. In rounders he can play as a batter or a fielder, without ever having to focus on the other players involved. As long as he can see the ball and the posts and has a fast turn of speed he will succeed. After the match, the same sports master who had laughed so heartily three years before, will come into the dressing room to congratulate Mark, shake his hand and clap him on the back. The score is 50–3.

Mark's favourite part of the school in the summer-time is the outdoor swimming pool. Watching Mark in the water one cannot help but be reminded of a frolicking young seal. Completely at home in this medium he appears and disappears at will – sometimes grubbing along the floor of the pool looking for likely coins; other times – surfacing for air – his head appears above the surface in the most unexpected places, often in the midst of a crowd of swimmers. There he will remain for some minutes before disappearing again to reappear perhaps at the other end of the pool. From the low diving board he "belly-flops" forward, throwing himself in with abandon. Other times, jumping backwards, he goes in feet first. The stronger the impact the better he likes it. Not for him the clean cleavage of the dolphin or the stately soundings of the porpoise.

The hard work of those patient hours at the swimming pool over the years has yielded handsome dividends in terms of water confidence, manoeuvrability and enjoyment. In this medium he can hold his own place with his peers. After swimming he pulls on his tracksuit jacket, proudly displaying his list of coloured badges – green 25-metre, blue 50-metre, yellow 75-metre – right on up to that red 200-metre badge. Each he has received from his coach on the day he first achieved that feat.

Weaknesses

And what of his weaknesses? At a practical level poor writing and presentation skills slow him down, hindering his progress. Academically he shows little capacity for logical reasoning at even the most elementary level. In mathematics he has learned to add, subtract, multiply and divide and is competent and interested in sums. This has stemmed from his Monopoly-playing days when he developed an interest in managing his own money, an area in which he is now very capable. However, apart from money management, on paper he can only apply his arithmetic skills in their most basic form – any twist or change in a question and he is lost. His old stumbling block, the application of knowledge, comes to the fore here.

It is as if he has got stuck in the groove of perception. As if he were still over-attending to scanning, storing and retrieving knowledge. He has made perception an end in itself rather than a means to an end and is not correlating and applying the data acquired by his senses, except, that is, on the very rare occasions when he is highly motivated as in the case of money management. *Then* he can do it. But in all other cases he is not moving significantly from perception to cognition and consequently in this area he is developmentally years behind his age-group. He can perceive knowledge and retrieve knowledge. Now the challenge is to achieve that vital central link of information processing and application on an ongoing basis. He will not be able to move forward without it.

This becomes most obvious in the field of social interaction. He does not understand what is involved in any but the most elementary social situations and therefore he is not able to deal effectively with them. As a result, he has received rejection from many of his peer group. I am thankful that at this age he is sufficiently unaware of his peers to be oblivious to this rejection just as he is indifferent to acceptance. He has, however, gained a reputation for fun, pranks and mischievous escapades, and having a great personal sense of the ridiculous he has become very popular with like-minded individuals. With this small group of mainly younger boys, he has gained acceptance and when there is mischief to be done, such as letting frogs loose during choir practice, he is delighted to partake and enjoys the resulting scene.

He is an accepting, unquestioning companion who will never seek companionship but now accepts it when it is offered. We have found that other children who themselves have difficulty making friends and being accepted will gravitate towards Mark, from whom there is nothing to fear. He is someone to be with who is not competitive, and with whom they can be comfortable and at ease.

But how does Mark, who to our knowledge has as yet never made eye contact with anybody or even looked them straight in the face (generally he will focus his gaze at some point in their left shoulder and stare through them), recognize any one boy or girl among a group dressed all alike in grey? Well, his recognition is based on voice and on hair colour and shape.

Fundamentally, however, he is a loner, preferring and indeed needing his own company – he needs to withdraw during free time to escape from the burden of overload. The vicissitudes of the past two years have been many for him and the sustained effort required to keep going has been Herculean. The white patch in the centre of his face is back and remains his constant companion during the school term. Often he has had to have a week off school just to recover from exhaustion and sensory overload. But always he has been willing to go back and try again and always he has progressed – gaining momentum as he goes. He enjoys school meals enormously, and is allowed to help out in the tuck shop opening boxes and stacking shelves, being rewarded in kind for his efforts.

Persecution

Unfortunately, because Mark is different he has become one of the targets of the school bullies and this has added greatly to his difficulty in coping on a daily basis. While he is oblivious to either rejection or lack of acceptance, he is very disturbed by the actions of these taunting youths who have inculcated into him their "code of dishonour" – "You must not tell; if you tell you are a snitch or a sneak." Or worse – "If you tell, we will beat you up."

Mark has never spoken about these episodes. We have only become aware of them thanks to an older boy who has befriended him and looks out for him. It is utterly reprehensible that children like Mark, who struggle so hard to overcome their innate difficulties, should have to shoulder this added burden of personal persecution – a persecution damaging to the perpetrator as well as to the victim. The school staff have been extremely kind to Mark and tolerant of his differences, and they have protected him in every way they can, but despite constant vigilance on the part of any staff bullying is a pernicious practice and difficult to stamp out. As I have written elsewhere:

> The fourth component in the school equation was the bully. There are bullies in all schools. Some act verbally, some physically. Sometimes they come in the clothing of lone wolves, other times like jackals they hunt in packs. In emotional and psychological terms the damage they do is incalculable. The impact of it can last a lifetime. They jeer; they mock; they kick; they punch; they steal self-esteem; they isolate; they segregate; they intimidate; they haunt; they stalk; they lie

in wait; they instil fear; they halt academic progress. Like the predators they are, they feed off the emotions of their prey and cause untold misery during the vulnerable years of formation. They roam the jungle of the school yard seeking whom they may devour. They pick on the weak; on those who for a number of reasons will not defend themselves and on those who stand out because they are different. In a society that requires conformity, to be different is to be a target.

What is it in the human psyche that causes one human being to prey on another? For too long schools have tolerated the persecution of one child by another. Going back in history, that caste system in public schools called "fagging" was regarded as a toughening-up process for life. Fortunately World War II put an end to it. Thirty years ago, one was expected to fight it out, or grin and bear it, leading to a survival-of-the-fittest policy. Why has there been so little political will in schools to deal effectively with such tyranny? Perhaps because bullying is in fact very difficult to deal with. It is so insidious that often attempts to deal with it may just drive it underground to reappear somewhere else, perhaps beyond the school grounds. But it is vital that it be tackled at an early stage. Any complaints of bullying should be taken up instantly at the highest level in the school and the pressure kept up until action is taken. Fortunately the damage it causes has at last been recognized and there are now official ground rules to deal with it.[12]

CHAPTER 9

The Thoughts
of a Mnemonist

A literal thinker

How does Mark – who obviously has the mind of a "mnemonist" (one with an exceptional memory) think? We look at the clues. At the age of five Mark watches a very wet visitor to the house shaking her umbrella in the porchway, saying in exasperation – "It's coming down in buckets".

Running to look out, he cries – "Where buckets, where buckets – no buckets?" At six he stands beside me at the cooker while I hold the frying pan in one hand and a piece of breaded cod in the other. I ask him, "Will we have fingers for dinner tonight Mark?"

Jamming his fists into his pocket he stampedes out of the kitchen to hide under his bed. At tea-time no amount of reassurance will convince him that the "fingers" were just portions of cod cut into finger-sized pieces.

At the age of seven, as he is washing his hands I focus on them thinking suddenly how like his father's hands they are. Without reflecting I say, "Oh Mark – you have your daddy's hands".

Greatly alarmed he snatches his hands away from me hiding them behind his back and shouts – "Not daddy's hands, not daddy's hands, daddy's hands in office with daddy." These and many other such conversational examples have convinced us that Mark's interpretation of language is entirely concrete and literal. This literal thinking means that he will understand words only in their narrowest and most stringent sense and that he will miss the real spirit and meaning behind the words. It points to a lack of imagination.

We adapt our language accordingly to keep it simple.

Word image inflexibility

Further clues appear. When Mark is eight new neighbours arrive in our area with a son the same age as Mark, a boy called Robin. I tell Mark – "Robin and his mother are coming over to tea." Mark runs out into the garden to watch the bird-table. I think – "He's withdrawing again".

But when they arrive he is back at the door gazing in blank astonishment at the shy, sensitive, dark-haired boy taller than himself, whose mother says – "Shake hands with Mark, Robin". Loud and clear I hear, "No feathers, no beak, no red breast".

I cringe with embarrassment only to hear Robin's mother laugh loudly – "I see there is a wit in the family; now you two go off and play outside while we talk."

This incident marks the culmination of a number of clues leading to a realization we can no longer ignore. It is that for Mark each word, whether bucket or robin, has a specific meaning and can only be used in one context. This one context has to be the context in which he first heard the word. In this particular case, the first time he had heard the word "robin" was when the small red-breasted bird had been pointed out to him on the bird-table. Because of his concrete literal thinking he has not the necessary flexibility to adapt to the same word having two completely different meanings. Leo Kanner, in his diagnostic paper, called attention to this facet of autism. He called it "word image inflexibility". He pointed out that a word once first heard in a particular context by the children he had examined could never be used in any context other than that original one.[3]

Consequently a word such as "fast" will cause Mark endless problems. A sentence that begins with somebody going "fast" (deeply) asleep can suddenly veer off at the word "fast" into who won the last race because he ran so "fast" (quickly), or why we have to "fast" (abstain) before a blood glucose test, or hold "fast" (tightly) to the rail when going down the escalator. If he delays too long on such a word he will find himself jumping to the wrong connection, losing the thread of what he wishes to say, and coming out with some uncomprehending sentence such as – "Last night Barry went *fast* down the escalator before a blood glucose test".

In conversation with others, such inflexible thinking results in his following a trail of words rather than the ideas under discussion. It also results in his interrupting the conversation around him by latching on to one particular word he has just picked up from it, then jumping in with a totally inappropriate comment based on that one word, which generally has nothing to do with the subject under discussion.

This practice has been dubbed in the family as "the conversation stopper"!

Then either all conversation ceases or else one of us has to intervene with some innocuous bridging comment that will get the discussion back on track until the next interruption. Somehow one can survive the first three or four interruptions, but after that a sense of surreal confusion takes over, with everybody losing track of their own ideas and of what they wish to say. Then they give up and there is silence.

When Mark is aged eight we have two established facts about his thinking. He is a strictly *literal* thinker. In addition this literal thinking is compounded by word image inflexibility.

Visual imagery

Three years later we can add a further established fact. Mark's thinking is based on visual images of words rather than the verbal words themselves.

He appears to have little verbal thought. In contrast he does appear to have a visual image in his mind for every word that has ever come within his knowledge. He will draw on these pictures then to give substance to the words when he hears or sees them. But the images he holds are not always the expected ones. For example if one tosses the word "spider" at Mark it will not invoke the image of an eight-legged creature weaving a web but instead it will invoke the image of an Alpha Romeo, *Spyder* sports car. Similarly, if the word "tree" is tossed at him he will not see a long trunk with branches and green leaves – rather instead he sees a drawing of a *family tree*. Personalize the tree a stage further and ask him for his image of a "poplar tree" and he will think of a Ford *Popular* car. These connotations are not the result of word image inflexibility because in all cases he has been familiar with the normal application of the word years before he has heard its adapted use. Rather, they appear to be the result of selective word imaging.

Thinking by association

When Mark reaches the age of eleven we have come to realize also that his thought processes work by association. For example, to hold the passage of time in his mind he will use pegs to hang it on. He compares the passage of time to the order of sequence of a totally different, unallied, set of circumstances from the ones in which he lives. The twenty-five days before Christmas are always compared to the twenty- five chapters of his school mathematics book. For each day he will announce the title of the chapter – "Today is equations and problems" or "Today is metric geometry" or perhaps "Today is indices and logarithms" and the events taking place in his own day will then be hung on the pegs of calculations explained in that particular chapter. This enables him to fix certain dates in his mind and also makes it easier for him to get through this period of time which for some reason he always finds difficult.

In a similar vein he will use the tracks of one favourite music tape to mark off the months of each year and will hang his own major life events on the individual tunes. Other music tapes will be used for more minor passages of time.

Time events can also be compared to journeys. During term time the routes chosen are large super-highways, with many lanes of fast-moving vehicles travelling at speed and encompassing major traffic junctions with under- and over-passes. During the holidays the routes chosen are those that run through towns, villages and sleepy hamlets with slow-moving traffic and many stops along the way.

Add, then, these four patterns of thinking – barren literalism; word image rigidity; recall by visual images, like running slides through a projector, and all context recalled by association to non-related events – and what do you get? Not surprisingly, they add up to conflict. Small wonder then that when Mark heard the words "Robin is coming to play" he visualized a red-breasted singing bird with feathers and a beak coming to play. Had he been told that a boy was coming to play he would have visualized a human voice, hair, clothes and limbs.

How can we reconcile four such non-complementary thinking patterns? We can use the strengths of his visual thinking to great advantage in explaining issues. For him personally it is a very important strength in education and self-expression. It is a valuable asset. But it does mean that all instructions and explanations must be visual. Fortunately, up to now our main approach to Mark's education has been a visual (seeing) rather than an aural (hearing) one.

Associational thinking, however, as we have discovered, is a two-edged weapon. It can be constructive if used as described above but there is a destructive element in it also because, as we shall see later, *Mark does not have a firm grasp of the principle of cause and effect*. Because of this weak link in his cause/effect relationship and his *modus operandi* of constantly associating unconnected, unallied sets of circumstances, he has put himself totally at the mercy of the random association of facts. Reason and logic do not appear to enter into his associations.

We will have to find him another way of learning and, if possible, teach him to think by another route – the route of logic and reason. This, however, is likely to be a long slow process, to be thought of in terms of years rather than months.

Important words

Words are very important to Mark and we continue the practice of always explaining the words we use and so making sure he has a firm grasp of the reality that lies behind each word. Rarely now is it necessary to explain a concrete word describing an object that he can see, feel, touch, smell or hear and rarely is it *not* necessary to explain an abstract word which he cannot. It is all too easy to assume that he knows and understands the meaning only to be brought up short when, on telling him to always try to "Be normal, like everybody else" one is suddenly brought face to face with the fact that his understanding of being normal is having a temperature of 37 degrees centigrade on the thermometer!

So, when Mark is twelve years of age, we begin with him a dictionary of simple explanations of words and every day we add some new words when they arise in conversation, always using visual imagery to get the meaning across. We pay particular attention to words with more than one meaning. Over the years the dictionary will grow as he grows.

Next we set out to break the constricting bonds of literal thinking by exposing him to the world of concepts, and introducing him to the abstract domain of proverb, idiom and metaphor. We begin with simple proverbs: "A stitch in time saves nine"; "You cannot put an old head on young shoulders"; "He who pays the piper calls the tune"; "It never rains but it pours". Choosing one, Mark depicts his interpretation of "He who pays the piper calls the tune", drawing the picture of a local piper sitting on the pavement and passers-by dropping coins into his hat, asking for special tunes to be played. Mark himself regularly does this, always asking for his own favourite tune on the pipes.

Sitting beside him, pencil in hand, I seek to interpret to him the broader meaning behind the proverb.

This process continues well into his teenage years as we work our way through every proverb, metaphor and abstract thought I can think of. Mark now begins to enjoy the challenge of such working sessions for their own satisfaction. Inertia has withdrawn off-stage. This pale spectre of the past no longer sits at his shoulder but watches now from a respectful distance. He is fast reaching the stage where the achievement of the work itself is the motivator. Although his writing and drawing skills are poor, he draws in perspective what he actually sees and the impressions are vivid. Somewhere along the way he moves away from word image inflexibility and barren literalism.

Global power

During these early teenage years I see Mark begin to integrate the overall power of his mind. Up until then his thought processes have been fragmented and divided as if different sections of his brain are isolated and working apart, with little cohesion between them. Now I see the beginnings of a coming together of these diverse sections and the start of a process whereby they begin to work as a united whole. Perhaps new pathways and nerve circuit connections *are* opening up within the brain itself. Whatever the reason, with it come the beginnings of generalization whereby he is able to move from the particular to the general. He can then apply his knowledge in a more global sense and, if told, "Robin and his mother are coming over to tea", he will not run to the front door expecting to see a red-breasted bird. Neither will he expect to see buckets of water falling out of the sky.

A self-conscious self

Arising out of this improvement in global cohesion will perhaps, in time, come the power to reflect and to think about his own thoughts and, following on from this, the ability to develop a self-conscious self.

Mark has never shown signs of self-consciousness in any sense of the word. Over the years he has attended day-based summer camps during the holiday months. Whenever volunteers are called for – to sing, recite a poem, play a tune, whatever, Mark, unselfconscious even at a superficial level, is first on his feet to volunteer while other, more aware children hang back. When he is twelve he is voted the Camp Champ Trophy. This reward is based mainly on his willingness to participate.

At a more profound level also it is clear that he has not developed a well-defined sense of self. The boundaries delineating himself from others and from his surroundings do not appear to be clearly drawn. *Mark automatically assumes that everyone else knows what he knows.* Consequently he never sees the necessity to preface his remarks, introduce a new topic of conversation, or give the background to an incident. Nor indeed does he seem to be aware of the necessity to inform someone if he intends to change his plans from those already agreed upon. He assumes they will know.

As already mentioned he cannot, due to a possible failure of proprioception, at times locate his limbs, having no intuitive feel for them. Always they have to be clothed so that he can see them.

Only once has he given a rare flash of insight into this phenomenon. Crossing a busy street in the city he suddenly comes to a full stop and stands immobilized. Going back to catch his hand I say – "Hurry up Mark – we'll miss the lights". I hear, "Who are you? Can't find your arms and legs – You're floating off into limbo again".

Putting my arm around him, I whisper – "Look down at your shoes and move them – lean on me – now let's sing together".

The physical and musical contact appear to break his isolation and he moves forward with me to the footpath on the other side of the street. Having crossed we go into the nearest café for coffee and something sweet.

This feature of autism, called "lack of the body boundaries", has been documented in the literature. One young man when writing about it documents his difficulty in keeping track of his body parts all at the same time. He refers to it as an "interface" problem. He writes of the terror involved in not being able to locate the connections necessary to find his ears, his eyes, his limbs – the feeling of being lost in a fog when he cannot connect with his own body. Neither, he tells us, can he on certain occasions connect to time or space. He is, however, he explains, always connected to his own self at his innermost core. This is what he holds on to and this is what keeps him going. He knows that even if it takes what seems an eternity he will find the connections and put them back together again.[13]

There is a link here between perceptual inconstancy, an inability to feel one's body parts and the development of a sense of self. Sigmund Freud held that before one could develop a sense of self one had first to develop a physical body self-image. This physical-body ego then, he considered, was the foundation for the ego of the intellect. He emphasized that the ego was first and foremost a body-ego.

It is well recorded by medical personnel that one of the biggest challenges facing amputees can be the loss of a sense of self. The deep disturbance of body image, caused by amputation, can lead to an identity crisis. One of the first lines of treatment by therapists in these cases is to re-establish identity by using mirrors.

We have not been able to introduce mirror therapy with Mark in order to improve his physical body self-image because of his aversion to looking in the mirror.

What does Mark see when he looks in the mirror? We have not succeeded in finding out the answer to this. It is still very difficult to elicit any really informative information from Mark about himself. There is some failure in his ability to monitor his internal environment, of that we are sure. It is as if all of his faculties are entirely preoccupied with the mammoth task of negotiating his outside environment and until he has mastered that he will not be able to turn his attention inwards.

So, in these early teenage years, still probing for answers, we turn back again to review the basic conditions we have set out to correct and to think once more about the three categories of sense and where Mark stands now in relation to them.

Space

Apart from some, at times, inconstancy in depth perception, Mark is now at home spatially in his environment. He moves about it freely, confidently and comfortably, as on a level playing field, except when using some types of staircases and all escalators (which he will avoid if possible), and crossing bridges. On crossing a wide bridge he perceives the sensation that the water is rising up to engulf him and will become terrified. We tell him – "Keep looking up and looking straight ahead." This advice is not very helpful to a youth who for a number of years has been using his peripheral vision to navigate his world. Consequently, we avoid crossing bridges where possible and lead him across, eyes closed, when we cannot avoid the situation. Later he will learn to canoe and will happily paddle down such rivers and under such bridges having no difficulty once he was actually on the water and not looking down at it from a height.

Time

Mark has brought order into his time-life and the events of the past by setting up a visual date calendar in his memory. Never having had even the hazy concept of "a few years ago"or "early last month" or even "last night", he has now developed a precise hold on time. He has related it specifically to date and the clock. Now, when recalling past events, he will say, "On the 20th of November 19— at four o'clock in the afternoon we went–" or "On the 29th May 19— at 10.30 p.m. we saw that plane landing–" or "On 4th January 19— at 9 a.m. the man came to fix the boiler and you said…".

On checking the bills we find he is always correct, although I can find it somewhat disconcerting to be reminded of the exact words I used at 9 a.m. on a given day four years ago! If my utterances are to be recorded for posterity I will have to exercise more caution!

For years he will operate this recall system and it gives him ready access, in a chronological order, to all important and incidental events of his life.

We continue to work on the sequencing of events in time, confining our pictures to non-social happenings. Sequencing of events in time is still a grey area for him but, as always, the more we work on an area the more his ability to see the drift of the sequence improves and the more progress he makes. This has been one of the most rewarding aspects of working with Mark. If one can tap into his difficulties and see where he is coming from – and it will require imagination, intuition, a lot of thought and sometimes the right flash of inspiration to do this – then the problem can be seen for what it is. Tackled in the right way then, real progress can be made.

He still wears his two dual-purpose watches, both now more appropriate to his age but still conspicuous. Both are worn day and night and very tightly strapped. Looking at the strap marks on both arms I am troubled concerning the possible constriction, but he cannot be persuaded to loosen them saying he could not feel his hands if they were looser. It appears to work because he no longer complains that "Hands won't do what they're told" and he has become much more dextrous in the use of his hands. In addition he wears a silver ring on each hand. Rarely will he pass a jeweller's shop without spending time gazing at the window display and after every jumble sale yet another clock or watch will be added to his collection.

Cause and effect

And what of that third category of sense – causality, the principle of cause and effect, often called the principle of common sense? Cause and effect are primary categories for the understanding of reality. Because we live in a cause/effect universe we need to belong to that reality with all its activities and challenges. But Mark is not overburdened by that reality.

It is somewhat sobering to realize that Mark, in all of his fourteen years, has never asked a why question.

A *where* question – yes –

"Where is your [my] school-bag?"

"Where did you [I] put your [my] shoes?"

A *when* question – yes –

"When is the train leaving?"

"When is the bus coming?"

A *how* question – yes –

"How high is the bridge?"

"How wide is the river?"

But a *why* question – such as – "Why does the fire light?"

"Why does the water flow?

"Why does the wind blow?" – never; questions that the constantly chattering Darren and the twins asked almost without ceasing in their younger years. Or their later questions of – "Why are the stars shining so bright?"

"Why is the aircraft flying so low?"

never appear to impinge on Mark's consciousness. Cause and effect do not appear to associate themselves significantly in his view of events. Dispensing with them, he will associate random facts.

One incident, which occurred about a year ago when Mark was thirteen, stands out in the mind. In the final of the inter-schools swimming competition, Mark, who has been watching the match but not competing in it, to his great annoyance is called away.

When he returns he finds that his school team has lost the match and the cup. Nothing will convince him but that had he been there they would have won. In his view they lost the cup because he was not there to watch. He is adamant about this and will brook no argument.

We have also noticed that one same incident, which can happen again and again, does not trigger recognition of the same antecedent in his mind. Each time he will look for a different cause for the same effect. This will become very obvious when, for example, the car does not start at the first turn of the ignition key. Instead of thinking logically and mechanically of the fault being due to an uncharged battery, or perhaps being out of petrol, he will associate it with some random fact such as it happened because he "did not get his home-work finished last night" or perhaps because he "has to return next week to the hospital for a blood test."

As previously mentioned the underlying culprit in all of this is his pattern of thinking by association. Images of one situation going wrong will conjure up the image of another totally different, unallied set of circum-stances going wrong. Then a chain reaction is set up as follows: a fear thought spreads in his mind; this in turn generates a surge of adrenaline which leads to racing heart, leaping pulse, churning stomach and the atten-dant high anxiety levels. If, as can often happen, there are too many such incidents during the day he will remain under stress all day, at the mercy of his overactive adrenal glands which are being constantly stimulated by fear thoughts.

At this point in his life any mechanical object which does not work per-fectly will set up such a reaction. Each time he sits into the car and fastens his seat belt he will tense every muscle waiting to see if the ignition will start "first kick". If it does he will relax immediately. If not he will remain rigidly tense for the journey.

How to deal with it?

Endless explanations, both visual and verbal, make no impact. So we return to the drawing board. Weary now with drawing images, and being conscious of Mark's interest in the game of Monopoly, I decide to depict the theory of cause and effect in the guise of a Monopoly game. Mark is enthusi-astic. "What colour will we use for the cause?" He chooses blue. Blue boxes are drawn along the edges of the Bristol Board. Each is labelled with a differ-ent cause. Many are based on the kind of everyday situations that are likely to cause problems.

"What colour will we use for the effect?" He chooses green. Green boxes are piled in a jumbled-up fashion all over the centre of the board. Each is labelled with a different effect.

"What colour will we make the arrows?" "Red of course." Rolling the dice, Mark sets to work matching cause with effect while I make tea and toast. Returning with the tray I see many red arrows attacking correct targets. Only a few are off target. Admittedly, the examples were simple such as – "What could be the cause when the car does not start 'first kick'?" He identifies five fact-based causes for this.

Over the next few weeks the cause and effect samples get more and more difficult and yet, under Mark's hands, many red arrows find their correct targets.

What we are seeing once again is another example of Mark knowing something in principle and yet not being able to apply it in practice. This gap becomes more evident with every day that passes. He may know something in the abstract but it is as if his capacity to understand, anticipate and judge the situation when he finds himself in the middle of it is not meaningful enough to apply this information. In any situation it is the minutiae of the situation, the non-essential details, that Mark will focus on. Consequently he will miss the main point at issue because he is concentrating on the parts rather than the whole. His tendency still is to fragment information rather than to draw it together.

However, it must also be remembered here that the skills involved in acquiring knowledge are processed in a different circuit of the brain from the skills involved in applying that knowledge. Thus the *real* problem may lie at a much deeper level.

One other factor involved in these situations is anxiety. Mark's stress levels in, for example, some social situations, can be so high that this alone will prevent him from applying his knowledge. In discussing the social skills of those with high functioning autism (HFA) and Asperger syndrome (AS) recently, Andron comments that many of the difficulties experienced by children when interacting socially appear to be because of anxiety and motor planning. She cites cases where children who were being taught social skills, when sitting in the group could identify how to behave correctly in a given situation. Yet when a similar situation occurred in reality, they were not able to apply these skills. When asked for the reason why, the children gave two reasons –

1.   fear prevented them from thinking and –

2.   they "couldn't stop their bodies."[14]

To sum up, then: in order to address this issue of cause and effect for Mark a radical change in the *modus operandi* of his thought processes will be required and any new way of learning will have to be based on strict logic and reasoning.

Meanwhile, it is of immense value to have an understanding of the manner of his thinking. One can then become more attuned to his difficulties and offer understanding, help and reassurance when necessary. Heretofore trying to make sense of his thought connections has been akin to wandering lost in a maze.

This innate impairment in understanding the principle of cause and effect gives the impression of an extraordinary absence of common sense.

Facts and figures

We look again at the dust gathering on the files of figures strewing the walls of the den, spilling onto the floors and tumbling out of grey folders in the presses, and we see opportunities that might interest Mark in the application of the results of perception.

Since Mark's fact-finding days there have been several thousand sets of statistics available for processing. They range from wall-charts of the detailed specifications of every car tyre on the market, through the minute diameters of several hundred drinking straws, encompass dozens of drawings of centigrade and fahrenheit temperature scales (toss any centigrade temperature figure at Mark and instantly he will give you its equivalent in fahrenheit and *vice versa*), take in the cylinder capacity and horsepower of every known make of car that he has seen on the road – all in addition to his special recordings of lighthouses, aircraft, and house and garden measurements. Every time Mark goes to a boat show, motor show, industrial fair or exhibition, he arrives home with yet another folder of figures which he will commit to memory.

Watching the dust gathering on the files daily, we think back to the parallel lines of toys that had lain permanently in the dust and were never used for constructive play.

We had waited then and it had never happened.

We had waited for him to sit at the controls of his self-made De Havilland control panel and simulate flight and it had never happened.

We know that the files of figures are destined for the same fate. But this time we will not wait, we will intervene and make it happen.

We buy him that novelty on the market – a calculator. He is enthralled. We sit around the table, he and I working together. I call out the figures. He adds the columns. We have a total. I write it down. He divides to get the average. He adds a second column. For every ten columns we get a percentage. He multiplies – then divides by 100 and the work goes on. Mark falls under the spell of information processing and its attendant bonus of shape. Around us the sheets of graph paper pile up on the table. They are decorated now with the radial symmetry of coloured pie charts, with the elegant black-and-white columnar outline of towering bar graphs, and the peaks, troughs and parallel lines of the trend graph.

Somewhere along the way I slip quietly away from the table. He continues, not even aware that I have left. Where processing statistics is concerned the needle on the dial of the want-to-do-it system is set fair at "steady as she goes". Mark has become self-propelling and committed to the processing of data. It is enough for now.

Later we will think about the application of the resultant knowledge and perhaps then we will be able to move towards thinking by reason and logic rather than by association.

CHAPTER 10

Restoring Equilibrium

We think about internal stress factors.

Mark's stress factors have changed over the years. To begin with they appeared to arise entirely from the environment surrounding him. By management (removal of sharp sounds, such as electric door bells and shrill phones, and disturbing visual stimuli found in fluorescent lights and their ilk), by organization (manoeuvring people and situations where possible to maintain a quiet household and escaping to the countryside when we could not) and by careful preparation for upcoming changes and events, we have contrived to reduce environmental stressors as much as is within our power. It is now obvious that his tolerance for these original sources of stress has improved.

This leaves the way clear to consider a new set of stress factors, this time coming from within. They show up in the form of:

- a sharp increase in overall free-floating anxiety

- intense irritability – always at its worst before meals

- disturbed sleep pattern

- hyperactivity starting up again and

- exhaustion (a seeming paradox – but it is as if his overactive mind will not let his tired body rest).

Mark is driven from within. We realize that much of this high anxiety arises from his pattern of associational thinking. But that is not the entire answer. There is more. Treading carefully around this question of internal systemic stress factors we focus on one that up until now we have had no occasion to consider. It is the factor of food intake, namely – diet.

Food, behaviour and learning

Around us there is much media focus on the question of what children eat and how it affects their behaviour and learning. We hear and read about hyperkinesis-learning disability (H-LD) the name given to physically over-active children with behaviour problems, who also have learning difficulties and who are lacking in concentration. This condition is also being called minimal brain dysfunction (MBD). Dr Ben Feingold, an allergist working in this field, estimated that about four to five million children in the United States alone may be affected to some degree by this condition. He also pointed out that an estimated half of these children take medication on a daily basis to manage the condition.[15]

In his work treating patients with allergies Dr Feingold had come to realize that certain individuals develop aspirin sensitivity and react adversely to aspirin, producing the symptoms of allergy. The active chemical ingredient present in aspirin is called acetylsalicylic acid. He further realized that certain foods, for example raspberries and tomatoes, contain naturally occurring salicylates. This salicylate group is very similar to the one found in aspirin and it can cause the same kind of adverse reaction in certain susceptible people.

How do salicylates affect the workings of the body? They act by inhibiting the production of some very important hormone-like chemicals called "prostaglandins". These prostaglandins are present in practically all body tissues including the major glands, such as the adrenal and thyroid glands, and in the brain and spinal chord. One of their many functions is to increase sensitivity to pain.

As his work with patients evolved Dr Feingold discovered that the artificial colours and flavours now added to a large number of manufactured foods could induce, in some susceptible patients, the same type of adverse reaction as aspirin sensitivity had. In other words, they could produce symptoms of allergy.

Putting the whole picture together he formulated the hypothesis that synthetic food additives might be interfering with normal brain and nervous system functioning in some genetically predisposed children. He treated his patients with a special diet from which all suspected foods were removed, that is, all foods containing salicylates and all foods containing artificial colour and flavour. He reported considerable improvement in many of these patients in both behaviour and in learning ability. In addition they were able to discard the drugs they had been taking. This elimination diet was popularly known as The Feingold Diet.[15]

Other areas being discussed in the current media focus on children's learning difficulties and behaviour problems, related to the over-consumption of white sugar and other refined foods.

Allergic reactions

We think carefully about the elements in Mark's diet. Does he show any evidence of allergic reactions to food?

- *Clue number one* – raspberries cause hives. This points to a sensitivity to naturally occurring salicylates.

- *Clue number two* – the only food that Mark has ever declined to eat is raw cow's milk and butter. From the age of about two-and-a-half he has refused to drink milk or any beverage to which milk has been added. He will however, happily eat milk puddings and custards made with cow's milk. It is quite possible that denaturing the milk by boiling it would render harmless whatever proteins or peptides were causing his aversion to it (heat will change the physical and physiological properties of proteins). To ensure that he does not lack calcium or other necessary minerals and vitamins, we have made goat's milk and cheese freely available to him. He eats both regularly. Goat's milk contains more calcium than cow's milk and has the advantage of being sulphur-free. There are some indications from the literature that sulphur is involved in allergic reactions. Butter is replaced by sunflower spread.

- *Clue number three* – recently he has been plagued with repeated bouts of constant sneezing which can continue for hours and are very debilitating. Despite the use of a controlling spray, at times he has to leave the house to walk by the sea or in the forest before the sneezing stops. This points to allergic rhinitis.

A simple blood test taken by his general practitioner reveals significant numbers of allergens in Mark's blood. A visit to an allergist is indicated. Here he receives the standard skin patch test for the twenty-five commonest substances known to be involved in allergic reactions. He tests positive for the house-dust mite, moulds, cat fur, dog fur, feathers, all pollens (trees, flowers and grasses) and eggs. He tests negative for all other food substances including cow's milk.

It is pointed out to us that this system of testing, while reliable for the positive reactions, could have a small failure rate on the negative reactions. In other words there might be other allergies present that would not be picked up on by this method.

Meanwhile we have sufficient information to begin with and much work ahead of us. We decide to begin with the dust mite and feathers which, we have been told, are most likely to be the cause of allergic rhinitis. Mark's bed is stripped and the mattress vacuumed and covered with protective material which will be vacuumed every day. Feather duvets and pillows are replaced by man-made fibre equivalents. Carpet and curtains are removed; the bare floor boards scrubbed, and metal venetian blinds fitted to the windows. Walls, ceilings and doors are vacuumed and painted and all unnecessary furniture is removed. The stripped room contains a bed, a chair and a locker.

The results are dramatic. Within two weeks Mark stops sneezing and is able to discontinue his medication.

One problem solved, we turn our attention to the other. In view of Mark's adverse reaction to raspberries, and keeping in mind his significant consumption of aspirin (to reduce fever, inflammation and pain) during the year of his treatment for Still's disease, we decide to remove all foods containing salicylate from his diet for a few weeks. These include many fruits and juices, a few vegetables, shop-bought baker's goods and some soft drinks. As he rarely drinks soft drinks he will not miss them, and home-baked products can be substituted for the shop-bought variety. It will be an easy and straightforward trial and to keep things simple the entire family will go on the diet. We begin. We keep a record.

After four weeks the diet is abandoned. No significant changes have been observed in Mark's behaviour. On reintroduction of the excluded foods he shows no adverse reaction to any of them. So it would appear that salicylates play no part in the conditions we are targeting.

What are these conditions? We consider them again –

- very high anxiety levels
- intense irritability, at its worst before meals
- hyperactivity
- exhaustion
- sleep disturbance.

Opposite them we write down everything Mark eats. Looking at the list one word leaps off the page. It is *caffeine*. We realize that Mark is addicted to tea – ten to twelve cups a day. Caffeine, being a stimulant, increases anxiety and hyperactivity, and causes sleep disturbance and consequent exhaustion. We have our first culprit. The caffeine will have to go.

Reactive hypoglycaemia

Continuing to look at our list we become aware of just how much of a sweet tooth Mark has acquired since his helping-out days at the tuck shop in school and probably since the early years when chocolate was our main motivator. Now it adds up to the consumption of a considerable amount of refined white sugar. Mark, without our realizing it, has become something of a sugar junkie. This is just the kind of situation that can lead to fluctuating blood sugar levels which could be the primary cause of intense irritability – particularly before meals. He is well on the way to *reactive hypoglycaemia.*

What *is* reactive hypoglycaemia? It means having an abnormally low level of glucose sugar in one's blood (*hypo* means low; blood sugar is called *glycaemia*). But how can there be a low level of sugar in the blood of someone who is constantly eating sugar? To understand this it is necessary to follow the path of what happens to white sugar and refined foods when they are eaten.

- *Step 1*. Because these foods are already refined they need little digestion and so they pass quickly into the blood stream and flood it with sugar in the form of glucose. This raises the blood glucose level too high.

- *Step 2*. Because it is now too high some of this glucose must be withdrawn for storage in the liver as *glycogen* (starch). To achieve this the pancreas secretes a chemical messenger called *insulin* (a hormone).

- *Step 3*. Insulin brings about the withdrawal of glucose for storage and as a result the level of glucose in the blood drops.

- *Step 4*. Then a craving for *something sweet* sets in and the individual reacts to this low blood glucose level by eating further quick sources of sugar. This results in flooding the blood with glucose again so the cycle repeats itself and a see-saw of fluctuating blood sugar swings is set up.

- *Step 5*. Every time the glucose level falls low other chemical messengers are needed to restore it because the brain must have glucose to function. One of these chemical messengers sent to the liver to release more glucose from glycogen is – *a surge of adrenaline*. *Adrenaline* is the anxiety-provoking hormone known as the "fight or flight" hormone (one either runs away from a fear-provoking situation or stands and fights it out, physically or psychologically).

This adrenaline is the hormone at the mercy of which Mark already lives because of his pattern of associational thinking and his dysfunctional sensory system. Over time any set of adrenal glands constantly forced to overproduce adrenaline will become exhausted, leading to all the conditions we are targeting. Much pressure could be taken off these adrenal glands if Mark's blood sugar levels could be stabilized. This will greatly help his recovery.

It becomes obvious that Mark's sugar diet is doing him no favours.

There would appear to be both an hereditary factor and a nutritional factor involved in reactive hypoglycaemia. Looked at objectively, the root of the problem lies in the swinging of glucose levels. If the blood stream were not being constantly flooded with glucose there would be no necessity to keep constantly storing it and then having to renew it again. Following on from this in turn, adrenaline would not be called on to release it again. There-fore a diet based on slow-releasing sources of glucose (wholegrain, unre-fined starches and fruit sugars) in conjunction with some protein (fish, poultry, meat), fats, vegetables and fresh fruit, should prevent this happening. The most important part of this food plan would be the removal of all white sugar, white flour and refined cereals from the diet.

We set to work, realizing that this time it will be more difficult and will only work if everybody gets involved in it. In addition, a decision is made to ban all food additives such as preservatives, colourings and flavourings – most of these in any event would have to be eliminated because the foods to which they are added contain refined white sugar.

Our first port of call is to the grocery store. Mark's brief is to research all ingredients listed by manufacturers on food labels. In the old days he would have swung into action with alacrity at such an assignment, but now energy and concentration are in short supply. So Dao helps out – checking each label and making the list.

In the kitchen I master the art of baking 100 per cent wholegrain, rye yeast bread – a dozen loaves at a time for the freezer. Added to these are cookies made with wholegrain rice, oatmeal, barley and rye flakes. They contain seeds, nuts and dried fruits to satisfy that sweet tooth.

By diligently searching in the health-food store I find an excellent caffeine-tea substitute – a brand of real tea leaves which have never contained caffeine, thus removing what was likely to be a stumbling block, the chemical removal of caffeine from tea. Vegetables as always will come from the garden as will much of the fruit. To cushion the withdrawal from chocolate, carob bars which do not contain sugar are substituted.

So we begin.

It is to be a slow substitution, gradually withdrawing from the old and introducing the new. Fortunately, it is holiday time and there will be no school lunches or tuck shop to contend with for the next three months. All food can be home-based. At the end of a month we take stock. Little change is seen in Mark. Realizing that years of damage cannot so easily be repaired we persevere. Now well into the second month the old foods have been totally discarded and, with them, much of the irritability, particularly before meals. By the third month his exhaustion is slipping away, he sleeps through the night and that sunny disposition and sense of fun we have not seen for some time are peeping out again. Also his excessive thirst appears to be coming under control. More and more often now we return to the house from an outing with a full, unbroached bottle of water.

By the beginning of school term he is much less hyperactive and less anxious. Eight weeks later in the half-term report we find encouraging comment, such as, "improved concentration", "improved ability to hold attention", "focused and alert" and "considerable overall improvement over last term."

The diet becomes a permanent feature of his food intake. He no longer partakes of school lunches, instead preferring to take in his own morning-break snack, and midday lunch-box. Now well buffered against swinging glucose levels, should the situation arise, he is able to tolerate the occasional infringement of the diet without any ill effects.

Today, when unpacking his school-bag, I find an extra lunch box labelled "Marks mums cokies". Inside there is a note:

"we LOVE your cokies please fil the box signed – 2nd form."

Scientific answers

So with equilibrium restored around us we are free to return again to tracking the course of autism in the scientific world, always looking for new developments in research. We find a paper which we consider to be second only in importance to that of Kanner's original diagnostic paper. Entitled "The syndrome of autism: A critical review", it was written by Drs Ornitz and Ritvo. In it they give the following twelve-point summary of their conclusions about autism. These conclusions were based on the results of "serious scientific efforts" and were arrived at in the light of the current state of the art in medicine. The authors avoided all studies based simply on opinion.[16]

1. Autism is a specific syndrome and it can be clinically defined by behaviour.

2. It is evident at birth or shortly afterwards and is life-long.

3. The symptoms of it indicate an underlying disorder which has an effect on the rate of development, on the regulation of perception, on language, on intellectual and cognitive abilities and on the ability to relate to others.

4. Autism cannot be caused by any known psychological conditions in the environment of the child.

5. Diagnosis is based on early developmental history prior to three years of age. This must indicate impairment in perception, language, rate of development and ability to relate to both people and objects. Many individuals show disturbances in movement (motility).

6. Autism can occur on its own, or in conjunction with other disorders affecting the central nervous system.

7. It affects children from all over the world, from all races and creeds, and from all intellectual and social backgrounds.

8. There is no cause-based treatment that will change the course of autism.

9. Correct diagnostic procedures involve a full medical and neurological examination. They must take into account the fact that seizure disorders can develop as the child grows older.

10. Behaviour therapy and special education programmes will help the prognosis in most cases. These should be undertaken by trained specialists and parents. All programmes should be periodically updated to take into account the clinical changes that will occur over time in most cases.

11. With regard to the outcome in autism they held that the intellectual impairments in about two-thirds of individuals are severe enough, unfortunately, to warrant their being classified as retarded throughout their lifetime.

12. Finally they concluded that further basic research into the organic process underlying autism is necessary if a reason-based treatment programme is to be developed.

We focus on two areas of this paper which have special interest for us. One is the *disturbance of motility* (movement). We look at it now in the light of Mark's night rocking and, previously unmentioned, his tendency from the age of about three to walk on his toes and later to flap his arms. We see less and less of these last two disturbances as he grows older. They are movements of which he himself is not conscious because, if brought to his attention – "Mark honey, don't walk on your toes" – he will look surprised and walk normally. If told – "Don't flap your arms, dear" – he will stop – not having been aware that he was doing it. More recently we have noticed an unconscious disturbance of his facial muscles. It appears that as one set of disturbances is being phased out another is beginning. We notice that all of these unconscious movements will be exacerbated or even brought on by stress or by extreme fatigue.

Ornitz and Ritvo write that their review of the literature has led them to conclude that these disturbances in motility can be best understood if thought of in terms of a dysfunction in the central nervous system. They point to the possibility of a relationship between them and the disturbance in perception. They list these disturbance movements that can take place. They involve the limbs, head and trunk – hand twirling and flapping, toe walking, body rocking and swaying, head banging and rolling and darting movements of the trunk. When they occur repeatedly they are referred to as "stereotypies."

The second aspect of autism discussed in this paper to which we pay particular attention is the *disturbances of perception*. The authors consider the inadequate regulation of sensory input to be a unique and striking aspect of the condition of autism, pointing out that it can show itself in the child as having too much or too little of any sensory stimulus.

They also comment that individuals with autism who have "normal" perception have been found to make poor use of visual discrimination when learning. In addition they have been shown to depend greatly on feedback from their motor (muscle) responses in order to make sense out of their perceptions.

Among their case histories we read of a young boy, aged nine, whose perception disturbances remind us of Mark. When asked why he rocked and had his hands before his face, he answered that he felt the walls were moving in on him and that the floor was moving up at him.

With regard to predicting the outcome in later life for children with autism, Ornitz and Ritvo cite two factors which predict poor outcome –

1. lack of ability to develop communicative language by the age of five

2. lack of ability to play appropriately with toys by the same age.

In discussion these authors are at pains to point out that *patience is the hallmark of management in autism* and that improvements and regressions will occur spontaneously irrespective of whatever treatment plans are being put into practice. Furthermore, they consider that parents are often best qualified to implement programmes of therapy and should be viewed in the light of professional helpers, working alongside the professionals. They completely disregard the old notion that parents could in any way be implicated in causing autism, pointing to many recent studies in support of their conclusion. In fact, they turn this old notion on its head by pointing to studies showing that the stress involved in rearing a child with autism can actually cause emotional disorders in parents.

In addition they state frankly that if a physician, consulted about a child with autism, assumes that there is "something" wrong with the parents and that this "something" has caused the autism, this physician, in turn, may produce an emotional disorder in these parents.

Although we have long since shrugged off that ghost of parent blame it has never *quite* exited the stage. Memory, always waiting in the wings, can stir it to take a fleeting curtain call at the most unexpected moments. Now, in the light of all the above, we feel somewhat exonerated and think that maybe we have not done so badly after all. Our equilibrium has been restored by the sound, scientific endeavours of Drs Ornitz, Ritvo and others. Perhaps it is now time to lay that ghost to rest for ever.

CHAPTER 11

Moving Forward

Changing times

C ontinuing to track the course of autism in the scientific world, we look back over the literature in order to trace from it both the concepts of autism, and the criteria for defining autism and we notice change. In 1943 Kanner had diagnosed autism on the basis of a narrowly defined set of symptoms. Subsequently, in the late 1940s and 1950s, attempts were made to broaden the concept and to include in it childhood schizophrenia and childhood psychosis.

In the late 1960s, through the 1970s and into the early 1980s there was a swing back again to a more narrow set of definitions. These were based on:

1. lack of ability to develop social relationships

2. delay in language acquisition (echolalia, reversed pronouns, and faulty comprehension) and

3. rituals and compulsions carried out in repetitive play routines.

All the above patterns of behaviour had to have their onset before 30 months of age.[17]

In the mid 1980s we see a widening again of the autism concept and definition. The work of Hans Asperger, originally published in German in 1944, comes creeping into the English-speaking literature under the title of

"Asperger syndrome". Asperger's concept and definition of autism is much wider than Kanner's cluster of nuclear symptoms. Consequently, it brings with it a more global view of autism – listing cases that showed severe organic impairment as well as cases shading into normality.[18]

Asperger called the condition *autistic psychopathy*. Like Kanner he was struck forcibly by the fundamental aloneness and isolation of the children he wrote about. As he described it, it is as if they were "alone in the world". He considers that the basic disorder in individuals with autism is defined by the limitation of their social relationships. He is at pains to point out that the entire personality in such children is decided by this limitation.[19]

He comments particularly and with great enlightenment on how peculiar and characteristic is their eye-gaze:

- of how rarely does this eye-gaze fix attentively on either people or objects in order to make contact (rather it slides by them into the distance)

- of how, when speaking to people, they do not look at the person; rather, the language is directed to the air around the individual

- of how mainly they use their peripheral vision for perceiving and of how in this manner they can process a large section of the world around them.

He contrasts all of this sharply with that of the average child who, from the age of three months, will make social contact on the basis of eye-gaze.

Over a period of about ten years Asperger observed over 200 children, all of whom showed autism to some degree. He was convinced that the cause of autism was organic or biological, that it "ran in families" and was due to genetic factors.[19]

Neither Kanner nor Asperger anticipated the fact that a considerable percentage of people with autism will also have intellectual disabilities. The figures for this vary from study to study, and show that something in the region of 70 per cent of all people with autism will also have intellectual disabilities.

Autism is now being classified as a developmental disorder. This means that from infancy onwards the entire pattern of a child's development will be affected. Consequently, all normally developing skills in the young child will be influenced by autism. More and more the words "developmental delay" become associated with the condition, indicating that there is a slowing down of all areas of natural development.

Change is also what lies ahead for Mark in these early teenage years – a change of place and direction. At the age of thirteen he bids farewell to the junior school – a farewell tinged with regret and sadness on the part of both pupil and teachers. He partakes of all the passing-out ceremonies and, complete now with school tie and crest, he is a fully accredited member of the Old Boys' Club. It is the parting of the ways for this group of fifteen who have cemented loosely together through the ups and downs of the last four years. Some are to return to their own countries, others move on to full-term boarding schools and a few, including Mark, will continue their education in day schools.

Some of these cemented friendships will last a lifetime – friendships often maintained across time and space to be renewed again in adulthood. Mark's two special buddies, Philip and Stephen, are leaving the country, one to return to Europe and the other to Africa. For them it will be farewell for ever because Mark, as yet, is incapable of forming the human social bonds necessary to establish and maintain the two-way contact that is friendship. Philip and Stephen relate well to Mark but Mark, in turn, is not capable of relating to them. He enjoys being with them when the occasion arises, laughs with them and enters into their practical jokes and mischief, but the sustained "burden" of the friendship is all on their side. Mark never seeks them out; he is not capable of initiating contact. Always it is they who have to come to him. When they leave Mark is alone again and will stay that way unless a parent, a teacher or some boys themselves set up the next encounter. When they leave the country, Mark, for them, will be just a memory. And for Mark? One wonders, will there even *be* a memory? As of now it is data and objects that fill Mark's memory.

For him people are still shadow and not substance.

So we will celebrate what we have been privileged to enjoy in friendship over the last four years and bring the era to a close on the occasion of Mark's thirteenth birthday.

We organize a party at the swimming pool for all fifteen of his classmates and a circle of other friends. Under the watchful eyes of two coaches and parents, the dome of the pool echoes to the rivalry and revelry of team songs and school anthems. Afterwards, on the way to the restaurant to blow out the candles on the birthday cake, when passing through the amusement arcade,

Mark stops to put a coin in the slot of one of the machines. He pulls down the lever.

A flood of silver cascades out – spilling onto the floor – clanking mechanically down the front of the machine to scatter in all directions. Mark hits the jackpot – a fitting reward for four years of endurance and endeavour – a fitting end to an era of achievement. His peers stampede from all quarters to help him collect and to share in the spoils.

The helpless chef, holding aloft his perfect confection of blue and gold on a silver salver, is trapped between the falling coins and the milling, searching hands. He struggles to keep his feet and his equilibrium.

The thirteen candles burn down unnoticed.

Change is the single most difficult aspect of living that Mark has to contend with on a daily basis. Even at thirteen his hold on his environment is still so tenuous that he will only navigate it successfully if every facet of it is predictable. At home he still clings daily, almost for survival, to sameness, ritual and routine. He can face out into the world each day and remain there successfully for a period of time only if, on returning home, he can slip back into familiarity with everything exactly where it should be and as it should be.

His rituals are still ongoing. The present one consists of building a replica of our village street with Lego building bricks. Some weeks ago on a visit to the city he saw and was captivated by a window display of prize-winning Lego models. On returning home he retrieved from the attic the never-used Lego presents he has been given over the years and set to work on the floor of the den. On returning to the house, from school or daily summer camp, each afternoon he drops on the floor and continues where he left off.

Change, then, of its very nature threatens his basic stability because it takes away from him the crutches he needs to build on to navigate the course of his day. For him, sameness is still sacrosanct.

Blueprint

How can we minimize the impact of this major change Mark faces in the autumn when he will begin all over again as a new boy – this time in an all-boys' school? We approach the preparation for this change on the basis of space and time. During the holiday period we will visit the school a number of times and let him familiarize himself with the layout of the sports fields, classrooms and all buildings he will need to frequent. From this he will draw a plan of the school for the walls of the den and think himself into it long before term begins. With this plan indelibly imprinted in his mind's eye he will navigate the buildings successfully on a daily basis. This approach will give him confidence and it proved very successful in his previous school.

In addition we will obtain a copy of the school timetable ahead of schedule. This also will go on the walls of the den where one or two glances will be sufficient for him to commit it to memory for the year.

Mark loves the predictability of a daily timetable – the structure and boundaries of it bring security and confidence. He can cope with the expected – he prepares himself for that. The unexpected – a class being switched, an outing postponed, a match cancelled – throws his *modus operandi* into grave confusion. We have noticed that one change in the day's schedule will affect every event after that. It is as if time events come to him in a block and if one is altered the remainder are no longer recognizable. It rather reminds one of his earlier years when a single change in an ornament in a room appeared to render that room unrecognizable.

It would appear that he relies on rigid subconscious time memory to navigate the events of the day rather than using his adaptable conscious mind, as if he still navigates by reference to a blueprint – in this case the blueprint of a timetable.

An adaptable conscious mind – looked at objectively this crystallizes the basic impairment in Mark. To navigate his world in time and space he is not using his adaptable conscious mind, substituting instead rigid subconscious memory. How can we move him from subconscious to conscious? Many of his thought processes are still fragmented and working in isolation. His islets of ability are strong but their focus is narrow and restrictive. An adaptable conscious mind of its very nature has to be global. Could it be that his islets of ability, because they are overused, are in fact contributing to his disability?

We mull over conscious *versus* subconscious, hoping to glean some insight into the fundamentals behind them. In the course of it we read an enlightening paper reporting on autopsy studies in autism.[20] This paper focuses on areas of the brain known to be involved with memory and emotion. Previous research showed that there is evidence for two memory systems in the brain. One is called *representational memory* and it is accessible to conscious recollection. It deals with learning and recognizing events and facts as well as all sensations. It depicts the use of memory in the normal everyday sense of the word and is thought to develop some time in the early years after birth. This paper reports finding abnormally developing cells in this memory system in the cases of autism that were examined.

The second type of memory system is called *habit memory*. This is a specific, rigid, memory system and it is not accessible to conscious recollection. In their research this team did *not* find abnormalities in the cells of this memory system. This led them to the conclusion that reliance on this rigid memory system, which they have found to be intact in autism, is consistent with the repetitive, stereotyped behaviour patterns found in autistic behaviour. They also point out that reliance on habit memory would explain why some children with autism can react "catastrophically" to small changes in their environment – for example, a piece of furniture being changed in a room. This, they hold, would be enough to render the entire room unrecognizable.

Second-level education

Wiser now and having gleaned more understanding we leave the issue of conscious mind *versus* subconscious memory to one side (and to time and nature) and return to the practicality of preparing for the school year ahead. Although Mark is the only pupil from his old school transferring to this new establishment, he is fortunate that Robin, also a new boy, will be in the same form. They will travel together and be a support for each other as we will operate a car-pool transport system taking weekly turns. In addition, Darren and the twins are old boys in the school and will look out for them both – being in a position to offer assistance if necessary.

What qualifications does the average adolescent of thirteen need to survive/succeed in a mainstream senior school environment? He will need a competent, educational peer-level standard on paper. Mark has already attained this level as demonstrated by the 50 per cent average result he obtained at the school entrance written examination grade. On the intelligence test he achieved an overall IQ level of 92. We are not over-concerned with his ability to cope academically with most subjects. We are, however, concerned about his poor writing and presentation skills.

Many hours of writing tuition have not produced clarity, legibility or speed in the vehicle by means of which he will have to present his knowledge. He now enters a six-year cycle of essay-writing in three different languages, English, Irish and French, in addition to comprehensive paper-consuming answers in history, geography and biology questions. The content of a first-class piece of homework is of little value if it is barely legible, unpunctuated and lacking in capital letters.

Also, because he writes slowly, the sheer amount of time involved in coping with this, for him, vast volume of written homework will defeat him.

We see only one possible answer. Mark will have to learn to type and we will endeavour to get permission to have some of his homework submitted in print. We find an old-fashioned, portable typewriter in the local auction rooms and with it he sets off to Saturday morning typing classes – happy at the thought of using this new machine with its intricate moving keys which strike, fall back and strike again.

Handedness

Observing Mark using his hands is an interesting experience. He has never developed hand specialization. He uses his right hand for work on the right side of his body and his left hand for work on the left. Also, he does not co-ordinate the use of his hands. When his right hand is in use, his left is either in his pocket or lying idle by his side and *vice versa*. Always being reminded to "use both hands together, dear", he will attempt to do so for about ten seconds and then fall back again into the old pattern as if he cannot sustain the effort required. Except on rare occasions (for example playing music or canoeing, when both hands have to work in unison) he invariably works single-handed.

We line up minor jobs in the garden for him to encourage the use of both hands together only to find, when he saws a small branch, that if the branch is on the right side of the tree he will use the saw with his right hand. If it is on the left side of the tree the saw will be used with his left hand. Meanwhile his free hand lies idly by his side. It does not seem to occur to him that he should use this free hand to steady the branch.

Overall, on watching him, one gets the impression that his left hand should be his dominant hand. He will post a letter, answer the phone, pick up his shoes and carry out all spontaneous actions with his left hand whereas learned skills such as eating, drinking, tooth brushing and writing are performed with his right.

The vast majority of people (90%) in the average population are right-handed and the ability to use each hand individually with equal skill (ambidexterity) is very rare. There is a correlation between handedness and the side of the brain that is dominant for speech (lateralization). Almost all right-handed people develop speech dominance and motor skills in the left hemisphere of the brain. This is the normal pattern of lateralization. By contrast, only slightly more than half of left-handed people develop speech dominance in the right hemisphere of the brain. In the developing embryo lateralization begins as early as twelve weeks into gestation (pregnancy).

A different pattern of handedness emerges in the autistic population where abnormal patterns of handedness have been found in almost all population studies undertaken of children.[21] The figures show that the incidence of left-handedness (20%), is about twice that in the average population. With regard to the incidence of mixed-handed dominance (as seen in Mark), it has been shown to vary from a low of 17 per cent to a high of 47 per cent across a number of studies with a mean frequency across studies of one-third (33%).

It is clear from the various studies that the children with autism who have established hand dominance, either right or left, will do better cognitively (intellectually) than will the mixed group. It is also suggested that these three patterns of handedness found in autism might have the potential for use as markers of different sub-groups or, indeed, for tracing different aetiologies (causes).

A very recent study compared handedness in two groups of high-ability individuals with autism. Group one had early language problems. Group two had not. The majority of group one showed mixed-handed dominance whereas the majority of group two had right-handed dominance. However, the proportion of mixed-handed dominance in group two was still significant when compared with a group of children who did not have autism.[22]

Motivation

One cannot, at times, but wonder to what extent motivation still plays a part in Mark's manual dexterity. At Christmas time he was given a present of a small electric Space Invaders playing machine. With his left index finger on the firing mechanism he performs a downward movement, co-ordinating it perfectly with a right to left movement of the joystick held between the index finger and thumb of his right hand. Lying on his tummy on the floor he spends hours shooting down the invaders with such success and rapidity that he can out-score, on a performance and time basis, every other individual, teenager and adult alike, who visits the house. His scores run into the thousands – theirs into the hundreds.

In music he now plays three instruments – clarinet, flute and panpipes. On the clarinet he has formal tuition in classical music. With the pipes and flute he indulges the great love of his musical life which is traditional and folk music. Watching his nimble fingers skilfully manipulating the keys – both hands working perfectly in unison – covering and uncovering the openings, co-ordinating embouchure, breath, note, hand and finger movements, one cannot but marvel at the dancing precision of these fine finger movements required to produce the sprightly beat of the reel or the haunting lament of the slow air. But then, perhaps, one should not underestimate the power of music to transcend movement.

This power of music to transcend movement is vividly portrayed by Oliver Sacks in the case of a patient with Parkinson's disease. This patient could be transformed from immobility to mobility by imagining the sound of inner music – music she had danced to many years before. With this spontaneous arising of inner music the power of movement would suddenly return to her and then she could partake of all that was going on around her until that inner music stopped. Then all power of movement would cease and "she would fall instantly, once again, into a Parkinsonian abyss". Sacks comments that this power of music to liberate such patients from immobility was fundamental and was seen in every patient. However, the freedom only lasted as long as the music.[23]

There is in the literature the story of six-year-old David who has autism and who, because of poor visual–motor co-ordination, cannot tie his shoe-laces. During music therapy it was discovered that he had excellent audio–motor co-ordination. So the therapist put the entire process of shoe-lace tying to music in the form of a song. David was then able to tie his shoe-laces without any difficulty using the beat (time) of the music to co-ordinate the process.[24]

The pitfalls of the system

Keeping in mind that all subjects require writing and presentation skills, what subjects requiring manual skills will Mark take at the school in the autumn? He will study art, musicianship, science and woodwork. We plan a four-week daily art course during the three-month holiday period, a course incorporating pottery, batik and ceramics as well as basic tuition in drawing and painting. Looking objectively at the remaining six subjects on the school curriculum – three languages, maths, history and geography – all should be well within his capability even allowing for his uneven intellectual profile. In this uneven profile the weaknesses, as would be expected, lie in the areas of insight, imagination, abstract thought and mechanical reasoning.

In English and mathematics he will take the lower-level course and will have the advantage of small class numbers in the region of about eight pupils. All other subjects will be taken at the level of a common paper competing at honours level (60%) or pass level (40%), and with full class numbers of twenty-four.

Our greatest concerns for the year ahead lie as always with the emotional, social and sensory elements of the school system. These, and not the educational content of the syllabus, are the factors most likely to defeat Mark. And these also are the elements over which we will have no control. We can do nothing to mitigate the effects of sensory overload at the school.

Nor can we have any input into the difficult social situations that might arise. We are aware that Mark's already high anxiety levels are going to be taxed to their utmost during the year ahead. Although we have built in what support structures lie within our power, when looked at objectively, even for the average young person, the stresses and strains of competing every day in a school environment can be formidable. It is true of most people that their school days did not fulfil that old adage of being among "the happiest days of one's life."

Any system which has to cater for so many diverse educational standards, so many conflicts of temperament, personality and backgrounds and such a wide scatter of natural talents and level of commitment is of its very nature bound to be flawed. How then can we best steer Mark through the pitfalls of the system?

- By thoughtful planning ahead (among other items a double set of all school books and sports gear were purchased at the beginning of term).

- By building in safeguards and fall-back positions (for example, emergency money, spare locker keys and telephone numbers stitched into a false inside pocket and replaced daily if they have to be used).

- By constant liaison with other parents (checking for unexpected half-days, changes of plans, last-minute cancellations and the like).

- By giving him occasional weeks off school (time out to recover).

- By relieving him of part of the load (at the beginning of term we will have him excused, on medical grounds, all team games for the first two terms).

- By giving him constant committed help to get him through the homework routine.

- By taking daily responsibility for the contents of the school- and gear-bags, thus making sure that he goes to school every day with exactly the right requirements.

Beyond that, eternal vigilance exercised with foresight.

And beyond that – *one day at a time.*

CHAPTER 12

Upwards We Snake

This Easter Sunday morning, an hour before dawn, we slip quietly out of the back door of the cottage and down the mossy slope to join the line of silent, dark figures moving purposefully ahead towards the mountain. Above us the stars shimmer – radiating their brilliance to earth against the inky blackness of the night sky. Our world is white – transformed by a mantle of hoar-frost. Beneath our feet it crackles, hardening the muddy ruts of the mountain track, filling the darkened pools with slabs of cleansing ice – beautifying the debris. Spiders' hammocks hang heavy, stretched out across the heather, etched in sharp relief – ermine fur transforming each sturdy upright – the more slender cross threads bejewelled with drops – a craftsman's dream of filigree.

Reaching the mountain we skirt the base, following the well-trodden path of centuries. The going is easy here, the turf firm beneath our feet. The sky lightens, blackness giving way to blue. The pace of the ascent is steady – set by the measured tread of the life-long pilgrim – muscle, sinew and nerve-fibre honed. We struggle to keep our place in the line, leaning heavily on our staffs.

Upward we snake.

No word is spoken – all breath and energy committed to the climb. Above us the stars grow dim – receding. We reach the scree. The going is tougher now. Loose craggy stones move underfoot. It takes only one false step to start a downward slide. Cautiously, we feel our way, testing each foothold before we advance to the next. The sky turns pale – that pre-dawn paleness of a vanishing night. The stars have gone – snuffed out. Time hangs suspended in that limbo between day and night.

Lifting our eyes from the scree we gaze upwards. The top of the mountain looms above us – the goal in sight. Dragging weary bodies on aching muscles we plod on – creeping forward over the rough ground. The line is broken and swallowed up ahead as the first of the pilgrims disappears over the top. Energy renewed we hold our place in line until our turn comes to pass over the rim of the summit and onto the flat plateau.

The first of the pale blue and yellow streaks spreads across the sky from the east. They deepen to azure and gold. Behind them, layer after layer of kaleidoscoped crimson light fans out to herald the rising sun now appearing above the rim of the horizon. Majestically it ascends, rotating on its orbit – a great globe of orange light. Behind us the ruins of the ancient ninth-century monastic church reflect its glory. Warmed and mellowed, the stonework covered in amber lichen glows. Illuminated – the recesses of its dark corners yield up their secrets.

We enter the ruins to watch and pray – awed before the splendour of this Easter dawn.

Long before noon we begin the downward descent. On reaching the lower slopes of the mountain we pass through the woodlands. Here we pause beside a stream and, filling the kettle, light a fire to brew up for our first meal of the day. Sitting stretched out on the mossy bank leaning against the silver birch trees, we eat in silence – listening – listening.

Many years later Mark would remember this woodland stop in the first of his poems.

Easter-day

Wish you were here
Under the dappled dome,
To hear the water in the liquid stream
Tinkling through its stony home.

To hear the crickets click,
To hear the song-birds chirp,
To hear the squeak-squeak of the hare
Leaping to its woodland lair.

The whisper of the wind
Straying through the trees,
The branches swaying softly
In the gentle breeze.

The bleating of the lambs in the fields nearby
And the wind moaning low with a pleasant sigh.

The blueprint fades

During the years that follow we will reflect many times on this Easter dawn as we watch Mark reach his own dawns. These past three years bring significant changes in him. He matures physically, socially and intellectually. He moves from isolation to integration, from the particular to the global, from object absorption to people awareness. He still does not make eye contact but occasionally now he will cast a fleeting glance with his peripheral vision at my face.

He inches forward from rigid subconscious memory to adaptable conscious mind and, as he does, so we see the islets of ability gradually sink below the surface of the lacunae. The transition is gradual, at times almost imperceptible, but it is there and it gathers momentum with each passing year. It is as if the weights are being slowly transferred from one pan of the balance to the other. For a time we wondered, would they reach equilibrium and the momentum stop there? But no, the upward swing of the conscious keeps pace with the downward fall of the subconscious and now we find that the conscious has broken through the surface. It would appear that for Mark it is not possible to maintain both islets of ability and adaptable conscious mind at the same time – that one can only be developed at the expense of the other.

A review of the literature on islets of ability indicates that anything up to one-quarter of children with autism have a cognitive skill considerably higher than the average figure for the general population. This particular cognitive skill will also be significantly higher than the child's own general cognitive level. Rarely, however, can these talents be put to constructive use because the subject matter occupying them, in most cases, has no practical application. This became obvious with Mark. There are, of course, very well-documented cases of autistic artists, musicians, and mathematicians with truly outstanding practical talents, but they are rare.

What is the nature of these islets of ability, also called bright splinters of the mind?[25] Studies from the research seem to confirm that they are "normal" intelligences, each with their own rules and probably with their own anatomical bases. They are, however, unpredictable and can disappear as suddenly as they appeared. They differ from ordinary intelligences by their separateness, by the fact that they stand apart and are not integrated with normal intelligence and personality, by being highly developed and by being autonomous.[10]

They have an untouchable quality about them and in Mark's case could not be influenced from outside or indeed from inside. They just seemed to come and take over. Their aloneness, their automatic quality, their obsessiveness, their sheer intensity, seem alien. Mark has never talked about these bright splinters of his mind; has never discussed the subject matter around which they revolve, as he will do with an ordinary talent like his musical ability. For him, we welcome their phasing out. For some time we have felt that they hinder normal development.

The sound of music

More and more the time that used to be given over to lighthouses, aircraft and their ilk is now being channelled into music. Mark has built up an impressive collection of folk and traditional tapes and on hearing a piece of music once he will pick up either the flute or panpipes and play the piece exactly as it sounds on the tape. He has been invited to join a group playing traditional and folk music. At the weekends, after the Friday-night classes, the group plays at the local club. Mark enjoys these sessions enormously. Musically, he is a well-integrated, accepted member of the group – socially, he remains on the fringes, not surprising perhaps as the average age of the group is twice his own age.

He remains anxious and tense before the music begins. But then, as he settles into the rhythm and beat, and as jig follows reel and polka takes over from slow air, his concentration is absolute. He "steeps" himself in the music – it wraps around him like an aura and for him there is nothing in the room but the sound of music. The sometimes hundreds of people sitting in a circle surrounding the group, perhaps clapping their hands to the beat, do not exist for him. He neither sees nor hears them. He is tuned only to the music in his head. Often the sessions run on into the small hours after midnight and still they play on – dispensing the magic. On occasion, visiting musicians from other countries join the group and the strange sounds from a didgeridoo or a sitar blend with the traditional Celtic notes, adding echoes of an ancient past. Mark is particularly excited about these special nights. There is a vibrancy about them, a vibrancy that extends his repertoire of sound – opening new vistas – sharing a different heritage – giving glimpses into the spirituality of another culture. He thrills visibly to these exchanges of sound just as he had thrilled to the sight of the elephant feeding when he was three years old.

At a classical level he gets formal academic tuition in musicianship and clarinet studies and has recently been accepted as a part-time, after-school pupil, for the next two years, at the City School of Music. Criteria for entrance to the school are strict and professional and only those with true musical ability gain acceptance.

Today, 21 June, marks the summer solstice. It has been designated International Music Day. To celebrate the occasion the headmaster of the school has organized an impromptu open-air concert. We arrive at the school in time to see the sixth-form stalwarts of the rugby team lifting the piano through the open window of the music room and out onto the lawn under the spreading branches of the beech tree. It has rained intermittently since early morning but the sky is now clearing. The junior school files out in line to sit cross-legged on the grass. Behind them the first-through-fourth-formers sit likewise – spreading out in circles around the piano. Mark, now a prospective fifth-former, takes his place with the senior boys, standing behind the rows of empty seats and awaiting the emergence of the staff. A small number of involved parents cluster in groups under the nearby trees. Precisely on time and led by the headmaster, the staff emerge and take their places.

The concert begins.

Mark is scheduled to play two clarinet pieces during the second half of the concert. I worry for him, hoping it will go well at this his first public solo performance. His turn comes. He moves smoothly into the piece to the accompaniment of the pianist. I think –

"Thank God, he's got off to a good start."

A sudden gust of wind tears the music off the stand whipping away the sheets. Blinded by the paper the pianist stops. Mark carries on – relying now on his memory. Faithfully it sustains him and he ends the piece with a flourish accompanied by a vivid flash of lightning and a resonating, ear-shattering peal of thunder. The thunder cloud bursts and the orderly group under the beech tree breaks up in disorder, running for cover.

Mark plays on – entering his second piece. He is scheduled to play two pieces, therefore he *will* play two pieces! Not thunder, lightning nor torrential rain will be allowed to interfere! – predictability at all costs. Behind him the piano becomes airborne again to disappear back through the open window of the music room. Holding the striped umbrella over Mark I stand beside him until the last note dies away. His first solo classical performance ends with an audience of one.

His second solo performance comes some weeks later. Over the last year the pupils of the chemistry class at the school have become members of a youth science movement set up to foster interest in the different disciplines of science. The individual groups have met weekly throughout the year. The close of the year's work is celebrated with an international youth science week – six event-packed days attended by similar young science groups from many different countries.

Mark has been asked to audition for the Thursday-night music concert. Passing the test, he is accepted and chooses the tin whistle as his instrument. He is scheduled to play a ten-minute medley of jigs and reels. Taking centre stage he begins – looking out over the heads of five hundred of his peer group. Enthusiastic, the young audience claps and taps to the beat. Mark finishes and bows. Calls of "aris, encore, mehr, more – we want more" rise up from the auditorium. Mark begins again, this time automatically slipping into the Friday-night session repertoire. The audience responds taking up the beat.

Thirty minutes later he takes a pause to begin the haunting lament of "The Londonderry Air". The hall is hushed, the mood changing with the poignant sound – the grieving cry of a mother lamenting the departure of her son to the war. The muted notes die away into the silence. The audience are on their feet – cheering – clapping. Mark bows to the standing ovation – to the calls of "May you always play the tin whistle!"

It is his finest hour.

One day at a time

And what of the last four years at the senior school? What of the vicissitudes of piloting an adolescent with Mark's impairment profile through the rigours of mainstream education? It has proved to be very much a question of *one day at a time*. We did not think beyond today – knowing that tomorrow would bring its own troubles – tomorrow would be anxious for itself. In addition to the expected sources of conflict/difficulty there was always the unexpected, ready to rear its turbulent head and knock events off course.

Mark's biggest challenge arose, as expected, from sensory overload. The school environment impinged on all his five senses. With his acute sense of tactility, the jostling that can occur while filing in and out of classes – while standing in line – while stampeding for the mini-bus on days out – whatever – upset him. The elbows, kicks, punches – deliberate or otherwise – hurt his skin, his muscles and his pride. With his emotional and social immaturity he was utterly incapable of deciphering whether a punch on the arm was accidental or deliberate, or maybe even friendly. To *his* sensory receptors they all had the same electrifying impact on his skin.

In the beginning he attempted to hit back at anyone jostling him but then he was reprimanded for being aggressive and fighting. Following that, his coping strategy became one of avoidance – avoid the situation by being last. This, in turn, led to being late and being reprimanded for unpunctuality. It was a no-win situation and was at its height during the first two years.

As the boys grew older they became more orderly and by this stage Mark had become one of a group of four who moved together and looked out for each other. This afforded him some protection.

His tolerance for sound bombardment improved over the years but he still reached maximum overload within a relatively short period of time. How did he cope then? His inner system took over and without his even being aware of it he went into shut-down. He had no control over this. It just happened. He compared it to a television screen going off the air. Everything just goes blank –

"As if somebody had pulled out the plug" (his words).

He feels nothing.

He hears nothing.

He sees nothing.

He is there in body only – oblivious to what is going on around him, until time has passed. Then he begins to feel a sense of coldness creeping through his body and this gradually brings him back to reality.

He then has to pick up the threads of what is going on around him (resource rooms for time out did not exist in the schools of the period). This is very difficult and of course he missed out on large areas of tuition. If he got one of these shut-downs during a period when they had to change classrooms, Robin or one of the group of four took over, gathered up his books and propelled him out of the room and on to the next venue. This change of scene always brought him back to himself.

His literal thinking pattern got him entangled in endless states of anxiety. On one occasion he was called up to the office to collect a letter. Running in from the sports field, through the building site for the new extension, he ran up the stairs leaving a trail of mud on the expensive, hand-woven carpet. He was severely reprimanded by the secretary for destroying a £2000 carpet. At pick-up time he sat, strained and tense, in the front seat of the car – the grey/white patch settled firmly in the centre of his face. Having read the signs, when we arrived home I made a pot of tea and toast and produced something sweet. He sat but did not eat or drink. I asked what I hoped would be the right questions –

"Now tell me what happened."

"I *must* have £2000."

"What do you want it for?"

"I *have* to buy a new carpet."

"A new carpet – for where?"

"For the stairs to the office. The secretary *said* I destroyed a £2000 carpet."

I looked down at his muddy boots and the pieces fell into place.

"Did you put mud all over the carpet – was that it?"

"Yes."

"Mark, if you put mud all over the stair carpet here, what would I do?"

"You'd clean it up."

"That's right – I'd vacuum it, wash it, then I'd let it dry and we'd walk on it again. Would it be destroyed?"

"No-oh I suppose it wouldn't – but the secretary *said* it was destroyed and it cost £2000 so I *must* have it."

"Wait a minute."

I went up to the attic and bringing down a square of old carpet handed it to him.

"Now destroy that piece of carpet for me."

Looking at the carpet in astonishment he used one of the stock phrases he would normally use when confronted with such a situation.

"I'm completely devoid of ideas at the moment."

"Right – let's see; I'll get the scissors; now I'm cutting it up into pieces. Is that destroying it?"

"Yes."

"Did you do that to the stair carpet?"

"No."

"OK. Now let's get the matches and go out into the garden. We'll put it on the grass and set fire to it."

Ten minutes later we looked down at the smouldering carpet.

"Is that destroying it?"

"Yes."

"Did you set fire to the stair carpet?"

"No."

"Well then, did you destroy the carpet?"

"No-oh I suppose not – but the secretary said –" His voice trailed off.

"Will there be people walking on it tomorrow?"

"I suppose so."

We went back inside leaving the smouldering carpet on the bonfire heap. Mark picked up a piece of toast and munched. I poured another cup of tea. There was silence.

"What will we do?"

"What really happened to the carpet, Mark, was it got muddy and in a sense the mud destroyed the *look* of the carpet because it made it *look* grubby. The secretary was annoyed by this and she exaggerated. But the carpet itself was not destroyed."

Another silence – Mark munched more toast.

"What will we do?"

"Suppose we write a letter of apology and offer to pay for having the carpet cleaned?"

"All right – we'll do that."

Mark reached for something sweet.

"And Mark – don't ever again walk up those stairs in your boots. Leave them at the bottom and walk up in your stocking feet."

Mouth full, he nodded. Another day's crisis had been averted.

Perseveration

Most of the anxiety-provoking crises are, however, not so easy to avert because they are not so obvious and easy for him to explain. Then Mark *perseverates*. Just as when he was younger he had perseverated in deed by lining up toys in parallel lines or by measuring the diameter of every match in a box, he now perseverates in word.

Perseveration is a common facet of autism. It is an outward expression of inner turmoil and anxiety. It takes the form of endless repetitive questioning relating to a specific topic and it goes on and on – *ad infinitum*. In Mark's case it is as if he is aware that there is an anxiety-provoking situation somewhere in his mind but he is not aware of exactly what it is or what is causing it. He cannot pin it down and this persistent "worrying at it" is an attempt to identify it. Just as in the past he could not locate his limbs – the concrete parts of his body – without outside help, so now he cannot locate the abstract – his thoughts – without outside help.

Perseveration then serves the purpose of calling in this outside help. Then one has to sit down, tease out all the facts surrounding the issue, get him to type them or draw a visual image of them and finally use one's powers of deduction to pinpoint the exact cause of his turmoil.

This is generally a process of trial and error and over the years I have jumped to many wrong conclusions. But Mark himself has an unerring instinct for the truth *when it is presented to him from outside*. He may not be able to arrive at it by himself but he will always reject wrong conclusions and instantly recognize the right one. When this happens the perseveration stops. Then the problem can be solved. However, if the situation is not dealt with immediately the wearisome repetitive questioning can go on for days or even weeks. When it is finally sorted out, in most cases the real problem at the heart of his turmoil bears no relationship whatsoever to the topic he was actually perseverating about.

Mark's perseveration then appears to be based on lack of insight. This lack of insight is the most disempowering impairment he faces at this stage of his life. It places him at the whim of every unusual situation, every exaggerated comment, every abnormal turn of events – whatever – and thus engenders fear leading to anxiety and, if severe enough, to panic. It is also the most formidable challenge we face in terms of how to deal with it. How best can we improve his insight into social situations? Any programme likely to succeed will have to be practical – but how? Closing my journal I walk away from the dilemma for now.

Some days later, watching Mark and Barry engrossed in one of Mark's favourite television programmes, I get the glimmer of an idea. Mark loves what he calls family drama television programmes. He will sit for hours watching these old serial programmes which chronicle the daily happenings in the lives of ordinary families and communities. He has a special interest in programmes which revolve around hospital situations such as *Country Practice* and *Shortland Street*.

Suddenly I realize that there is a wealth of suitable material here for use in role-playing. Mark has an *interest* in the situations that arise. Now perhaps we can take it a stage further and give him some *insight* into the situations that arise – insight into how and why people react and interact as they do, and into the thoughts that lie behind the words.

Setting up the video recorder I tape the programmes. Barry cleans out half of the den. Dao hangs a curtain to section off our stage. We prepare our lines and dress up in stage costume, using wigs and liberally applying the grease paint. Every facet and action must be exaggerated to get our meaning across. We must appear larger than life.

Mark sits in our auditorium; our audience of one. The first episode involves a hit-and-run accident. We act out. He watches. We ask the why questions, why questions that Mark still does not ask. We mime the answers. He watches. We play and replay. Settling into his seat, he becomes involved and the show goes on.

CHAPTER 13

Over the Rim
and Onto the Plateau

September dawns bright and sunny, bringing with it the new school year. Mark, now a senior boy, enters the fifth year – the beginning of his last two-year cycle. Today, Friday, is a day of anticipation. The results are coming out. The mood in the car this morning is sombre and silent. No chatter disturbs the smooth purr of the engine. The three passengers sit tense and absorbed. Three months ago the fourth form, in conjunction with seventy-five thousand others of their peer group, sat the first of the two State examinations undertaken as part of their educational cycle. The results today will determine whether they advance to the next level or repeat the fourth-year programme.

Parking by the gate I watch them file in for assembly.

Turning the car, I drive home to wait.

Returning at lunch-time for the expected half-day closing, I sense the atmosphere. It palpitates with tension and excitement. Around the grounds groups huddle in corners – scanning white slips of paper. Others walk alone holding brown envelopes close – afraid to open them, afraid of what they might see there. One breaks out of a huddle and turns cartwheels, yelling – "I got an A in maths!" Another runs in circles around the sports field throwing his books in the air, catching them as they plummet – "I passed! I passed!"

He gets a flying tackle from behind accompanied by a wild –
"Whoopee – I got three honours!"

Locked in combat they do a war dance around the goal post. They are
joined by a third chanting – "I got two Bs – I got two Bs!" They go into scrum
mode trying to gain possession of an imaginary ball. Watching, I see the
scrum grow larger.

Over by the headmaster's office a tall boy slips around the corner of the
building, a hint of tears in his strained white face. Running to catch up with
him a more successful friend claps a comradely hand on his shoulder –
walking in step to show solidarity. From behind the windows the present
fourth-formers look out. This time next year it will be their turn.

But Mark – where is Mark?

Turning I see him standing by the car door. He is alone. His aloneness
rivets me. It hits me like a tidal wave. Knocked mentally off-balance, I
struggle for my mental breath and think "Oh no, please no, not after all his
hard work." Slowly I walk over to him trying to formulate in my mind the
words I will use.

The door of the headmaster's office opens. He steps out. He is accompanied by the form-master, smiling broadly and holding a brown envelope in
his outstretched hand. "Mark, you forgot to collect your results – congratulations – well done." Mark takes the brown envelope and shakes both outstretched hands. They move on to congratulate others. "I'll open it at home
over tea and toast and something sweet," he says. I think, "He has at least
passed."

At home, sitting munching toast, he hands me the brown envelope. I
open it and together we look down at the white slip of paper. The letters rise
up to meet us. They leap off the page – six honours and four passes!! Not a
single failure in ten subjects and an honours grade in science, music, art,
French, Irish and history. He has succeeded beyond all our wildest dreams
and has come twelfth in a class of twenty-four. His future in the school is
now assured and his place among his peers secure.

This achievement is something he has gained entirely by his own Herculean effort and commitment. It is something for which he has fought hard
and won. It is his victory of concrete tangible results and it can never be
taken from him. He has climbed his own personal mountain and his dawn is
blazing across the sky.

We celebrate – driving to the cottage for one last week of September
holiday and sunshine.

Seeing faces

Sitting on the beach watching Mark rowing the dinghy along the shoreline I consider what a handsome young man he has grown into – tall, strong, well built, his body moving gracefully to the pull of the oars, his dark hair bleached by the sun – bright grey/blue eyes fixed on the island ahead.

Mark's eyes – I wonder what they see now at this age? What kind of a picture does the world present to them? We are fairly sure that the cracks in his fragmented vision have knitted together and that his world is now visually more solid, tangible and whole. There is, however, one exception to this.

It is the human face.

Mark's lack of eye contact has been one of the strangest aspects of his autism. From infancy, all through childhood into adolescence, endless effort has been expended in trying to entice him to make eye contact, but it was all to no avail. So it was decided to leave it to time and maturity. Recently he has moved from looking at a point on one's shoulder and staring through it, to casting fleeting glances at faces out of the corner of his eyes – thus using his peripheral vision.

This means that he is using the rod cells in the retina of the eye to process facial recognition. These rod cells are distributed around the periphery of the retina and are the cells we all use for vision in low light intensity, for example at dawn and dusk. Because of this they have poor visual input and will detect movement of people and objects, their shape and outline, but will not be able to process their finer details.

The other type of light sensitive cells in the retina are called cone cells. They respond to colour and function best in bright light. They have high visual input. They are essential for recording clear accurate images. The area of the retina where the greatest number of cone cells is located is called the *fovea*. This is the point of keenest vision. It is quite obvious that from infancy Mark has used to great effect the cells of this fovic area in scanning and recording the minute object details of his environment. But what about the human details? In view of this use of peripheral vision rather than fovic vision when viewing faces, is it possible that Mark either cannot see faces or sees them so poorly that they are unrecognizable?

The clues are there. Family relationships are indecipherable to him. Outside his immediate family he appears incapable of recognizing whether a grown man of average height is someone's husband, son, brother, father or even grandfather. Within the extended family he cannot decipher by sight which group of children belong to which group of parents.

In the neighbourhood if he sees dark-haired Mrs X driving away in her car and then on coming into the house sees dark-haired Mrs Y sitting in the kitchen he will say, "But I saw you drive away a few minutes ago". That is unless she speaks first. Then he will recognize her by her voice. More and more he tends to wait for people to address him first before he speaks.

Over the last twenty years there has been much written in the literature about abnormal face perception in autism. It has been documented that autistic children do not treat people as people; rather, they treat them as if they were objects. We saw many examples of this in Mark's early case history when he used other people's hands to get what he wanted. Conversely, there are examples of children with autism treating inanimate objects as if they were real people. We also saw examples of this in Mark's earlier years when he "peopled" his world with objects.

One recent study gives an account of an adolescent patient with autism who has been preoccupied with collecting Kanji characters (Japanese ideogram/alphabet figures) from childhood. She perceives these Kanji characters to be real people and substitutes them for the faces of the figures she draws. The figures will be perfectly drawn but in the place of the face these Kanji characters appear instead. One set of characters will depict tears, another laughter and yet another anger. The author of that report is familiar with other autistic patients in her practice who have a similar attitude to inanimate objects. She points out that this practice would seem to be delusional to us but might, in fact, be based on perceptual inconstancy.[26]

Going on to discuss what might be the basic disturbance in autism she quotes Hobson. Hobson questions the whole concept of how the normal infant or child recognizes a person as a person. Following on from this he considers the question of what has gone so "badly awry in autism" that the child with autism will treat a person more like part of the furniture. He concludes by suggesting that basic to the disorder of autism, in many cases at least, may lie a "biological perceptual-affective" impairment.[27] Kanner, it will be remembered, used that word *affective* in the title of his original paper on autism ("Autistic disturbance of affective contact"). As previously explained, it relates to the *emotional* element in a psychiatric condition.

Other research has tested face perception in children with autism using photographs and video recordings of faces and has matched their results against peer groups of non-autistic controls. Rather than relying on facial expression, as their peers did, the children with autism sorted the faces on the basis of the hats or glasses worn by the participants. In addition, they performed worse on a task of finding the "odd face out" than did the control group. On the other hand, they performed much better on matching upside-down faces. All these results indicate that piecemeal facial processing does occur in some people with autism and that such people do not use the configurational contour of the face as a whole when given the task of identifying faces.

Groups of children with autism have also been found to be impaired in recognizing facial expressions: expressions, that is, of anger, laughter, happiness, sadness and other basic emotions. This raises the question of *prosopagnosia*.

Prosopagnosia – what is it?

Prosop means face. *Agnosia* means that a person cannot correctly interpret sensations even though their sense organs and nerves are functioning in a normal manner. The fault lies within the brain itself. People with prosopagnosia can neither recognize faces nor recognize emotional expressions. For them there is no distinction between familiar and unfamiliar faces because for them there is no such face as a familiar one. They lack that vital capacity to develop familiarity. This is thought to be based on a lack of the vital capacity to respond emotionally to faces.

A recent paper documents the case of a young man of nineteen who was diagnosed with both Asperger syndrome and prosopagnosia. He reported that his recognition of people was based on hairstyle, clothing, manner of walking and such accessory items as beards and spectacles. "Faces in the flesh" (real people) were used to test his reactions to facial recognition. He could not recognize the members of the clinic staff, with whom he was familiar, when he met them outside the clinic in the street, in shops or when they were sitting posing as patients in the waiting room. When asked to identify members of the clinic from photographs he could not do so, explaining that he listened to voices to identify people and there were no voices in photographs.

The author of that report suggests that prosopagnosia may be an essential symptom of one of the autism spectrum disorders, perhaps of a specific sub-group of Asperger syndrome. She draws a parallel between Kanner's view of autism as an *affective* condition and Hans Asperger's consideration of it as an inborn defect of *emotion*. She then considers these in the light of the symptoms of prosopagnosia, commenting that autism and prosopagnosia converge and overlap in this area of impoverished visual "emotionality".[28]

Here one is reminded again that Hans Asperger in his original paper drew attention to the fact that the average infant, from the age of about three months, makes social contact through his eye-gaze. Asperger contrasts this with the peculiarity of eye-gaze found in the cases of autism which he examined, commenting on the absence of such eye-gaze which instead of making "contact" with the person spoken to, simply slides by him. All of which is very reminiscent of Mark who never, as far as we are aware, has actually gazed into another person's eyes.

Could Mark then be suffering from prosopagnosia? Or is it just that he cannot actually *see* the human face?

It is time to find out.

Some days later we row across the calm sea to the island to picnic in the shallow cove. The tide is on the ebb. It ripples lazily in and out of the rock pools, the sun glinting off the wavelets in a myriad of multicoloured spectra. Sitting at the base of the cliff we spread the cloth on the spotless white table of sand, settling our backs against the black limestone of the rocks to absorb the heat. Out to sea a school of dolphins is heading our way. Leisurely they dive, leap-frog and dive again – always in harmony. The hum of the trawler sweeping the bay attracts them. Curious, they come to investigate. Below us, the brown oarweed stands poised upright – ready to change direction. Watching it I see the fronds wave towards us.

The tide is turning.

"Mark, what colour are your eyes?" Sitting beside me, eating the last of the sandwiches, Mark darts a quick glance at my face out of the corner of his eyes and a second glance at Dao sitting on my left. I have dark brown eyes. Dao has grey/blue eyes. "Brown," he answers. Mark does not know the colour of his eyes. Dao sets up a distraction. "Look, the trawler is coming around. They must have located a shoal of herring. Come on Mark. Let's go around the back of the island and watch the fishing." They leave me to my thoughts. I have now established two facts. Mark was able to see my eyes and he does not know the colour of his own.

Over the months that follow I try to piece together the facts I can glean from him. He still has difficulty with monitoring and elucidating the functioning of his sense organs. It is as if he cannot be quite sure that they *will* work, therefore he cannot give a positive answer to any question about how they actually *do* work. Perceptual inconstancy is obviously still a significant factor operating in his world of faces.

Slowly and with perseverance a picture begins to emerge. Going into the den one evening I pause to watch the family drama programme Mark is engrossed in. Not for the first time my eyes rebel at the intensity of the depth of colour Mark insists in tuning the set to. Mentally I compare it with the normal tones of the colour setting on the average television. Could there be a clue here? Pretending I have mislaid my spectacles I ask Mark to interpret the faces of the characters, with questions such as – "Is that the actress with the blonde hair and blue eyes – what's her name?"

"No, this one has brown eyes and dark hair."

"Isn't that the face of the chap who plays James Bond?"

"No, it's an old, lined face."

Then I ask a very direct question.

"Mark, can you see these faces clearly?"

"Oh yes, on colour television a person can always be viewed in the whole context without fragmentation."

I am astounded! I find myself speechless!

It is one of the rare occasions when Mark is able to volunteer clear, concise, accurate information about his senses – albeit delivered in one of his stereotyped phrases.

I now have a large piece of the puzzle falling into place. Mark can see faces clearly on television provided the colour is set at maximum intensity thus establishing that the images are being recorded on the retina by the cone cells. But what about *faces in the flesh*? I am about to ask but am forestalled by his usual signing out statement – "No more questions – too much interference – system overloaded."

Medical investigations

We decide to enlist the help of the professionals. Mark agrees to undergo some medical tests. We pay a return visit to the eye specialist who had examined Mark in his earlier years and discuss the situation with him. He warns us that it is unlikely they will be able to pinpoint where the difficulty is. Their present equipment and knowledge is just not advanced enough. However, we decide to forge ahead. Mark undergoes a comprehensive eye examination and no fault is found. His eyes and vision are found to be perfect. The problem is more likely to lie within the brain.

We are referred to a neurologist. Here Mark undergoes a computerized tomography (CT) scan. No structural abnormalities are found. The neurologist informs us that research has shown that brain abnormalities that might be characteristic of autism do not show up on a CT scan and that scanning techniques are at present not sophisticated enough to detect such abnormalities. They have performed the scan to exclude the possibility of the presence of co-existing disorders that would show up, but not to exclude the possibility of the autism itself. In our process of elimination we have now established that Mark does not have any of the co-morbid (co-existing) disorders of autism that would show up on a CT scan.

Our third referral is to an endocrinologist. The tests undertaken in this department are to rule out the possibility of a metabolic disorder by investigating the results of all standard blood tests and undertaking 24-hour urine analysis. The present state-of-the-art scientific techniques are used, but no errors of metabolism are found in Mark's system. All his endocrine glands (thyroid, adrenal, etc.) are found to be functioning within the normal range and all standard and non-standard blood tests show up nothing outside the normal range. It is emphasized that only a very small percentage of people with autism show up with a metabolic disorder.

Finally Mark undergoes 24-hour EEG testing to investigate any possibility of seizure activity. An *electroencephalogram* (EEG) is a recording of the electrical activity from different brain areas. It is a measure of brain activity. There is a firm body of research on EEG studies in autism but, in common with much of the research in autism, the findings contradict each other and positive conclusions cannot be drawn. Consequently, all that can be said is that abnormal EEGs do occur in some people with autism and that this abnormality may be associated with co-morbid organic syndromes. Mark's EEG does show some abnormalities but the findings are inconclusive and no definite pattern can be established. There is, however, no evidence of seizure activity.

Epilepsy (seizure activity) has a stronger than normal association with autism. The peak times for seizures to occur are in early childhood and again in adolescence. By adulthood their estimated prevalence is of the order of 20–35 per cent.[29] This contrasts sharply with a prevalence of 0.5 per cent in the general population. Intellectual disability co-morbid with autism is a significant risk factor for the development of seizures in individuals with autism. However, epilepsy also occurs relatively more frequently than normal in high-functioning autism/Asperger syndrome. It has been shown to be of the order of a few per cent.[30]

Looked at professionally, then, we have taken the question of Mark's face perception problem as far as it is possible to go within the present parameters of medical technology. Until more sophisticated methodologies become available we will not find the answer. So we return to our detective work and our now well-honed tools of observation and deduction.

Mirror image

We caretake a friend's house while the family are on holiday. Visiting every day to check and turn lights on and off, I notice Mark hurrying past the large floor-to-ceiling mirror in the hall. He never looks into it. What is he afraid of?

I take him to the store to buy a replacement mirror for over the bathroom sink.

"Mark, how does my face look in this one? Does it make me look pretty?"

"Don't know."

"What do you see?"

Mark stands in front of me with his back to the mirror and glances at me out of his peripheral vision.

"Two dark eyes and lips moving."

Surprised at being able to elicit so much information from him so easily, I think, "Piecemeal processing – my face is fragmented – he cannot see the full contour of it". Grasping the opportunity, I catch him lightly by the shoulders and turn him around to face the mirror.

"Now look at us both in the mirror and tell me what you see?"

"Nothing."

"You mean you cannot see our faces?"

"Yes."

"But – ?"

Mark is gone. Whenever my probing questions become too much for him he will either tune out or walk away. This type of close question-and-answer session is very hard work for him and I am well aware that his tolerance of it is strictly limited. For him it entails concentrating intently to hear verbal information with no visual aids to help him. Then he has to hold the question briefly in his memory while he processes the answer in his mind. Finally he has to transfer his answer from his visual, associational speech, which comes readily to him, into our neurotypical speech, which does not.

This is the most difficult aspect for him because it involves searching for the right phrases among his repertoire of learned language and adapting these phrases to deliver his answer. It is akin to translating it into a foreign language. And he is not yet fluent in this foreign language although he improves constantly.

In these types of information-seeking situations which are set up to elicit specific information he cannot use his repertoire of learned-off phrases because the information is too personal and specific. He has to delve deep to find it. Therefore, I must always be aware of how difficult it is for him. I must choose my timing carefully and, above all, keep the sessions short and never ask such questions when he is tired; always then after a few questions give him his own space to "unjam the switchboard" (his words).

Enough then for today. I have elicited two very important facts –

- he was able to see only two isolated features of my face and

- he was not able to see either of our faces in the mirror.

Mark is incapable of making up a story, telling a lie or using his imagination to cover an incident. He can only tell the truth as it appears to him because the kind of inventive, abstract imagination needed to make up a story does not come within his experience. At this point in his life he can deal only with concrete facts.

Walking through the store in search of him I find him looking at electrical shaving units in the next room. He is enthusiastic about them saying he would like one for his forthcoming birthday. Mark loves shaving. Always shaving by touch he will spend a long time each day going over his face with a battery-powered razor.

During the next few weeks I make an exhaustive tour of the auction rooms until I find what I am looking for. Eventually I do. It is an antique shaving table of rosewood, with its small, adjustable round mirror beautifully mounted and rising above it to face level on a long slender brass pole. Just below the mirror there is a miniature barometer attached to the pole. The entire piece is badly in need of repair and restoration but the basics are sound and Dao will accomplish the transformation. It will stand in the corner of the den and on the wall behind it Dao will fix the new electrical shaving unit with its attached light.

On birthday morning the shaving table and unit are a huge success. Mark is enthralled with the barometer and the table – even commenting on the satisfying shape of the mirror. He spends time adjusting it at different angles. It is clear that this is one mirror he is not afraid of. It is too small and intriguing to be threatening.

Dressing up for the small family birthday party that evening, my ever-active mind flits back to the past – to previous parties. It pauses at the children's Hallowe'en party we had when Mark was six. I remember Mark's bewitchment at the sight of the painted faces of his young peers. An idea presents itself. Reaching for my rarely used make-up box, I apply some of the contents liberally and emerge looking somewhat like an over-decorated circus clown. "Mark will you help me with the chairs please?" He comes and moves the chairs around. He does not look at me. "Tell me, is my hair all right?" Looking up, his glance travels to my hair and stops at my face. He looks at it using his full vision.

"Your face – what happened to it?"

"It's make-up. I put on rather too much I'm afraid."

"It's like the faces on television."

I have my answer. Mark can see my full configurational face provided there is enough colour on it.

CHAPTER 14

Descent and Dissent

Faceless people

Thinking about faces confronts us with the strange and difficult world in which Mark has had to grow up. A world without faces. What image does it conjure up? Occasionally, on television, one sees people sitting, moving, walking, talking – people whose faces have been blotted out for anonymity – whose faces have been replaced by small flickering three-dimensional coloured squares. It is a strange experience to watch such people. They lack identity, expression, familiarity, even definition. They appear alien. One cannot make contact with them. There is an inevitable *disturbance of affective contact* because there is nothing tangible there to connect with.

One can empathize with their voices and the content of their stories but one needs a face behind the voice to make that affective contact. One needs the expression in the eyes, the quivering lips, the worried lines on the forehead, the tension in the jaw muscles. It is these that give definition to the person behind the words. One needs the human being behind the story and the expression of that can only be found in the face. *A face is what defines a person as a person.* It is the focal point of being. Lacking a face, there is nothing there for someone to focus on.

One wonders at what age Mark began to realize that those tall (to him) objects with hair, limbs and voices, seemingly coming from nowhere, were beings with faces. Quite possibly his first experience of seeing faces was those painted faces at that Hallowe'en party when he was six years old.

As radio was always our medium of choice, in those early years the only television set in the house was a small black-and-white portable set. Mark never looked at this; he never seemed conscious of it. The rare visits to a cinema or a circus, or perhaps the equally rare opportunity to see colour television in a neighbour's house, would have been the only occasion on which he would have come into contact with coloured faces. And even then one wonders if his strongly fragmented vision of these early years would have prevented him from seeing them. We bought our first colour television set for the den when Mark was thirteen and he has always been its main user.

Confronted now with what we have managed to piece together, can we do anything to improve his ability to perceive *faces in the flesh*? Because one's senses are all integrated it has long been established that if one sense fails the other senses can become more acute to help compensate for this failure. For example, in a darkened room one can find one's way around it more easily by following a trail of perfume. Smell will help to compensate for sight. Touch will also help to compensate for sight. Perhaps if Mark were to become more familiar with faces using his sense of touch then perhaps this, in turn, would help to bring them into focus.

We organize a course of professional aromatherapy massage for him – a half-hour session twice a week for a period of three months – twenty-six treatments in all. Part of this treatment involves training in using the tips of his fingers in order to apply pressure to both his own face and the faces of others and so become familiar in a tactile way with the face concept.

He emerges from this treatment with an improved sense of proprioception, announcing that he now finds it much easier to feel, and therefore locate, his arms and legs. He finds that he no longer needs the second wristwatch. Gradually he will move to wearing short-sleeved shirts – no longer having to rely on sight to locate his hands.

He is pleased with the results of these aromatherapy sessions saying that he feels "more together", "more grounded". He also reports a big improvement in "that feeling of floating off into limbo". It is less frequent and less intense. We plan another course in three months' time. Meanwhile, he continues his facial exercises.

Over the months that follow we watch him very slowly orientating his vision to include faces. He begins to make very fleeting eye contact with my now somewhat heavily made-up face. Going into the den one evening I find him looking into his shaving mirror while he runs the razor over his face. I wonder what he sees there. I ask no questions. It is enough that he at last looks into a mirror without fear. The development of a gaze reflex will take a long time – possibly years. He comes to it very late in life – developmental delay. For now, however, it is sufficient that he has begun.

The first leg of the descent

Mark's last two years of school are slipping by and he continues to work hard – always with a view to that final examination which will decide his career options at the age of nineteen. Other than the end-of-term athletics, he has opted out of all school sports, being now at the age when he has the freedom of choice to do this. It allows him more time to concentrate on his music and his new-found interest in canoeing. Always happy both in and on the water he has joined a canoe club and this year takes part in the first leg of the annual city-river descent.

On an autumn day of torrential rain we set out for the upper reaches of the river, canoes firmly lashed to the roof rack and passengers and gear stowed to overflowing in the wagon. Reaching the set-down stop, we watch the heavy flow of a river in spate, with grave misgivings. At our feet the dark foaming, swirling water circles and eddies before pouring over the slippery boulders to the peaty blackness of the pools below. A few days before we had stood in this same spot in the September sunshine, listening to the bright water murmur and meander as it lapped a leisurely way along its timeless course. From upstream now the rumblings of an ominous growl grow deeper and still the rain pours down swelling the volume of the river. We watch what seems to be a sleeping giant gathering its forces for a terrible awakening.

Fear gnaws at me – biting deep as it did of old.

Unless the event is officially cancelled Mark will go. The same Mark who still clings to the perseveration of sameness and routine will not adapt to a voluntary change of plans. I know this. His inflexibility and resistance to change will win and if we attempt to intervene we will have a mutinous Mark on our hands. Better that he go with our blessing than without it. Despite all our training and admonishing we have not managed to instil into him any real appreciation of danger. It is a lethal combination – this insistence on following a set plan at all costs and a lack of the awareness of danger. He will go and we will have to stand idly by. The rigidity and intransigence of this condition that is called autism is borne in on me one more time.

As the river rises we watch and wait for the rain to ease. One by one the cars with their occupants turn for home. Most of our passengers hitch a ride with them. A small group of canoeists – mainly the very experienced – and Mark, who is but a novice by comparison, take to the overswollen river and set off along the four-mile stretch to the lower reaches of the mud flats – the end of the first leg of the descent. We watch Mark wobbling in the water, his canoe spinning out of control. We watch him struggle with the paddle to right it before being pushed side-on towards the bend. A rush of water – he is hit and capsizes. Two of the leaders race to his side. They flank him – uprighting the canoe. Mark paddles again. All three are propelled out of sight towards the first of the rocks now turned into mini-rapids.

Heads bent into the driving rain and feet squelching in the mud we follow the course of the river on foot.

It is our longest day.

Four hours later we arrive at the rendezvous on the road by the mud flats. Many times on our downward journey we have had to leave the river bank and take to the road when the terrain became unnegotiable. By noon the rain had stopped and the sun shone but still the river swelled and rushed headlong, filled now by the rivulets from the feeder streams of the mountain.

Nowhere do we see evidence of the canoeists or of a landing, but then a river in spate does not leave such evidence. Forced once again to take to the road for the final stretch, our anxious thoughts propel us onwards through the last half-mile. Rounding the bend we come suddenly on the meeting place – an enclave cut into the rock. Before us, etched out with all the clarity of the high-powered lens of a microscope, a group of figures is brought sharply into focus. They appear stationary and then with the resolution of the lens they move – changing out of wet gear – mugs of strong coffee and dark chocolate changing hands – canoes and paddles lying abandoned on the tarmac – a scene of sane normality after the turmoil of the river. My eyes search among the dripping forms for Mark. White-faced and subdued he gives me the double thumbs-up sign. In his language it means – "I did it – I did it."

Exhausted and spent, I sit on the nearest rock and take a cup of coffee from an outstretched hand.

Judgement

We had tempted fate and once again Providence was kind to us. Ever since Mark's early teenage years, when we had sat together processing the results of his years of data collecting, Mark has become self-propelling. He has become a trier. A trier who will push himself to the limits of endurance and beyond. This is what has brought him so far – what has brought him out of the isolation and aloneness of autism. But this great strength has to be tempered with the flexibility to adapt to changing circumstances – with the ability to recognize danger and use common sense in the face of it, neither of which have been brought into play on this day of the river descent.

It could have ended in tragedy but, *Deo gratias*, it has not. Nothing like this must ever happen again and we must ensure that it does not.

For years we have walked the fine line between allowing Mark as much freedom and encouragement as is possible in order to develop to his full potential and to carve out for himself an interesting, fulfilling life, and the calculated risks of so doing. Mark's ability to judge a situation is impaired. Judgement is based on insight and Mark's insight, although improved, is still rudimentary. He has made the first breakthrough and the foundation is laid but, as with all his progress, momentum is slow and is gathered through the years rather than through the months.

Now, at twenty, does Mark qualify for a diagnosis of autism on the basis of the more modern criteria on which the diagnosis is founded? These criteria are centred around the triad of impairments:

- impairment in communication

- impairment in socialisation

- impairment in imagination.

This last is allied to repetitive patterns of behaviour and insistence on sameness. The diagnosis of autism has always been based on behaviour and there is, as yet, neither a medical test nor a biological marker which will unequivocally diagnose it.

Mark can no longer be considered to be actually impaired either in communication or socialization, although his language is somewhat lacking in spontaneity and delivered in a monotone with little inflection. But the impairment in imagination with its attendant inflexibility is still firmly entrenched. Imagination and insight go hand in hand. Being deficient in both and clinging rigidly to set routines takes away from him the free will to judge a situation impartially and consequently places him in danger.

Can Mark envisage danger now any better than he could when he was three years old and ran out onto the road to touch the lights of oncoming cars? Could he have imagined the many hazards of the river descent today? I think not. Had he been able to foresee them he would never have undertaken the journey. He is aware of them now, having experienced them dramatically at first hand, and has already stated that he will not undertake the challenge of the second leg of the descent. He is aware now that he is not yet ready for it. This has been a significant but highly dangerous learning experience and it has been the pattern of his learning to date. He has to experience at first hand the dangers and disadvantages of every situation before he becomes aware of them.

Mark has concrete imagination. He can write very descriptive essays about subjects he has personal experience of. Topics such as "The day we won the cup final" or "My first driving lesson" come easily to him because they are based on personal experience. He is describing events he lived through. But the kind of abstract imagination that arises out of a global-ranging mind does not seem to be readily available to him. Lacking this ability to look ahead, to foresee the unknown, to envisage the alternative, to take into consideration "what might happen", he lacks the ability to make a sound judgement.

Living with Mark has always involved anxiety. As he grows older the anxiety does not lessen; only the focus of it changes. It is easy to protect a young child but much more difficult to protect a young adult. Young adulthood is, of its very nature, an assertive phase and Mark is showing all the spirit of assertion and need for independence common to his peer group. We have always been tempted to protect him and for us to do this would have been an easier option to choose – an easier road to travel. But that would have been to opt out of our responsibilities to him and would not have prepared him for independence, nor for carving out a niche for himself in society, because we must always envisage a future when we will not be here – a future when if Mark is not capable of managing his own life, he will become dependent on others. These are the vital breakaway years and if the opportunities are not grasped now, the chances may never come again.

And yet – and yet – as we have seen today, Mark is not ready for these responsibilities. He is not ready for the decisions involved.

So this, then, is the dilemma with which we have to live. The dilemma of how to temper the still-limiting aspects of his autism with freedom and safety.

To live with autism is to live with change. All forms of autism may look alike in the early years but, as we have seen with Mark, the pattern changes as the child grows older. The basics will remain, although they may be modified, and outwardly they take on a different form. As I have written elsewhere:

> This picture of a fixated, obsessive, child can represent autism in the early years. But the picture is not static. Any artist depicting an impression of autism will need different canvases and different brushes. On his palette of primary colours he will need to mix many shades of colour; many nuances of tint, tone, and hue, because autism is not a condition that reveals itself uniformly. Rather, it runs the gamut of many facets and behaviours, all of which shade into each other and change over time and environment, pointing to multiple causes.[12]

Compromise

There is enormous variation in the autistic condition and people with autism can be as different from each other as are people in the general population. Autism may change over the course of a lifetime but it does *not* go away. One can forge a compromise with it, but that is all. Behaviour can be modified, communication improved, socialization skills learned and applied. Some people can achieve significant compensatory skills and find a productive niche in society. But autism does not go away.

It has been my privilege during the course of my work to become acquainted with a number of people who have high-functioning autism/Asperger syndrome. They range in age from eighteen to eighty. All are academic people. All are successful (some highly so), or about to be successful, in their chosen careers. Some of the older people are married, some have chosen to stay single. All have managed to find that niche in the workplace where they can use their particular talents – talents in some cases founded on childhood obsessions/fixations. All are respected for these talents and consulted for the scope of their knowledge in their chosen field.

But all have in common that aura of tangible aloneness and those who confided in me confided their awareness of their difference – their awareness of their inability to make that affective contact. They felt their aloneness.

They felt their disconnection. Compensate as they might, they could not surmount it.

Superficially, their difference is most obvious in communication. They speak to share outside facts but not to share inner thoughts and ideas. There is no richness in their communication – a dearth of inner self. Try as one might one could not establish a two-way interactive communication process with them. They speak *at* the person rather than *to* the person. That *link* that forges the connection is missing. Mostly one listens while *they* speak. One could spend half a lifetime communicating with them and yet, each time, would come away having got no closer to the real self. On the next occasion one would start all over again at the beginning. At times one wondered, is there a real self behind that persona? Or is there just the persona?

They are different. They have a different mode of being. And they are fortunate in having lived in an era when "to be different" was more accepted – in an era when a scatter of behavioural differences and non-conformity was tolerated by society as being part of the wider whole and indeed valued for its diversity.

And their difference is also obvious, if more subtly so, in their lack of imagination. Perhaps one follows on from the other. But one wonders which was basic: surely it must be imagination.

In discussing autistic communication, Peeters and Gillberg describe autism as a problem in the development of imagination – imagination, that is, in its most embryonic form.[31] This, they consider, is what is needed to transcend the literal and develop the scope to reach beyond it in order to invest sounds with meaning and so develop language, and, following on from this, what is needed to attach meaning to what is observed in social situations and thus develop social behaviour. Here one is reminded of a highly intelligent young man with autism who explains that he did not use speech to communicate until he was twelve years of age simply because he did not know that words have meanings, and therefore saw no reason to learn to produce them as sounds.[13]

Peeters and Gillberg also point out that parents and people who work with, or interact with, autism require a considerable effort of imagination in order to try to appreciate the concrete, literal world that is autism.[31]

Genetic factors

Autism is currently classified under the diagnostic umbrella of autistic spectrum disorders or pervasive developmental disorders, both of which have almost the same meaning. Two of the sub-groups classified under this diagnostic umbrella are autistic disorder and Asperger disorder (syndrome). It is generally acknowledged that the wide variation and complexity of symptoms to be found within the autistic spectrum point to, not a single disease entity, but multiple aetiologies (causes) similar only in that they end up in a final common pathway of behaviour.

Over the years it has become clear that genetic factors play a very important role in the cause of autism. Autism is genetically complex and the most likely model on which to base it is one in which three or four genes interact together to produce what is called the *autism phenotype*. The phenotype of an individual is the physical expression of the genes he or she possesses; in other words, it is what he or she turns out to be like owing to the interaction between genes and environment.

To be genetically complex means that no single gene or even a combination of genes will determine whether an individual will have autism or will not have autism. Rather the autism will result from the interaction of the genes that confer risk with certain environmental factors yet to be determined. Environmental factors cover anything from the basic nutritional environment of an individual to the presence of toxic factors. The task of future scientific work will be to determine what are these environmental risk factors involved in autism and, having found them, to seek to modify them and so reduce or eliminate the risk of developing autism. It is thought that all mental illnesses and behavioural disorders are genetically complex.[32]

Drawing on the limited evidence available it would appear that autism, Asperger syndrome, and the broader autism phenotype (i.e. a person with some symptoms of autism occurring in a mild form, such as having an excessive reaction to sensory overload or having a preference for solitary activities) are seen to aggregate in the same families. In some family members the condition will show up as classic autism; in others, for example parents of an autistic child, only one or two traits may be present, and in others again it will show itself in the form of Asperger syndrome. As will be appreciated, the severity of Asperger syndrome falls between the expression of the broader phenotype (mild) and the expression of classic autism (severe).[33]

CHAPTER 15

All On a New Year's Eve

Seeking to widen his horizons even further, Mark joins a hiking/ hostelling club. The invitation to join has come from some members of the Friday-night music sessions who are active club members. We suggest that he start with the easier day hikes, hoping to stave off the long weekends away from home for another year. These day ventures turn out to be very successful. He leaves early for the city on some Saturday mornings, equipped with hiking boots, packed lunch and rain gear, to join the special coach with some thirty or so others. He returns content, if exhausted, in the late evening having climbed a mountain, walked the hills, explored the forests or travelled long sections of the sand dunes by the sea – drumming up for tea and sambos (sandwiches) along the way – and munching carob to keep the energy supply flowing. Mark's tin-whistle is always at the ready to join in the impromptu music sessions that spring up – in the coach, on the mountain or wherever they stop for a rest.

During these outings he meets and gets to know many of the event leaders whom he learns to recognize by voice, hair and general appearance. This lays the foundation for the long weekend trips away from home of the future.

Although his eye contact improves slowly and with it his ability to perceive faces, for much of the time he sees them only in piecemeal fashion. He finds it much easier now to talk about his face perception and if asked – "How are faces today?" will answer "not great" or "I see eyes shining, a forehead wrinkling, lips smiling" or "I see an outline but everything else is blurred" or, very occasionally, "I see your face clearly". If asked – "Mark, what do you see when you look in the mirror?" he will answer – "Sometimes I see a face, sometimes I see nothing". Then he will walk away to avoid further questioning.

Anxiety

We are beginning to discover that Mark's anxiety levels impinge greatly on his ability to see faces. On days of high-anxiety levels his face-perception problems are at their worst and, conversely, on days when he is calm, relaxed and not over-fatigued, his ability to see faces is much better. This inconstancy of face perception significantly hinders his ability to deal with the world. At times it brings with it a disturbing sense of unreality.

Briefly we consider the question of medication to help reduce the debilitating effects of anxiety but just as quickly we reject it. We have always shied away from using medication to control or reduce these associated features of Mark's autism, preferring instead, if at all possible, to manage these conditions with alternative methods – in this case a caffeine-free diet, yoga, meditation and relaxation. Having been introduced to yoga at a young age Mark will undertake a work-out in times of stress. He uses his meditation and relaxation tapes daily, finding them of immense benefit. This regime of management does not cure anxiety but will help greatly to alleviate it. Because of his associational thought processes, leading to weak logic and a slender grasp of the principle of common sense, Mark's anxiety tends to be self-perpetuating. Much of it responds well to reassurance.

The four key factors considered to be of importance in managing anxiety conditions are – reassurance, relaxation, recreation and occupation.

How common in autism is anxiety and its attendant companion fear?

The answer to be found in the literature is that it is very common indeed. Most of the studies looked at (and there were many) showed that anything from one-quarter to three-quarters of the people under investigation were found to have symptoms of anxiety and fear. One study, investigating a large group of high-functioning people with pervasive developmental disorders (HFPDD) (including Asperger syndrome (AS) and high-functioning autism (HFA)) found symptoms of anxiety in over half the individuals in their sample.[34]

There are also suggestions from other studies that rituals and routines are used by children and adolescents to relieve these high anxiety levels, and that in times of stress a big increase can be seen in the incidence of these behaviours.

With regard to people with AS, it has been found that overwhelming anxiety can give rise to phobias about speaking in social situations and that this can lead to what is called "elective mutism".[35] This latter is a condition where the person speaks only in certain situations, or speaks only to certain selected people or may remain completely silent because the anxiety generated by taking part in a conversation is just too great. It becomes overwhelming.

Another worker in the field of AS, in discussing anxiety and panic disorders in his patients, points to the severe anxiety states that may occur, particularly, for example, in the face of the threat of a substantial life change. Such anxiety states can lead to psychotic episodes with symptoms similar to schizophrenia.[36] These, however, when treated with medication, are reported to have had a good outcome.

To sum up then – anxiety states are prevalent in autistic spectrum disorders and can, in certain people and under certain conditions, at times be very severe.

College days

To return to the story of Mark – how is he now that he is approaching his twenty-first birthday? Having left school at nineteen with sufficient credits to enter college, he is now a first-year student undertaking a two-year broad-based foundation course in business studies. This course is well within his capacity and does not tax his ability to any great degree, thus allowing him time to enjoy college life and continue with his music and outdoor pursuits. He is fortunate in his choice of college and has entered what he describes as "the happiest year of my life".

He becomes one of a group of twelve – six young men and women who "hang out" together in cafés, bars and discos, who walk the hills and valleys together or perhaps just hitch a ride into town to see a movie. The group actively sought him out and invited him to join them.

His days are full.

The hierarchy and discipline of the school years have been left behind and with them the necessity to conform to social norms and standards or else run the risk of intimidatory tactics and scapegoating. Mark now has the freedom to be himself – to be what he is and to build on the plateau at which he has arrived. In the atmosphere of acceptance that prevails in the college, he no longer has to look over his shoulder.

Hostelling

During the Easter vacation Mark announces his intention of going on his first weekend-hostelling trip – a two-day pony-trekking venture in the north. This will involve travelling over 200 miles by coach with some fifty people, most of whom he has never met, making two overnight stays in two different hostels, and pony-trekking by day and participating in traditional music sessions in the local bars at night. It will also involve minimal hours of sleep and arriving back in the city long after midnight. Then, as the group disperses, he will walk to a taxi rank and accomplish the final leg of the journey home on his own by taxi. He has worked out his itinerary and is determined to go.

While Mark sleeps soundly at night over the next week, we lie awake pondering the pros and cons of such a trip, weighing up the benefits against the deficits. With some trepidation we give our permission, building in what safeguards are in our power. We speak with the leaders briefing them on Mark's impairments. They are reassuring, volunteering to look out for him and to appoint a buddy to be at hand and befriend him on the trip.

He sets off early on the Saturday morning. We drive him to the depot, seeing him safely onto the coach. We have demanded one concession: that on return we pick him up at the depot rather than his risking an early morning search in the city for a taxi that might not be available. He departs and we return home to wait.

And so begins the first weekend of waiting and listening. Listening for the phone and hoping it would not be a cry for help.

There is no cry for help that weekend and at 5 a.m. on the Tuesday we watch him jump down the steps of the coach as day-light spreads over the city. The coach had broken down and was five hours behind schedule. We fill the wagon with as many of the weary travellers as we can accommodate and drop them off one by one on our route home. At home we brew up tea and toast and add something sweet while an exuberant Mark tells us of his adventures.

The weekend had been a resounding success. I am dispatched with the roll of film to get it developed. Already, too excited and over-tired to sleep, Mark makes plans for the first weekend in June when the group will stay overnight on an offshore island to birdwatch and to gather at daybreak in time to hear the dawn chorus. The first-year college exams take place in May and vacation begins before 1 June.

Nightwatch

It is midnight on New Year's Eve. The phone shrills beside me. Already alert, I pick it up quickly.

"Mum, I'm very ill. Can you come and get me?"

Mark is 300 miles away on a four-day hostelling trip.

"Where are you calling from? Is it the hostel?"

"I can't hear you. Can you shout, Mum? The noise is terrible here."

At the top of my voice I repeat my question. "Where are you calling from? Is it the hostel?"

"No – we're having a New Year celebration here in the local bar."

"Give me the number there? Call it out slowly?"

Scribbling it down I think – now when he runs out of coins I can call him back.

"What's happened, Mark?"

"I've been throwing up for 24 hours. I feel terrible. Can't keep anything down. Come and get me."

"Have you seen a doctor?"

"No – we're miles out in the countryside – in the middle of nowhere. Come and get me, Mum."

"Mark, can you get hold of Joe or Conor [group leaders] for me?"

"But can you come and get me?"

"Let me talk to Joe or Conor first."

"I'll look for them but there's hundreds here."

I think of how he struggles to see faces and his obvious high anxiety level which will make it much worse. How will he recognize any one person in what is obviously a milling mass of people?

The phone goes dead – no sound.

Dialling again I ring the number. No answer.

I put down the phone and dial again.

Again no reply. The buzz-buzz of the dialling tone resonates in my head. A crisis like this is what we have always feared. Now it has happened. Thoughts of a perforated appendix and dehydration float around in my mind.

And he is so far away.

Somebody answers. The background noise is deafening.

I can't make out the words. Loudly, I shout – "Get me the bartender please. It's urgent – very urgent."

I hear the metallic sound of the receiver being put down on the coin box. I wait. The minutes tick by.

"Hello" – a different, stranger's voice.

"Is that the bartender?"

"No. He's busy."

"Who are you?"

"Can you speak louder? Who do you want?"

My voice is beginning to crack – my vocal cords strained. "Is there a young man called Mark there near you?"

"Anybody here called Mark?"

"Anybody by the name of Mark here?"

I wait – the voice barely distinguishable against the din in the background.

The phone changes hands. It's Mark!

I breathe a prayer of thanks.

"Mum, I found Joe. Here he is."

"Joe, Mark tells me he has been throwing up all day. How is he?"

"Yes, he has been very sick. We thought it was maybe too much to drink. We told him to slow down a bit on the jar."

"Joe, Mark doesn't drink alcohol – just soft drinks. Put him on to me."

"Mark, have you been drinking alcohol? Because that would – "

"I have not."

"Tell Joe that."

The background noise blots out everything. I am conscious of the strains of "Auld Lang Syne" and a hundred hoarse voices surfing through it. On the fringes of it the peals of the church bells home in – sonorous – heralding in another year. I had forgotten it was New Year's Eve.

I shout again. "Joe, Joe, are you there? It's not alcohol. Can you get a doctor for him?"

"I'll try. Hold on. I'll be back in a minute."

I hold. I hope the connection does not break. My anxiety rises.

"Hello. The nearest doctor is forty miles away. The coach driver will take us. Katy and myself will go with him."

"How can I contact you?"

"What time is it now?"

"Almost one o'clock."

"I don't know exactly where the doctor is. Say an hour and a half with the coach on these country roads there, and another back. We should be back at the hostel, which is in the opposite direction, at about 5 a.m. Ring us there then."

"Thanks Joe. Put Mark on to me."

"Don't worry. We'll look after him. Here's Mark now."

"Mark, Joe and his wife and the coach driver are taking you to the local doctor. He'll look after you. You'll be fine. It would take me too long to come down and get you. I'll ring the hostel at 5 a.m. and we'll talk again then. Off you go now and don't worry. Talk to you in a few hours."

"Bye, Mum."

"Bye, love."

He is gone. I put the phone down.

Four hours to wait.

The silence of the house rises up about me. I hear this silence as loudly as I hear the reverberations of the cheering, celebrating crowd, three hundred miles away. Conflicting they clash in my head. I think of Mark. But I must not think of Mark. I have delegated my authority and now I will have to depend on others.

The spectrum of life

Will Mark always have to depend on others? Clearly he could never have coped alone tonight with this crisis. When we are no longer here, will he be capable of managing his own life? Getting out my journal, I try to gather my thoughts and put the next four hours to some constructive use.

Opening a new page I write – "Mark at twenty-two."

Where on the *spectrum of life* is Mark at the age of twenty-two?

I pause, recognizing the need to go further back.

Yes – but first – where on the *spectrum of autism* is Mark at the age of twenty-two?

That is a much easier question to answer.

Mark has moved along the spectrum from the severe end of classic Kanner-type autistic disorder to the HFA/AS end. This in turn, at its higher end, will shade into normality. He would now occupy a place about halfway along this spectrum between HFA/AS and normality.

Any stranger meeting Mark now for the first time would not associate him with the word *autism*. He would apply such terms as "different", "immature", "shy", "anxious", "unusual voice – somewhat metallic sounding", "little small talk", "difficult to have a two-way interactive conversation with but is a mine of interesting, relevant, information on topics that interest him such as sport – rugby, soccer, formula one motor racing – motorbikes, cars, aircraft, weather conditions – watches all national and international sport matches and can hold his own in a discussion and an exchange of information on such topics."

This stranger would probably sum him up overall as of average intelligence, but overprotected, with poor adaptive skills and certainly not street-wise. But this stranger would not think of the word *autism*. For Mark has shed the embryonic amnion of his aloneness. Like a skin it has peeled off and should never re-form.

Tests for adaptive skills and cognitive intelligence skills – what do they measure?

Intelligence tests (e.g. WAIS-R), measure such factors as verbal and non-verbal reasoning power, memory, ability to solve mathematical problems and overall ability to process knowledge, as well as the time taken to do so. The problems put forward are highly specific and the test is highly structured. Mark's WAIS-R showed a verbal IQ (VIQ) of 98 and a performance IQ (PIQ) of 74 – thus giving him a full-scale IQ of 86. This lies within the average range.

Some sub-groups of strictly defined AS individuals (using a definition of AS close to that used by Asperger himself) have been found to show this pattern of higher verbal IQ and lower performance IQ. However, in the same study, this pattern was not found among the comparison group of individuals diagnosed with HFA. In this latter group both IQs were in a similar range.[37] It has been suggested that this fact could have the potential to distinguish AS from HFA.

Adaptive skills tests, on the other hand, measure how an individual copes with the demands of everyday living in the environment in which he finds himself – how he moves around his world with competence. This, of course, includes social skills.

Mark has had much tuition over the years in the area of adaptive skills, and coping strategies have been established to cater for all the usual and unusual events that are likely to arise. But, as previously explained, while he may learn and know what to do in a given situation in the abstract, when he is faced with it in reality he is not always readily able to apply this knowledge. Rather, he learns by doing. Common, predictable, everyday situations have been learned by the constant repetition of doing until they become habit. But unpredictable situations like the current crisis have to be lived through before the pattern of coping becomes established.

The opportunities to grow in everyday adaptive living skills, opened up for him by becoming part of this hiking/hostelling group, have been enormous and we are grateful to the movement who have accepted him and accommodated him so readily. Allied to which is the great joy and fulfilment he derives from being under "the day and night sky of the great outdoors". For Mark draws his energy and revitalization from this world of mountains, valleys and vegetation. At times one will hear him say "I am starving for the countryside".

And what then, in view of all the above, of that second question – where on the spectrum of life is Mark at the age of twenty-two? Looking back over the years to the beginning, he has come a very long way but there is still much ground to cover and the terrain at times like tonight is not easy travelling. Perhaps this is a question we will leave for another day.

Four o'clock – another hour to wait.

For now it is time to check on Dao. Turning the handle of the door softly I slip noiselessly into the room. I hear his even breathing. Quietly he sleeps. I am thankful that he did not wake up at midnight when the phone rang. Just a week home from hospital following his second coronary by-pass operation, he needs sleep.

Five o'clock – I dial the number and ask for Joe.

"They're not back yet," the voice tells me – and then – "I think I hear the coach now, hold on, I'll check."

I hold.

"Yes they're coming into the yard now. I'll call him."

I hold again.

"Hello, is it Mum?" It's Mark's voice.

"How are you, Mark?"

"Much better, Mum. The doctor said it wasn't my appendix. It's a bug. He gave me an injection and it's working. I'm much better. I had half a bottle of lemonade. It stayed down. We're going to bed now."

"I'll call you in the morning."

"Bye, Mum."

"Bye, love."

My watch is over.

I can come off-duty now.

CHAPTER 16

Darkness Falls

The old year has died away and the new one faces into the cold of what will become a severe winter. With it Mark returns to college to prepare for his diploma examination in the forthcoming June. This will end his first two-year cycle in the college. Then he will decide whether to go on to further education or to join the workforce. Meanwhile the "happiest years of his life" look set to continue as he moves forward with his college friends, his music group and the now occasional hostelling weekend.

A few weeks into the college term Mark falls prey to various infections – colds, influenza, a repeated low-grade fever and recurrent kidney infections. As a result he misses out on most of the winter term lectures and assignments, as well as the first half of the spring term. Consequently, he will not be in a position to sit the diploma examination in June. He will have to repeat the entire year.

The blow is a severe one and his disappointment is acute. Now his close-knit group of eleven companions go forward to higher studies while he has to remain behind and break into the upcoming class of (to him) unknown students and the new curriculum of a changing course. The prospect of this imminent change weighs heavily on him. In any crisis in Mark's life his two great needs come heavily to the forefront – his needs for

1. predictability and

2. structure.

Now both had been swept aside leaving him floundering.

What can we do to help? We have little power in this situation. We can offer reassurance, advice and encouragement. We can listen and be there for him. But we cannot do what we did all through his developing years because Mark is now an adult and is expected to advocate for himself in his world. We are no longer players but have been relegated now to the sideline.

There is, however, one area in which we can still take an active role and that is his current health problems. We look objectively at what has brought him to this impasse. It would appear to be a badly functioning immune system because he is not clearing these viral/bacterial infections in an immuno-competent manner. In the course of our research we have come across a number of studies reporting on irregularities and dysfunctions in the immune systems of people with autism. The first of these studies dates back to the early 1970s.

The immune system and autism

We have essentially two systems of defence against disease. One produces T cells. The other produces white blood cells called B cells. T cells and B cells have a powerful ability to deal with all foreign substances entering the body.

The immune system abnormalities found in autism research include the following:

- abnormality of B cells

- a reduction in T cell number and activity. This was found to be correlated with the severity of the autistic symptoms; the greater the reduction in the T cell activity the greater the extent of symptoms.[38]

- reduced natural killer cell activity, which leads to reduced protection against viral infections.[39]

- a deficiency of immunoglobulin A (IGA).[40]

- an abnormal response by the body to its own brain tissue (autoimmunity).

Most of the above abnormalities are involved in *autoimmunity*.

What is autoimmunity?

Autoimmunity arises when one's body loses the ability to distinguish between what belongs to itself and what is in fact a foreign invader. In other words, it loses the ability to tell what is self from what is non-self. Then, for no apparent reason, it turns on its own tissues and begins to attack them. It is not known why this happens. Here the trigger factor, antigen, is not a foreign substance but part of the body itself. Quite obviously, autoimmunity is harmful.

Mark has already shown an example of autoimmunity in his severe illness due to Still's disease. This disease was caused by the inflammation and destruction of his cell tissues by his own body's antibodies (called autoanti-bodies – "auto" means *against self*). His early rheumatoid arthritis (namely Still's disease) is an example of autoimmune disease. Rheumatoid arthritis has been known to occur in some members of his paternal family line.

The literature shows that autoimmune disease characteristically clusters in families. There is general consensus that this points to a genetic predisposition being involved in autoimmune disease.

One study, conducted of sixty-one families with children with disorders of autism, found that almost half of the families had two or more members with autoimmune disorders. This was greater than in the control group. It was also found that if the frequency of autoimmune disorders increased in these families, so also did the risk of autistic disorder.[41]

Several studies have found evidence of autoimmunity affecting the central nervous system (brain and spinal cord) in different samples of children with autism. One group of researchers looked at a number of these studies in a critical review that they undertook. They comment that, taken together, these studies provide circumstantial evidence for the idea that anti-bodies produced by the body tissues against its own brain cells (autoantibodies) may be a causative factor for the development of autism.

They stress, however, that the results from all of these studies need to be confirmed using larger groups of patients. They also point to the range of different behaviours found in autism as well as to the variation in degree of impairment found in autism. Following on from this, they consider that groups of patients currently diagnosed as having autism may in fact be repre-sentative of a number of varied disorders arising from different causes and different diseases.[42]

Treatment

Is there any treatment that can be given to improve the functioning of a defective immune system?

In the general population intravenous immunoglobulin (IVIG) has been used since the early 1980s to treat several autoimmune disorders and this has resulted in beneficial effects. It is also used to treat immune deficiencies.

Have there been any reports of the results of IVIG treatment in the autism population?

Yes – in the 1990s a few studies have reported on treating children with autism with IVIG. The first of these treated ten children (with known immune system abnormalities) for a period of six months. The improvements, noted by clinical observation, were described as consistent, although variable. They were seen in terms of calmness, better eye contact and social behaviours, and loss of echolalia. Two children from the group showed marked improvement in speech, thinking and attention span. A few patients showed a reversal to features of autism once the six-months' treatment schedule had finished. However, they improved again when a new course of treatment was started.[43]

A second investigation, this time of five children, also carried out a six-month trial of IVIG. They reported "no statistically significant changes" in any of the children when measured professionally on four of the standard autism rating scales. Immunologic testing had not been performed on these children prior to treatment.[44]

A third study reported results from an IVIG trial of ten children, all of whom had immunologic abnormalities. Half of this sample showed no detectable change after treatment, a further four showed mild improvement, but one child showed a dramatic response, becoming fully normalized over the period of four infusions.[45] However, over the following five months after treatment, this child reverted back to his previous autistic state.

In discussing the results of the above three studies Krause and colleagues point out that it is important to keep in mind the "risk of transmitting potential blood-borne pathogens" by IVIG treatment. They also point to the necessity for a controlled double-blinded, placebo-controlled study to be undertaken on a large group of "carefully diagnosed patients" in order to ascertain whether IVIG has a role to play in treating autistic disorder. In addition, they consider that widespread use of IVIG as a clinical treatment should *follow* the controlled trials and not *precede* them.[42]

Solitude

For now, however, we decide to leave the complexity of IVIG treatment to one side and in an effort to find some help for Mark, we consult a general specialist/physician asking for advice on how to improve the capacity of his immune system to deal with these recurrent infections. Having ascertained that Mark has no organic illness he prescribes a regime of rest, good nutrition, restricted activity, sleep and freedom from stress. So we repair to the cottage for the summer months hoping that the sun, sea and sand will work their magic again.

As the months slip by we notice Mark withdrawing. He becomes solitary, spending long hours in his room and wandering the hills and seashore by himself. It is as if we had turned back the clock through all of the past fourteen years to his tenth summer when he had slipped away from us yet again to some unknown plateau where we could not reach him in the land of his retreat; only this time it manifests itself in different behaviour. I look at the parallel lines of shells and stones cemented into the floor of the patio and memories of that summer stir vividly. With affection I think of Barry, now living abroad. With nostalgia I think of Mark as he was in that year.

I watch Mark now. He has become withdrawn, inactive – alone again. And yet – this is not aloneness. It lacks the tangible feel of the aura. This is not a regression – not a reversion to autistic-like behaviour. I am too familiar now with the aloneness of autism to mistake it for anything else. This has the feel of solitude, the feel of someone who wants to distance himself – of someone lost – preoccupied with searching. This is something different – something disturbing – but different.

It is not the crippling inertia of lack of motivation. Rather it appears more in the guise of the desperation of someone who cannot motivate himself. This is not "I will not". This is "I *cannot*". For Mark has become a perfectionist. From his mid-teenage years he has become very intolerant of his own shortcomings. He will not tolerate self-failure and often defeats himself by expecting too much of himself – by his own very perfectionism.

Watching him now it seems that he has lost his zest for life. Is he giving up the fight? Has this one more blow been just one too many? Has he lost the will to continue the struggle?

We have never used the word *autism* with Mark. We have never discussed the fact that he has autism, simply because it has just never come up. We decided that should he ever ask why he was different we would have dis-

cussed the whole concept of being different with him and would have talked
of autism. But he has never asked. Because he was happy with himself and
largely was unaware of his differences we decided to leave well alone. The
only time he has ever questioned me about himself in relation to others was
when he was ten years old. Returning from an afternoon spent with Darren
and the twins in their home, he walked into the kitchen, stood directly in
front of me, caught my hand and asked what was to be his first abstract
question.

"Why have *you* [I] got only *I, me, myself* [you]?"

It took me some time to work out that he was asking me why he had only
me and had no brothers and sisters! He accepted my reply that God had not
given us any. He had instead kept just one very special boy called Mark for
us.

So, largely then, Mark has accepted life and particularly people as he
finds them and that includes himself.

Was this present picture an image of someone coming face to face with
his differences, confronting them and coming to terms with them? Or was it
simply the picture of a weary body and a tired mind debilitated by recurrent
illness and years of extending his resources too far? Mark needs rest, of that
we are very much aware. But he does not seem to be able to take that rest as
he would have of old. We need to talk with him but he does not seem to be
ready to talk with us. So we wait out the summer wishing we could turn back
the clock to the earlier years when we could confront each difficulty as it
arose and work out a formula for dealing with it. The problems then were so
much easier to contend with. They always seemed to be within our capacity.

As autumn sets in it becomes clear that Mark is reaching a crisis. His
mood is changing and he sinks more and more into apathy. With it comes a
quality we have never seen before in him – the quality of irritability. He
announces that he will not be returning to college. We agree with his
decision, realizing it is the right one. We have come to the same conclusion
ourselves. We have slowly come to the realization that the change in Mark's
behaviour is ominous. We need professional help.

What if?

Mark agrees to see the psychiatrist he saw some twenty years before when he
had been discharged from hospital following his recovery from Still's

disease. He had felt at ease with this kindly father/confessor figure then and he now shows no distress at the prospect of seeing him again.

Sitting in the low chair in the corridor outside the consulting room, I hear the murmur of the voices behind the closed door – Mark's slightly higher and more pressured than that of the consultant. Wearily, I lean my head against the wall, awaiting my turn to be called. Wondering what lies ahead now, closing my eyes, I think back over the last twenty years. Have we followed the advice given then – the advice to "Keep Mark happy and keep him on target?" Have we kept Mark happy? We have certainly kept him on target.

The "what ifs" arise in my mind – what if we had taken a different route? – what if we had never subjected Mark to the rigours of mainstream education? – what if we had instead accepted his autism, educating him at home and keeping him within the family circle? – what if we had not fought autism in the hope of a better life for him? – what if we had never encouraged his plans for college, his canoeing ventures, his outdoor pursuits and hostelling? – if so would we never have arrived at where we are today?

Perhaps if we had not expected so much of Mark he would not have pushed himself so hard nor expected so much of himself. Perhaps then he would not have reached this stage of breakdown.

The what ifs trail off. Their futility is wearying. I face the reality of that alternative route and the bleak picture it conjures up – an isolated Mark trapped in the alienness of aloneness and in neverending rituals and routines, forced to spend a lifetime dependent on the good will of others – and knew we would do it all again. That picture has always been our most powerful stimulant. When that picture is brought into the equation there is *no* alternative route.

At any one point in life a decision can only be taken based on the facts as they stand. We have taken our decision and have achieved much more than we had ever expected. Yes – Mark has experienced rejection, unkindness, intimidation, bullying, extremely hard work, undue stress, exceptional fears and anxieties. But Mark has lived a full life within his capacity and he has experienced great joy in his successes and great pride in his achievements. He has experienced the closeness of friendship and comradeship, and has enjoyed and reciprocated the warmth of care and affection. For Mark has grown into a warm, generous – both in kind and spirit, affectionate, very likeable young man. He has carved out for himself a life and up until now he has largely enjoyed it.

For now we can only speculate as to what might have caused this present impasse. Whatever it is we will see it through. We will work with it and we *will* get through it.

The voices behind my head cease talking and I hear movement in the room beyond the door. It opens. My name is called.

"You can come in now."

Squaring my shoulders, I get up to join Mark in the consulting room.

CHAPTER 17

So Deep is the Night

In the consulting room the atmosphere is positive and friendly. Mark appears visibly more at ease. The doctor suggests that he come into hospital for a few weeks. He explains that this would be the most satisfactory situation in which to treat Mark's illness. Because there are complications due to his basic autism, screening and evaluation will take time and can best be achieved in a hospital setting. He is, however, fairly sure that Mark has a psychiatric disorder co-morbid with his basic developmental disorder of autism. But in order to identify which one, others need to be eliminated, as symptoms can be overlapping.

He outlines the advantages of the hospital régime. Mark will undergo an initial period of bed-rest to deal with his present state of exhaustion. In conjunction with this he will be treated with a system of medication targeted and tailored to his specific needs. This requires monitoring to establish the correct dosage and to take into account the possibility of side effects, so that the medication can be discontinued or reduced should adverse reactions arise. He will have daily visits from the consultant and/or members of his team. Then he will be given the opportunity to discuss his worries. After this initial period, which should take a week or two, Mark will move on to the next phase.

This includes a specific diagnosis, followed by education about the condition of his illness and learning how best to cope with it. He will be encouraged to attend the daily lectures given on different categories of mental illness, their causes and treatments. In addition to this there will be daily participation in group therapy under the direction of a trained therapist. Within these groups, patients are encouraged to explore their inner thoughts, feelings and attitudes, are helped to identify problem areas and are guided towards working for change. This phase also includes classes in anxiety management and relaxation and some forms of physical work-out.

The final part of the programme involves individual therapy sessions with a cognitive psychologist in addition to occupational therapy in art, music, drama, pottery, wood carving, creative writing and other such self-expressive leisure activities. Allied to this will be role-playing sessions devoted to developing positive self-image, social skills and qualities of assertiveness.

Listening closely I am impressed, realizing that Mark would benefit greatly from such a régime. It is suggested that perhaps we should talk about the possibility of Mark's admission over lunch and then come back and see the doctor afterwards. There will be a bed available later in the day.

We make our way to the busy cafeteria and sit at a secluded table in the shade of the potted palm trees. I feel a sense of relief mingled with apprehension — apprehension about what lies ahead and yet relief that the long, helpless watching and waiting of the summer months are over. That forced inaction has taken a numbing toll on all of our senses — most of all on Mark's. Numbed as I am, the thought of what lies ahead is compelling and frightening — a psychiatric disorder now superimposed on his basic autism. It scarcely seems real that this could have happened and if it were not serious the consultant would not have asked for hospitalization. This is obviously no simple episode of depression. This is beyond our scope. It is time now to leave Mark to the care of the professionals. But will he be prepared to enter hospital?

Across the table from me he toys with his food, pushing it around the plate. I wait for him to speak — letting the silence drag on — actively preventing myself from rushing in with either reassurance or advice. This must be his own decision.

Around us the clatter of crockery blends with the hum of conversation. I look through the glass wall to the patio beyond. The scene is a bright patch in a sombre setting. The mellow sunshine lights up the reds and golds of the autumn flower beds — beautifying the carpet of fallen leaves that soften the angles of the old, grey, stone building. They lie there — quiescent — in all their shades of yellow to brown. As I watch a sudden puff of wind swirls them up.

Like ballerinas they twirl and twist – dancing across my vision. Rising higher they float and then cascade slowly to earth to pile up in a corner – harbingers of the end of a season and the onset of decay. My mind harks back to Mark's other hospitalization and to that early Sunday-morning drive through the empty streets of the city almost twenty years ago. Then we were at the beginning of our journey. Had we now come to the end? Was Mark's season to be so ephemeral; so full but yet so fleeting?

"What should we do?" Mark asks.

I drag myself back to the present and away from my morbid thoughts to find Mark looking at a point in my shoulder. I allow myself an inner smile – "What should *we* do?" It means that Mark, who has fought so hard for his independence and the right to manage his own life, is now willing to take advice again. It augurs well for his co-operation, which would make his present situation so much easier. I choose my words carefully.

"I suppose it could be managed from home but the treatment would be much slower. Coming into hospital has certain advantages. It would greatly speed up getting established on the medication. Also you would see the consultant or his team every day instead of just once a week. This would lead to a much quicker diagnosis. And Dao and I would be in every day to see how you are doing. And remember, Barry comes back tomorrow. He also will be in."

Silence again – I wait. Looking around the cafeteria I register for the first time the large number of young patients, of similar age to Mark, sitting at tables inside and out on the patio. Watching their body language, the comradeship and solidarity between them is evident. They obviously draw support from each other. Idle thoughts flit through my mind – thoughts of friendship and how it can be cemented in the most unexpected settings; of how often it is adversity, and not prosperity, that binds people together. It surprises me this preponderance of young people in a psychiatric hospital. In my inexperience of psychiatric illness I had thought the preponderance would have been in the middle to older age group.

Following my glance Mark observes, "There's a lot of people like myself here, so I suppose it can't be that bad."

"Yes, I noticed that."

The minutes tick by.

"All right – I'll go in."

Slowly I shudder, something halfway between a breath and a sigh welling up. I sink back into my chair, releasing the strain on my tensed muscles.

The way back

It's later tonight and I sit beside Mark's bed. He weeps silently: a great watershed of pent-up up tears pouring down his face. It is as if all the tears he has never shed in his life have broken the wall of the dam and are flowing free. I have never seen Mark cry. In all of his twenty-four years there have been no tears. I watch now – struggling to keep my own detachment – struggling to keep my equilibrium. I cannot afford to get caught up in this. I cannot let myself be swamped. For his sake I must keep control.

Slowly I come to see it for what it is – the beginning of healing. As the dam bursts perhaps it will sweep away whatever darkness has entered his soul. In time the storm passes, leaving in its wake a measure of peace. He sleeps. Towards midnight I slip quietly out of the room and down the long corridor to the exit. The echoes of my tapping heels on the tiles invade the whispering silence. Around me the hospital lies sleeping – only the shadowy, white-clad forms beneath the lamps keep the watch. Removing my shoes I walk on – the distance endless. I do not look back. There *is* no going back now.

I open the door and pass out into the darkness.

Almost without visibility the hospital routine moves into gear, and inevitably Mark is carried along with it. He is content to be ferried by the slow, methodical, predictable pace of the treatment – meals in the ward dining room at set times – medication administered afterwards – clinical observations taken and recorded, four-hourly to begin with, twice daily thereafter – consultant rounds in the morning, visitors in the afternoon and evening – night staff taking over from day staff, and alternating again at the chime of the clock. And in between, the all-important factor of bed-rest: a protected world requiring no effort; a system that turns on its own wheels: and Mark sleeps, cocooned by the medication and the predictability of his surroundings.

Moving on, he is encouraged to dress and leave the sanctuary of the ward. When we visit now we sit downstairs in the cafeteria where Barry will join us, or walk in the sunlight and sit at the base of the old oak tree. And Mark talks – talks of his depression, and of how it seemed to creep up on him on that New Year's Eve almost a year ago, intensifying since then until it took over his every thought and he could not talk about it. We listen as haltingly the words come out and we glimpse the darkness within. In between there are days of long silences. These are the not-so-good days; days when his thinking is slowed down and every word is an effort. Then we wait in silence – conscious of his agitation. We have been told that it will be some weeks before we see the full effects of his anti-depressant medication.

In time he attends the first of the morning lectures and begins a process of discovery of what will become for him a vital interest in mood disorders and in the categories of drugs used to treat them. Having been a student of chemistry and biology he has enough basic information to apply this and will soon commit to memory the generic and specific name of each drug, its target illness, recommended dosage, side effects, contra-indications, drug interactions and warnings. (Later he will commit all to the computer to chart, graph and process for reference.) The old Mark and his capacity for stockpiling information is coming to the fore again. Or, rather, perhaps he is retreating back into the comforting confines of ritual and routine – withdrawing into this facet of autism in an effort to relieve anxiety. A dictionary of medication is to become his favourite bed-time reading.

After six weeks he shows no response to the medication and is changed to a different anti-depressant. The dosage is increased slowly. We meet with the team in the consultant's office for a discussion of his case. They are not yet ready to give a diagnosis. There is a depression component to Mark's illness, of that they are aware and that is what they are targeting at the moment. But it is not the full picture. However, they are satisfied with his progress to date and feel he is now ready to join in group therapy and to begin returning home for the weekends.

We settle into this second phase of treatment.

Co-existing psychiatric disorders: How common are they?

There is time now to return to the research and take a look at what information is available concerning the psychiatric disorders that can co-exist with autism and Asperger syndrome (AS). We find many references to such psychiatric disorders occurring in the high-functioning autism (HFA)/AS population, and to the fact that this population can show wide-ranging psychiatric symptoms. Most workers in this field agree that the greatest problem facing them is in trying to establish which symptoms are an integral part of the basic core of the autism syndrome, which symptoms are actually part of the acquired psychiatric disorder and which are overlapping.

This is echoed again and again. There is little research in this area and what little exists is not always based on properly structured procedures. Consequently, most workers emphasize the need to undertake well-planned studies using strict methodologies in order to evaluate whether these so-called co-existing psychiatric disorders are actually *acquired disorders* or simply *different aspects* of high-functioning people with pervasive developmental disorders (HFPDDs). The answer to this will, in turn, have serious implications for treatment, particularly in the area of medication.

Neither, at this present time, are there any epidemiological studies in this area (studies of the incidence of co-existing psychiatric disorders in general populations of autism and AS). The only information available comes from referred cases. Because these cases are referred for treatment, and come to the attention of the medical profession in this manner, they are more likely to contain a higher incidence of co-existing disorders. Consequently, they do not represent a true picture of the prevalence of psychiatric disorders in the autistic population. However, they give some pointers and indicators to the overall general pattern of occurrence.

Referred cases

One study (combining the results obtained from eight different series of cases) reviewed the results of seventy-four such cases. The following were the results:

- The commonest disorder reported was depression; over half the patients suffered from this unipolar affective mood disorder.

- Slightly more than one-tenth (12%) received a diagnosis of bipolar mood disorder (manic depression) with mania occurring in a further seven per cent of cases.

- Schizophrenia-type disorders occurred in over one-tenth of patients.

- Hallucinations were diagnosed in eight per cent of the cases.

- Other disorders reported included anxiety, catatonia, paranoia and schizoid disorder.

Generally speaking, the overall impression given from the studies reviewed in this report is that the HFA and AS population has a substantial risk of developing disorders of depression and anxiety.[46]

Schizophrenia

The author of the same review[46] comments that it is unusual to find first-rank symptoms of schizophrenia (SCH) in cases of autism, but a number of studies and clinical reports have found evidence of auditory hallucinations, paranoid ideas and delusional thoughts in the HFA and AS population.

The situation with regard to diagnosing schizophrenia in conjunction with autism is complex because of the ambiguities involved in the diagnosis of HFA/AS. In fact there are incidents of people with AS/HFA being mistakenly diagnosed as having SCH. The negative symptoms of SCH particularly overlap with the negative symptoms of AS. A recent, well-ordered study investigated the overlap of symptoms in two groups of men (14 in each group, age range 17–39). One group had a diagnosis of SCH and the other group a diagnosis of autism. It was found that half of the autism group met the criteria for SCH whereas none of the men with paranoid SCH met the criteria for autism.[47]

These authors also emphasize a point that keeps recurring in the literature concerning psychiatric disorders co-existing with autism. It is: *these additional disorders are indicators of a poor long-term prognosis (forecast) because they can contribute greatly to a worsening of outcome.*

Hans Asperger himself reported an incidence of SCH of one per cent among his patients.[19] This is the same rate of occurrence as in the general population. Other workers in this field point to the fact that it is the high-ability people (the words high-ability and high-functioning are used interchangeably throughout this text) with autism who are more likely to show some of the characteristics of SCH – SCH, that is, of the disorganized subtype rather than the paranoid subtype. A study was carried out recently of 41 people with autistic disorder who were suspected of having SCH. When they were tested for the full syndrome of SCH, a rate of less than one per cent was found. Based on chance alone an incidence of one per cent would be expected.[48]

It becomes obvious from all the above that the situation with regard to diagnosing psychiatric disorders co-existing with autism is by no means clear-cut. Rather, it is fraught with considerable difficulties and much work is required in this area.

With regard to other conditions associated with HFPDD, in the preliminary results arising from a case series study of 99 individuals with AS, attention deficit hyperactivity disorder (ADHD) occurred in slightly over one-quarter, obsessive-compulsive disorder in one-fifth, and depression in slightly less than one-fifth of those studied. It is interesting to note here that there was an age factor involved because ADHD occurred more frequently in the younger age-group whereas mood disorders occurred more frequently in the older age-group.[34]

Treatment

Research has shown that there is no medication that produces significant behavioural improvements in most individuals with autism.[17] To what extent, then, is medication used to treat these co-existing conditions of autism?

An extensive review of this question was undertaken by Martin and colleagues when they reviewed the "small available" literature on this topic and also described a study of medication use patterns in over 200 individuals with AS and related conditions.[34] They begin by pointing out that even though almost one-fifth of the autistic population falls into the non-disabled range of IQ, this group has routinely been excluded from studies on the use of psychotropic medication (this is the name given to the drugs used to treat mood disorders). They then point to the ambiguity that arises when one considers the lack of such studies and the consequent lack of empirical evidence for the use of medication, and contrast it with the increasingly common practice of prescribing such medication in the clinical management of people with AS and related conditions. ("Empirical" means relying on experiment or experience or observation and not on theory, reason or logic.)

In their own research into the use of psychotropic medication they carried out two surveys. Both surveys found "widespread use" of such medications in separate samples of over one hundred individuals who were awaiting screening and assessment for AS. In the first survey over three-quarters had received stimulant drugs at some period in their lives, over one-third had received SSRIs (selective serotonin reuptake inhibitors) and less than ten per cent had received neuroleptics (antipsychotics). Looking at the overall pattern they found that lifetime psychotropic medication use was common. Often more than one drug agent had been prescribed and the prescribing rationale was obscure.

In their second survey, this time of 109 individuals (aged 4–43) they found that over half were currently taking psychotropic medication, and that half of this group, in turn, had been prescribed two or more drugs at the same time, thus indicating that the HFPDDs are, all in all, a population of people who are heavily medicated. In addition, more than two-thirds of the group as a whole had received psychotropic medication at some time in their lives. They contrast all these figures with a large-scale study of individuals with autism where it was found that less than one-third were taking psychotropic medication.

They consider that the high rate of clinical prescribing in the HFPDD population is all the more significant when it is considered against the fact that there have been "no psychotropic medication studies specifically designed for individuals with HFPDD".[34]

Infantile autistic bipolar disorder

I have previously mentioned that the wide variation and complexity of symptoms found within the spectrum of autism do not point to a single disease entity. Rather they point to many different causes and are similar only in that they end up in a final common pathway of behaviour. Some workers in the field consider that autism is a syndrome or sequence of syndromes and that these, in turn, are caused by a number of diverse unconnected individual diseases.

One of these disease entities of autism has now been described. It is called infantile autistic bipolar disorder (IABD). The criteria which define it are:

- regression after an initial period of normal development

- classical criteria for autism must be present

- the core autistic symptoms must show a cycling pattern

- there must exist among first- or second-degree relatives a family history of bipolar disorder or major depression

- an absence of abnormal features, seizures and neurological dysfunction.[49]

IABD is reported to be "not common" but very small numbers of people with it will have been seen at specialist autism clinics.

The authors of this report on IABD stress that this is one disease only and that the cycling pattern occurs in the basic core autistic symptoms themselves as they become exacerbated and then die down again. The condition presents within the first thirty months of life and obsessive traits and special abilities are a feature of it.

They emphasize that it should not be confused with later onset bipolar disorder which develops in children with autism who have depressive episodes and sometimes manic episodes as well. In this latter case, they point out, there are two disease entities involved, namely autism and bipolar mood disorder.[49]

Scattered throughout the literature we have seen well-documented, single case histories of children with autism who received an additional diagnosis of this later onset bipolar mood disorder. In two cases the onset of this had occurred at as young an age as six years. When successfully treated with a mood stabilizer (lithium) and an anti-psychotic medication (neuroleptic) both cases showed a marked improvement in both the bipolar symptoms and their condition of autism. They were followed up closely for four years. During this period any attempt to lower the dose of either drug resulted in deterioration of behaviour and the rapid return of bipolar symptoms.[50]

Neurotransmitters

Having gained considerable insight by now into the psychiatric disorders that can attach themselves to HFA, we can look at Mark's condition in a different light. We appreciate the difficulties of diagnosis and the all-importance of correct diagnosis because on this will hinge the decision of which medication to use. So we take a look at how medication works.

To understand this we need to get some insight into how different parts of the brain and nervous system communicate with each other. This is done by sending electrical signals along nerve cells. These nerve cells are called *neurons*. Neurons are not joined on to each other. Instead there are minute gaps between them called *synapses*. In these synapses there are important chemicals called *neurotransmitters*. There would appear to be over a hundred different neurotransmitters in the brain. These chemical neurotransmitters are implicated in changes of mood because they are involved in the degree of brain arousal, in ability to pay attention and in all emotional activity. They are also responsible for attaching significance to the cold hard factual information that the brain has to interpret.[32]

Three of the most common of these neurotransmitters are *serotonin, dopamine* and *noradrenaline.*

Decreased serotonin transmission across the synapse is thought to be involved in depression. This is the rationale behind the use of some drugs which work by boosting the level of serotonin, as they are designed to increase the level of that particular neurotransmitter at the synapse between neurons. An increase in the level of neurotransmitters can be achieved in any of the following ways:

- by increasing the manufacture of that particular neurotransmitter

- by blocking its breakdown

- by preventing it from being taken up from the synapse and in this way retaining it there longer. The SSRIs work by this method

- by mimicking the action of the natural transmitter. This type of drug is called an *agonist.*[32]

The precise way in which these anti-depressant drugs (which target both anxiety and depression) work is complex and is not fully understood. Many anti-depressants affect more than one neurotransmitter and it is thought that their ability to relieve depression probably involves a number of different therapeutic actions on more than one neurotransmitter system. Depression tends to go hand in hand with anxiety. Studies have shown that about half of the patients with a diagnosis of major depression also have an anxiety disorder. Many of the medications used to treat one condition are also effective in treating the other.[32]

There are four major groups of anti-depressants and which one should be selected for any particular patient is often a matter of trial and error. In Mark's case the first anti-depressant he was treated with belonged to the TCADs (tricyclic anti-depressants) and as we have seen it produced no therapeutic affect. He is now being given a trial of one of the SSRI group and, six weeks into this treatment, he begins to show a response. His low mood is lifting and his days and nights are not so dark.

CHAPTER 18

Storm Tossed

The club

Mark has been discharged from the hospital and his mood continues to improve. He attends the third phase of the programme as an outpatient, travelling in to the hospital on a daily basis. This is a special programme geared to the needs of the patients aged between eighteen and twenty-six who have developed psychiatric illness. It is run along the lines of a club. As his special occupational therapy Mark chooses to take art, pottery and wood carving. He appears to have forsaken music. His instruments have been lying idle for over a year.

He is committed to the club and when we visit now he will be found sitting around a table in the cafeteria drinking coffee with his peers, while working on plans and scheduling events for the club. On days out the group travels around the city, to cinemas, art galleries, exhibitions, or perhaps to go ten-pin bowling in a nearby arcade. The pace of the programme is consistent but fluid. The group regulates itself under the benign guidance of a panel of therapists and sets up committees to organize fund-raising events in the hospital function rooms – events such as concerts, discos and even a very successful ball held on St Valentine's Night. Alternatively, they may cook lunch, thus improving their culinary skills, and invite paying guests. All of which help to make the programme self-financing.

Basically, the club is constructed as a forum for peer interaction, to encourage initiative, to teach social skills, to learn appropriate self-assertion techniques, to build up self-esteem and to deal with the myriad of other social and emotional demands that can be made on a now-vulnerable population struggling to come to terms with psychiatric changes. Incorporated into the day will be classes in anxiety management, in challenging false beliefs, in planning time management and in overall rehabilitation in preparation for returning to life in the community. Whatever areas require special attention are singled out and given professional attention. For Mark one of these areas centres around speech therapy to improve the quality and tone of his over-loud and somewhat monotonic voice.

Speech therapy

All through the years, whenever Mark was encouraged to lower the tone of his voice and speak more quietly, he would do so, but within seconds his voice would automatically rise again to its former pitch. When asked why he could not keep it within the normal range he always gave the same reason although the older he got the more eloquently was he able to express it. When asked a similar question by the speech therapist on his first visit he gave his usual response:

"I have so much noise in my head that I can't hear what I'm saying unless I force it out on high power. If I can't do this I don't know what I'm saying because I can't hear myself. Speaking doesn't come easy to me like it does to everyone else. I have to work hard at it. I have so much of this – what Mum calls 'white noise' – in my head that it drowns out my own speech. That's why I have to boom it out."

It has become obvious over the years that, although the white noise was always present in his head, it was greatly exacerbated by two factors – one – a sharp increase in the surrounding noise level – and the other – an increase in his own internal anxiety and stress levels.

Clearly then, it is not going to be possible for Mark to reduce the volume of his voice to any great degree so, on reflection, the therapist decides to approach his speech therapy from the angle of getting some inflection, nuance, rhythm, tone, pauses and emphasis into his sentences in order to create a more natural effect and to act as a vehicle for expressing some of his inner feelings (such as anger, self-assertiveness, surprise and other everyday emotions). This, in turn, will help Mark to understand and take note of the subtle nuances of feeling in the speech of others.

A series of speech recordings are set up and Mark listens to his voice on tape for the first time, thus hearing the differences in the manner of his speaking from outside. On tape he practises letting his voice rise at the end of a sentence, emphasizing certain phrases, altering the flow of others, pausing to give weight to a certain word and generally using his musical ear to lilt his voice. With conscious effort he succeeds well but it becomes clear that while he likes the idea and is quite capable of putting it into practice in the abstract, the effort required when in normal situations is considerable and other communication needs take precedence – needs such as deciphering the essential details to respond to in interactive speech and the ever-present basic effort of manipulating learned tracts of speech and using them to put his thoughts into words.

Mark's ability to communicate in this way improves with every sentence he utters and his speech would now appear quite spontaneous, were it not for the tone in which it is uttered.

Perhaps at a more opportune time he may continue these voice production exercises and apply them, but for now all his energies are committed to getting well and completing the programme.

Laughter

The club committee decides to produce a magazine to advertise the programme and to exploit whatever budding talent might be available. Each member of the group gets a specific appointment, from editor to publisher (Mark becomes assistant publisher) and all are expected to contribute in some form – to write feature articles, produce art work, undertake interviews of staff members or contribute works of humour or imagination. Mark decides to enter in this last category and to exploit his new-found interest in medication. He entitles his story:

The human element in medication

It was a dark night and a thin pall of mist hung around the mountains. A car pulled up outside the committee-room entrance to the rear of the hotel. A tablet popped out, followed by its counterparts, until a long line of Fentazin, Domitol and Cogentin had entered the building. The tablets settled around the table. The chairman got to his feet to address the meeting.

"Ladies and gentlemen, welcome to the meeting. As you know our mission is to cure Mental Illness. There has been some trouble in Russia. Dopamine, the rogue, has been causing delusions and hallucinations. Also, in China, Manic Depression has been seen moving rapidly across the country leaving a trail of chaos. Where are Laroxyl and Triptozol?"

"On sick leave, sir," answered Cogentin, "Dr Ativan had to see them yesterday."

"Tell them our plans then. Fill them in," ordered the chairman.

"Can you describe the delusions?" asked Fentazin.

"No," replied the chairman, "but within 17 hours and 21 days I want to see all symptoms gone."

"Right," said the tablets, all answering together.

"One final question, who is leading the operation?" asked Orap.

"Dr Priadel," replied the chairman, rising to his feet to close the meeting.

Later that night Orap telephoned Clopixol to discuss the delusions.

"Pretty scary, isn't it? Imagine: one person thought he was a wood-pigeon."

"Oh dear," said Clopixol. "Maybe we should abandon the project."

"No!" said Fentazin, coming in on the other line. "We will go ahead. Twenty milligrams should work."

Five days later Orap, Fentazin and Cogentin were eating lasagne in a café in St. Mark's Square, Leningrad. They heard a newsflash on the radio. Dopamine was loose and was spreading false beliefs. Depression was getting worse thanks to that slippery customer Serotonin. Through the window Cogentin suddenly spotted Dopamine getting into a Lada 1600. The neuroleptics sprinted down the street after him. The chase for Dopamine was on. Swerving on two wheels Dopamine took the corner at speed and hit a post. Orap was first on the scene.

"Freeze, Dopamine," he growled.

The gun fired and Dopamine was dead – killed by twenty milligrams of Orap.

Within hours the tablets had cornered the slimy Serotonin and put him safely behind bars.

Instantly all delusions died away and hallucinations vanished. Then Depression went and all phobias and irrational thinking disappeared. Then all was well.

Ten days later the chairman addressed the meeting again.

"Congratulations tablets. You have killed Mental Illness. We will celebrate."

And the next day the tablets got a write-up in the *Medication Times*.

Mark's time on the programme comes to an end and he prepares for discharge. Over the last few months some time and guidance have been given over by the therapists to discussions of career options and, where possible, to provide opportunities for work practice in chosen areas. Mark had opted to work in the hospital gardens and greenhouses. He liked the outdoor work and, based on his experience there, he has decided to change course from the academic atmosphere of business studies to the more leisurely paced, less intensive, world of landscape gardening and horticulture. He attends an interview for a place on a three-year horticultural course and gains acceptance. Mark's depression is now well controlled and he is ready to move on.

We meet with the consultant for what we know will be our final visit as he retires shortly. He takes us back over the years to the first time he had seen Mark at six years of age. He tells us he had been struck forcibly then by Mark's classic textbook presentation of Kanner-type autistic disorder. In all the intervening twenty years he had not seen a more perfect example. He tells us he had been equally impressed by our commitment to Mark and our searching approach to his condition. He had deliberately withheld his diagnosis of autism because he did not wish to take away our hope nor colour our vision. Now, coming to the end of a long medical career, he tells us that he learned very early on in that career that hope must never be denied because to deny hope is to deny life.

He has seen the medical profession confounded more often than it cares to admit. Looking at Mark now he considers that medical prognosis has been confounded one more time. He would never have expected, twenty years ago, that Mark would reach the plateau on which he now stands. Nor is he now going to choose between labels such as high-functioning autism or Asperger syndrome, adding that Mark does not need labels. He has proved that he can do without them.

Commenting on Mark's depression, he considers it would be a wise precaution to discontinue taking anti-depressant medication now because there are atypical features to his depression. His experience with other patients has shown that these atypical features could lead to a development of unpleasant moods if anti-depressant medication is continued for longer than necessary. He gives instructions for phasing it out slowly, adding that the depression has now almost remitted and should give no further trouble. He recommends that Mark slowly ease himself back into his former life-style.

Shaking hands we part, saddened that his retirement will deprive us of a wise counsellor who has become such a good friend to Mark.

A month later Mark begins his horticultural course. Slowly his energy returns and with it his enthusiasm for this new career. The organizers are aware of his condition and are prepared to make allowances and phase him in gradually. The outdoor life-style suits him and soon he becomes involved in all aspects of the course. Within three months his anti-depressant medication has been phased out. He takes his first hostelling weekend away from home.

Tears

Within a month of discontinuing medication we notice changes in his behaviour. They are low grade. Short periods of agitation and irritability alternate with good spirits, high energy and unrealistic planning ahead – plans to live in another country. This is followed in turn by weeks of normal behaviour. Then short periods, often just a few hours, of fatigue, withdrawal and slowing down of activity occur, to be followed again by weeks of normal behaviour. These changes are at times so fleeting and low grade that one wonders if they are just a reaction to outside events.

We consider that they probably result from the withdrawal of the anti-depressant medication. Any psychotropic medication will bring about adaptive changes in the brain while it is being taken because this is how medication works (and also how cognitive and psychological therapy, the so-called "talk therapy", works). They actually alter the structure of the brain. Consequently then, when discontinued, the structure of the brain will adapt and change again. We tell ourselves that he is going through a rocky period and that it will take time for his nervous system to settle again on an even keel. This should happen when the last of the chemicals have left the receptor sites in the synapse – a process that could take anything up to six months or indeed perhaps longer. Mark himself does not seem to be disturbed by these moods or perhaps even aware of these changes in his behaviour.

As the months go by we see a worsening of these changes. They come in faster cycles, the disturbed moods last longer, are more intense, and the periods of normal mood in between become shorter, lasting days now rather than weeks. Mark later describes these periods of normal mood as "short pearly glimmers of sunlight, visible between thick, black, oily thunder-clouds."

If this pattern continues these mood swings will become kaleidoscoped, running into each other and joining up. Because it becomes obvious now that this is what they are. They are mood swings and they are harbingers of a major storm ahead. We remember the warning of the consultant that in Mark's case unpleasant moods could develop following some anti-depres-sant medication.

His work practice deteriorates. There are days of low mood when he struggles just merely to get out of bed – the leadenness of his body self-evident. They alternate with days of high-energy when he is first into work in the morning tackling all the most difficult practical assignments of the day but leaving most of them unfinished – with days when his racing thoughts fly ahead of his unstoppable speech and prevent him from concen-trating on lectures, or listening for long enough to take instruction. But the days we dread most are the days of intense agitation, frustrated anger and iri-descent irritability. On these days we walk around him as if barefoot on broken glass. In between there are a few days, or perhaps hours, of oasis-like calm when he seems to be in the eye of the storm. Then we can communicate.

On one of these days he agrees to go back to hospital saying he will seek the sanctuary of the ward hoping for release from the chaos of his thoughts – the thoughts that race uncontrollably through his mind and exert such pressure in his head that at times he feels it will explode.

We wish our former consultant was still in practice but he has left the country, so we set up an appointment, for four days hence, with his successor, who will have Mark's case notes to hand. While waiting out these four, short, seemingly endless days, in order to keep ourselves occupied we search for information on rapid cycling mood disorder in an effort to explain why Mark is swinging between high moods of euphoric elation, low moods of depression and in between the very unpleasant moods of dysphoric elation.

In the average population we find that the term "rapid cycling" is used to refer to those who have four or more episodes of mood swings in a year. But we find little information on these very rapid cycling, fast-changing mood swings we see unfolding in Mark, other than a passing reference to the fact that in some susceptible people anti-depressant medication can accelerate the frequency of such mood swings. It becomes clear that genes are implicated in the basic mood swings of bipolar mood disorder (BMD), so much so that the evidence is sufficiently compelling to justify setting up the large-scale molecular genetic studies which are now under way.[32]

We learn that the incidence of the illness in the average population is one in a hundred and the average age of onset is seventeen to eighteen. As previously mentioned there are no figures for the incidence of it in the general autistic population other than that reported from case histories. These case histories make no mention of the type of fast-changing cycles that Mark has become caught up in.

The four endless days pass into the shadows and tonight Mark is back in his old room in the ward. Tonight there are no tears. Instead, there is a feeling of security and sanctuary.

At midnight I walk again down the long corridor and listen to the whispering silence. Alone now in the dim light and attuned to the shades of the sleeping building, I make no effort to hold back the tears – the tears I have never shed in all of Mark's twenty-six years. Opening the door I pass out into the twilight and the soft summer rain.

The tidal zone

For two weeks Mark remains storm tossed in a tidal zone of ebb and flow. Then gradually the storm recedes and his moods begin to stabilize. The stabilizing force is lithium – a common element of nature, found in rocks, water and plants, as well as in ourselves.

How can a simple element of nature control the storms of the mind so readily? The answer is that lithium is no ordinary element. It is one of the most reactive in nature, requiring very little energy to move in and out of the barriers across cells and between cells. Carrying a single positive charge it can rapidly change the composition at the interface of neurons (nerve cells) because it belongs to that family of metal ions responsible for causing electrical signals to sweep down through the axon or nerve fibre and so send messages along nerve circuits.

Lithium is thought to act in the brain by increasing the production of brain-protective compounds. These compounds protect the neurons which are involved in recurrent mood swings and return their overstimulated reactions to normal. This action of lithium is not a temporary one. It is continuous, provided the dosage is correct and the blood level is kept within the therapeutic range. Up-to-date research has shown that the longer a patient is taking lithium the better will be its therapeutic effect. After four years it will be more effective than it was after two.

However, while lithium has been proved to be very effective in treating standard bipolar mood disorder on its own, it has not been proven to be as effective when it is the sole agent in the treatment of rapid cycling mood swings. Consequently, in Mark's case it is decided to add a low dose of the atypical neuroleptic medication. Research has shown that this neuroleptic medication has been found to be the single most important agent in the treatment of recurrent psychiatric disorders. It targets both serotonin and dopamine receptors and blocks their action. In addition it binds to an array of other common neurotransmitters and is associated with a high success rate. This combination of lithium and neuroleptic medication proves to be the key factor in Mark's recovery.

As he improves he rejoins the club, settling into the routine again and for the first time in his life he begins to question his condition of autism and his now co-morbid mood swings.

"Why me? Why was I chosen? Why not Ted? Why not Simon?"

Knowing that he has issues to resolve he requests and is granted a year's leave of absence from the horticultural course. Talking through his difficulties with him we become aware that this illness has changed his way of viewing himself and consequently his relationship with his world. Up until now he has largely been happy with himself and tolerant of the shortcomings of others. He has always looked kindly on his peers and on those he interacted with. He did not seem capable of envy or dissatisfaction. Now his self-image and self-esteem have plummeted, his future is uncertain and he has to reach acceptance of who he is. Mark has to find himself all over again. To do this he will have to work through all the negativity that now dominates his thinking.

How can we find our way through this impasse?

We search for a clinical psychologist experienced in the field of autism and are fortunate enough to find an erudite professional who is prepared to share her considerable expertise in this area with us as a family and with Mark as an individual. Some weeks later we meet with her, and Mark undergoes his first session of cognitive behaviour therapy.

What is cognitive behaviour therapy?

Cognitive behaviour therapy involves getting insight into how we think. It sets out to change patterns of faulty or negative thinking and to replace them with thoughts (cognitions) and self-statements that promote positive and more realistic ways of looking at situations. Perceptions, mental attitudes and beliefs are looked at and disputed to show that they do not always represent a true picture. Then the individual can be encouraged to adapt to different ways of looking at a situation by disputing his own thoughts. For example, a statement such as "I can never get anything right", can be disputed by "That's just not true, I get a lot of things right."

Over time, with practice, permanent changes can be brought about in thinking patterns. This in turn will alter moods, increase self-esteem, change the way an individual views his own life and influence his interaction with others.

In the course of Mark's therapy one incident stands out in the mind. He has become very conscious that he now has two medical conditions – a developmental disorder and a co-existing psychiatric condition. In his own estimation he has two labels and this is a big issue for him. Listening to his concerns, his therapist decides to tap into his strong capacity for visual imagery. Some days later he wears a smart, new, grey jacket which he loves and feels good in. As he leaves she says – "Mark I'm admiring your jacket. It's a wonderful colour and beautiful soft material. It must be very comfortable to wear and it's such a smart up-to-date style. You look so well in it. May I have a look?"

Mark slips off the jacket to show her. Turning it inside out she finds the labels – two small discs of innocuous black cloth stitched on to the inside of the lining.

"They're just the labels," says Mark, looking at her in puzzlement.

"Yes, they're *just* the labels. Are they part of the jacket?"

"No – not really I suppose."

"Mark, when you go home this evening will you do something for me? Will you measure the area of the jacket and compare it with the area of the labels. Let me know what percentage the labels are." Showing his surprise he nods, wondering: does she need the measurements to make a similar one?

This evening he spreads the jacket across the dining room table and running the measuring tape over it section by section he jots down his figures. Then he measures the labels and with calculator in hand he works out the answer. The labels are 0.0001 per cent of the jacket.

He knows now why he has been asked to do it.

It puts the question of labels into perspective for him. He views them now as something which may be necessary because they give information and they give insight. But they form no part of the jacket *per se* and the jacket is what matters. Compared to it they are infinitesimal.

Mark reaches the beginnings of acceptance.

CHAPTER 19

Landfall

The present

We sit in the third row of the lecture hall surrounded by other parents. Across from us Mark sits with his peer group. One by one their names are called and they mount the steps to the platform. A firm hand-clasp, a scroll of parchment changes hands and they turn to face the hall. The cameras flash, the applause rises, and they walk back proudly to their seats, conscious of what they carry with them – a testimonial to hard work and achievement and a passport to the future and to the work force. For Mark has completed his studies in horticulture. Today he graduates and so ends the third and final part of his education. He has arrived at his planned destination.

The journey has been long and arduous. There were obstacles to be overcome, unexpected stops and delays along the way and unforeseen complications. Then there was excess baggage to be taken on board – to be stored and accommodated. But today Mark has reached the place he set out for.

At lunch, staff, parents and graduates mingle and share anecdotes of the ups and downs of the past three years. There is much laughter and a few nostalgic tears and promises to keep in touch. We walk around the grounds and Mark poses for group photographs – mementos for the future. Slowly the chatting groups break up, the good-byes are said and one of the most important days in Mark's life draws to a close.

But it is not over yet. Later tonight Mark returns to the hospital. He was admitted a few days prior to this for a short period of adjustment in his medication. As he enters the ward, one by one patients and staff rise to their feet and clap. I stand back, merging into the shadows. Looking straight ahead, Mark walks on – on down between the two rows of applauding figures, each in turn rising to his feet as Mark passes.

Around me the ward resounds to the wave of spontaneous applause and Mark receives his second standing ovation. It takes place in a very different setting from the first. But it is a measure of respect and acknowledgement of success and achievement from a population of people who know what it is like to challenge the odds in the hope of winning. Because of that it is all the more profound.

At the end of the ward Mark turns the corner and walks to his room. The sound dies away into the silence.

It is his crowning moment.

The past

Leaving the present we return to the past before we look to the future and ask ourselves that, had we had just one wish to be granted in the past in coping with Mark's autism, what would we have asked for? We have no difficulty in choosing between wishes. We would have asked for the gift of wisdom. The wisdom that comes with knowledge. The knowledge that was *not* there then but *is* there now. Because, with the advent of molecular biology and the application of the tools of neuroscience and molecular genetics to autism, answers are appearing and slowly a pattern is emerging. This pattern revolves around faulty circuits of neurons occurring in the autistic brain (cross-wiring) which leads to messages not being delivered to correct brain centres and thus not mapping onto areas of the brain specific to that stimulus. Instead, they map onto an area of the brain specified for dealing with a different stimulus and so the message either never arrives at its correct destination or is misinterpreted at its wrong destination. It becomes clearer that these processes appear to be under genetic control.

Brain research

The study of the brain is hugely complex and the processes underlying its structure and development are probably among the most complicated on this planet. It is certainly the most complex structure ever to be investigated by the mind of man, and yet in the last five years alone some giant steps have been taken in unravelling the mystery of what is going on in the autistic brain.

I previously mentioned that nerve cells are called "neurons". In the brain there are thousands of different kinds of neurons and they are grouped together to form circuits. These circuits are the underlying basis of behaviour and of mental life. The study of the organization of these circuits in the brain reveals that "the brain is a massively parallel distributed information processor" (p.33).[32] This brain design recognizes patterns of markings in parallel streams. For example, one stream will analyse colour while another will analyse shape. These are then subdivided into further parallel streams. These parallel circuits are so organized that they mark out different regions of the brain for different functions. This type of brain design is capable of coping with degrees of failure in the individual elements that go to make it up. All of which makes the brain a very efficient information processor indeed – better and longer-lasting than a computer. In addition (and this is of vital importance in the case of autism) if there is damage to any particular area of the brain it may be possible to adapt undamaged circuits to re-route messages to areas of the brain spared such damage and so pick up functions which would otherwise be lost. *The younger the developing brain is the more likely it is to respond to such adaptation of function.*[32]

Autism is now thought of in terms of being a disorder of higher-order intellectual abilities which are involved in information processing. In the quest for where in the brain the fault might be located, research up until recently has focused on the *structure* of individual cells, looking for pathology (disease). This pathology centres around cell loss, or cell increase or cell damage, and a wide range of these types of abnormality *have* been found in both imaging and autopsy studies. This is not surprising when one considers the individual variation of symptoms found in the autism population.

These findings however, though significant, have provided little insight into, or understanding of, the pathology underlying autism. In very recent research, attention has shifted from looking for single cell pathology to examining the manner in which cells are assembled to form the small basic units of circuits within the brain. This research has found abnormalities in the assembly of these circuits in autism and in Asperger syndrome. As the authors of this investigation point out, their research emphasizes the role of information processing within the brain and may lead to a novel approach to future research, resulting in possible therapeutic interventions.[51]

Other significant recent findings have emerged from two large-scale studies of individuals with autism, ranging in age from two to forty-six years old. It was found that in the younger age-group, in early childhood there had been an increase in total brain volume. This early increase in growth was, however, not maintained and by later childhood had fallen back to the same size as was found in the normal control group. Furthermore, brain size in these autistic children had been normal at birth and this accelerated growth had taken place after birth, it coinciding with the emergence of the symptoms of autism in the second year of life. This is the time when the circuits in the brain which support intellectual abilities are becoming estab-lished, and excessive growth during this period will naturally disrupt this very intricate, delicate, procedure. In addition, the increased head circumfer-ence, found in this research among the adults and adolescents in the autism sample, points to the fact that they also had increased total brain volume in their early childhood. This paper records that, in a minority of children with autism, the brain, after some delay, can again pick up the threads of normal development and make some degree of progress. This progress, they hold, in some cases may be large but is never complete.[52] In this connection it is inter-esting to note that old photographs of Mark confirm that he also had a sub-stantial increase in head circumference early in the second year of life. This first became apparent at about fifteen months and it was obvious and com-mented on at the time, but of course, the significance of it could not have been foreseen.

Allied to findings in this particular brain area is a discovery of major importance made in the first year of this twenty-first century. One important autism laboratory undertook research into the levels of eight brain growth factors in new-born blood samples from infants who subsequently devel-oped autism (the people concerned are now in their late teenage years). Four of these brain growth factors were found to be increased in the infants who later developed autism and in the infants who later showed intellectual dis-ability without autism, but the factors were *not* increased in infants who later showed normal development. These four brain growth substances are known to be involved in regulating the production of brain cells, in the orga-nization of them and in programming cell death or cell expansion. An increase in the presence of these factors at birth would be in line with the increase in brain volume found in very young children with autism.[53]

Some of the most promising results from recent brain imaging studies relate to face perception (promising, that is, in terms of possible treatment). It is well documented in imaging studies that the area of the brain which responds preferentially to face discrimination in normal individuals is the *fusiform gyrus* (FG), a temporal lobe structure. Two recent studies (using functional magnetic resonance imaging (fMRI)) have found that individuals with autism and AS showed either reduced activity or no functional activity in this area (FG) of the brain when viewing pictures of faces. Instead they showed activation in a part of the brain (inferior temporal gyrus) normally associated with object discrimination. This result was in sharp contrast to the control group who showed robust activation in the FG when viewing pictures of faces.[54, 55]

All of which suggests that the perceptual processing of *faces* in people with autism spectrum disorders is more like the perceptual processing of *objects* in the general population. These and other studies of face perception in autism suggest disturbances in the specialization of the local brain circuits in face perception.

Mark has shown evidence of disturbance in brain circuitry in three different areas:

1.   in perceiving "faces in the flesh" and in black-and-white pictures

2.   in his lack of hand specialization and, not previously mentioned,

3.   in his synesthesia.

Synesthesia (derived from the Greek word meaning "union of the senses") is thought to be due to extra circuits in the brain which should have been pruned away during development but were not. It results in two or more of the senses becoming intertwined and is often referred to as "having a quirk in the senses". The commonest two senses to be so affected are those of sound and sight with the result that when a synesthete hears a particular sound he will see a particular colour at the same time. He will actually *see* the colour before his eyes – he will not just visualize it – and the same colour will always be associated with the same sound. For example, in Mark's case, the sound of a wood-pigeon cooing always produces sharp spikes of a brilliant purple/grey colour which dominate his vision, while at the same time he feels the needle-sharp spikes with his hands. Thus, three of his senses clash together and he finds the sensation very real and very disturbing. In other synesthetes the senses of taste and sound become intertwined (they will actually taste sounds) and others again have the experience of all five senses clashing. Synesthesia has been documented in medical history for over two hundred years. There is considerable interest now in research into synesthesia because it has been realized that there is a possibility of using it to obtain insight into how the brain works – into how in fact the brain can become the mind. Originally thought to be very rare in the general population, recent research into cognitive neuroscience shows synesthesia to occur in about one in two hundred individuals. It has been documented quite often in the autism population.

Application of research findings

Looking objectively then at these findings from modern brain research and applying them to Mark, we come to the conclusion that the single most disabling factor of Mark's autism has stemmed from the sensory deprivation involved in his inability to see the human face and so become initiated from early life into the human experience. This deficit has deprived him from birth of the opportunity to partake in social interaction and has consigned him to years of aloneness. Even today Mark's own face is curiously untouched by the experience of living. In some undefinable way it does not appear to have recorded the full passage of time. He looks years younger than his age-counterparts and shows few of the signs of ageing seen in the average thirty-year-old. The years have left him physically unmarked, as if his lack of affective social contact through eye-gaze (which comes naturally to the average infant from about three months) has somehow slowed down the ticking of his internal biological clock and consequently the record of the passing of time is out of alignment with reality. For so long Mark has been in the world but not of it. Because of this, his social and emotional development have been delayed and, although he constantly makes gains in this developmental delay, there is still much ground to reclaim.

Had we been aware from babyhood that Mark could not see faces would it have been possible to do anything to alleviate the condition? The answer is *no* – not then. But in terms of present-day research the answer is *yes*, because fMRI studies are now sufficiently advanced to find out whether or not intensive training/treatment in face viewing in children with a face perception deficit will be followed by improvement in these originally poorly functioning brain areas. Or to put the question another way – will the FG show normal levels of activity after intensive face training? If the answer to this is yes, it would indicate that it is possible to normalize functional activity in brain areas in autism. On the other hand, if the answer is *no*, but it is found that useful functioning had developed in a different part of the brain in response to these exercises, then this, in turn, would hold out promise for redirecting lost functioning to new brain areas.

The potential now for devising neuroimaging studies to find out about brain learning mechanisms in autism and using them to map out individual biological interventions to improve social, language and other skills is considerable.[54] One of the first testing grounds for investigating this potential will be the use of fMRI techniques in the area of face perception. Such studies are already under way.

These recent brain studies also give new insights into why intensive early intervention programmes have been found to be beneficial for children with autism. It has been known for over twenty years that such applied behaviour treatment methods have achieved significant results in increasing communication and the ability to learn, in guiding appropriate social behaviour and in reducing inappropriate behaviour.[32] It has also been shown that the earlier these programmes are begun the more progress can be made. Children between the ages of two and four have been found to make greater gains than do children over four years old. This suggests a plasticity to moulding development in the very early years in autism which may be unique and which may indicate a critical time-span for intervention.[56] This suggestion correlates well with what has been previously written concerning new findings relating to the disturbances in the specialization of nerve circuits in the autistic brain.

It brings to the fore two important points about early intervention treatment. The first of these concerns the vital necessity of early diagnosis so that treatment can be started without delay. It is now possible to diagnose autism midway through the second year of life and ongoing research points to the possibility of diagnosis at an even earlier age.

The second point relates to the content of these early intervention programmes. There are few studies available showing which ingredients of a treatment programme are likely to be the most effective. For example, IQ tests are not usually good criteria for measuring change as they are least likely to show change over time because they have been developed to show stability.[57] The treatment variables that need to be examined are the extent of the curriculum, the theory underlying it, teaching approaches, the focus on language development, strategies for developing social skills and special targeted areas, e.g. handling unacceptable behaviours.[56] Much co-ordinated, comparable, research, using strict scientific methods, is called for in this particular area. Meanwhile it is of interest to note that in these early intervention programmes significant emphasis is already being placed on a *look at me* approach when the teacher will reward the child for every effort made to look in the direction of her or his face.

The future

Autism has had a bleak and troubled past and the fates both of autistic people and the parents of autistic people have suffered because of it. It is now sixty years since Leo Kanner first diagnosed the condition and for half of that period of time autism has been a victim of the mother did it/parental culpability controversy. In fact there are still some parts of the world today where its ghost lingers on and professionals still subscribe to this view.

On moving into the 1980s and 1990s, more rational views of autism began to appear when research moved forward into the expanding fields of genetics and brain studies. However, the fate of autism still remained dogged by controversy. Because of the lack of clear fundamental answers as to its aetiology the field was left open for the growth of sometimes questionable treatments, based mainly on anecdotal evidence and not on sound scientific analysis. Many of these controversial treatments have become divisive.

More recently still, the measles, mumps, rubella (MMR) vaccine has been implicated as a possible factor in causing autism and again serious controversy has arisen on this issue. To gain insight into the background against which this controversy arose we go to a comprehensive report produced on this issue by the National Disease Surveillance Centre and the Department of Public Health, Southern Health Board, Ireland. In asking the question "Does the MMR vaccine cause serious diseases (e.g. autism, Crohn's disease)?", the report answers it with:

> In 1998, Dr Andrew Wakefield and colleagues at the Royal Free Hospital in London published a paper in the *Lancet* describing 12 children with developmental and bowel problems [ref.[58]]. Eight of the children had autism, which the parents reported began soon after vaccination with MMR. The hypothesis put forward was that the MMR vaccine caused a leaky bowel; this allowed a toxin to enter, which affected the brain and caused autism. This hypothesis is not proven, and the researchers themselves stated that they had not proven a link

with MMR vaccine. Experts from the WHO concluded that the study "fails at every level to make a causal association" [ref.59].

Going on to discuss other studies undertaken to investigate this same issue, the report further states:

> A study published in the *Lancet* in June 1999 by Taylor *et al.* looked at the immunization records of 498 cases of autism, born between 1979 and 1998 [ref.60]. They found no sudden "step up" or change in trend after the introduction of MMR; no difference in the age at diagnosis between vaccinated and unvaccinated children; no association between the onset of autism within 18 months after MMR; and no clustering of developmental regression in the months after vaccination.

And again:

> In December 2000, Patja *et al.* published the results of a Finnish study that reviewed adverse drug reactions (ADRs) reported after 1.8 million individuals were immunised with 3 million doses of MMR, since 1982 [ref.61]. No case of inflammatory bowel disease or autism was linked to the vaccine during a long follow up (1982–1996) of those specific cases.62

All the above-mentioned controversies slow down the progress of work on the cause of autism and its treatment, because they divert time and much needed resources away from where they are most required, which is in the arena of solid, scientifically structured, research. In addition, controversial treatments can compete with medical treatment options and the ensuing differences of opinion can set up tensions and stresses, the impact of which causes unnecessary burdens to both families and clinicians – to families who may, among other considerations, have to agonize over the lack of necessary resources to fund such treatment – to clinicians who may find themselves being forced to take sides and thereby become drawn into unwelcome controversy.

Throughout Mark's growing years, every so often we would hear or read about some new miraculous treatment that would cure autism. In the beginning, in spite of the fact that many such treatments did not stand up to even common sense, let alone scientific sense, we somehow suspended our critical faculties and "went for it". As one parent has so succinctly put it, "Credulity is an elastic limit, capable of stretching in proportion with need".63

Somehow when the neon lights flash *cure* it is hard to resist; somehow if one is doing something about autism or is seen to be doing something about autism one feels better about it. Then there is hope and the placebo effect of it to keep one going. (*The placebo effect,* "placebo" meaning "to please", is commonly recognized in medicine as a treatment in its own right even though it is based only on the patient's faith in the treatment. It is not unusual for a placebo effect to occur in about half of the patients in any study of a medical treatment.) Standing helplessly by, listening to the relentless ticking of a biological clock (one's own and that of one's child) can bring with it a most overwhelming sense of powerlessness. Then one feels the need to take action and do something about it.

So in this very questionable process we found ourselves chasing rainbows down endless cul-de-sacs which led nowhere. As time went by we became older and wiser and more disillusioned with each unfulfilled expectation. We also came to realize that some of these alternative therapies had, of their very nature, the potential to cause harm to Mark. While one may waste time and resources, one needs to think very carefully about any treatment that has the potential to cause damage. Until such time as much more is known about the cause or causes of autism and they can be related directly to any alternative therapy that is offered, then it is a wise precaution to keep an open mind and think very carefully about any such therapy before undertaking it.

There has been a lingering tendency in autism to keep harking back to the past. This is particularly true of that other controversy regarding whether the children described by Kanner and Asperger are the same or different. Much emphasis has been placed on searching through the original papers of both these pioneers of the autism concept in order to shed light on this issue. This has been proven to be of limited value. Kanner and Asperger were experts of their time but that era is now past and time and research have moved on. There is a move afoot now to look forward from this position and to assess the usefulness of different diagnostic criteria on the basis of issues such as genetic factors, neurobiological/neuropsychological findings and nature of outcome, so that whatever diagnostic concepts are arrived at will be subject to "external validation".[64]

The 1990s was the decade of the brain and significant progress was made in brain research during this period. Because sufficient resources were applied to other neurological disorders, such as Alzheimer's disease, striking advances were made in the understanding of the biological basis of these disorders. Thanks in part to parent involvement, these necessary resources are now being applied to autism and, as we have seen, the first few years of this twenty-first century have already yielded very significant answers. As a result of progress in the fields of genetic and brain research the future for autism looks bright. There is still some way to go but the road ahead is more open now.

And what of the future and the road ahead for Mark? Mark's case has been complicated by the development of co-existing bipolar mood disorder. As we have seen, these co-morbid psychiatric disorders of autism are not particularly well known about, nor are they particularly well understood. One fact that is well documented, however, is their potential to contribute to a poor outcome. Much of this will depend on how quickly they are picked up on and how successfully they are treated. There is a growing realization from the literature that, while there is a general consensus that psychotherapy is of benefit in conjunction with medication in disorders such as depression and schizophrenia, this initiative has not generally been applied to bipolar mood disorders.[65] This is despite the fact that the few studies undertaken in this area have shown a good clinical outcome when psychotherapy treatment was added to medication.

Mark's mood swings are well controlled due to the combination of medication and psychotherapy. He now shoulders his two medical conditions lightly and considers that he has come through the vicissitudes of autism and its co-morbidity unscathed. He feels at peace with himself and in harmony with his world. In some curious way, possibly helped by appropriate medication, the experience of the mood disorder has somehow "softened the edges of his autism". He is no longer driven but goes at life more calmly – looking outwards and taking more cognizance of the *human* world around him. Rarely does he turn to the inner one. Now, people are interesting to him for what they might say and think, rather than what they might do. His observational comments on himself and on those who impinge on his day-to-day life are astute and sometimes very accurate. I smile when he suspects my ulterior motives in making certain suggestions and says, "Mum – no hidden agendas please!"

Insight has grown and the twin principles of cause and effect have forged a link, so life becomes more predictable. All of which helps to reduce anxiety.

He has returned to his music after some years of absence and under Barry's motivation and guidance has taken up the clarinet again. He and

Barry play duets together – harmonizing clarinet and alto-sax. This is opening up new vistas and opportunities for him.

After much thought and reflection on his past and present he has now arrived at a very positive attitude to his life. Somewhere along that journey he became conscious that there are other people out there who are more challenged by the circumstances of their lives than he himself is and he now devotes time and energy to lending support where needed.

But most of all Mark has reached acceptance of who he is –

"So I have autism/Asperger syndrome and I have bipolar mood swings. That's all right by me. I get ninety per cent of everything and that's not so bad."

And that also is Mark's gift to us – acceptance. For nigh on thirty years we have fought autism, concentrating only on its negativity. Now, seeing Mark as he is today, we feel we can lay down the cudgels and accept it. We can go even further and appreciate the qualities of autism. For autism is honest – it does not cheat or steal, nor seek to defraud – nor is it responsible for the pain it inadvertently causes. Autism is just and has no guile, nor does it lie or manipulate. Autism is kind – it does not bear malice or victimize, nor does it prey on others – rather it seeks to forgive. It is not motivated by self-interest but has a shining simplicity and integrity about it that is rare in the world today. These are some of its strengths and Mark has them in full measure.

References

1. Piaget, J. (1953) *The Origin of Intelligence in the Child*. Translated by Margaret Cook (1993) London: Routledge and Kegan Paul.

2. Piaget, J. (1962) *Play, Dreams and Imitation*. New York: W.W. Norton.

3. Kanner, L. (1943) "Autistic disturbance of affective contact." *Nervous Child 2*, 217–50.

4. Kanner, L. (1962) "The child is father." *TIME Magazine*, 25 July. (p.64).

5. Roberts, J. (1989) "Echolalia and comprehension in autistic children." *Journal of Autism and Developmental Disorders 19*, 2, 271–81.

6. Baltaxe, C.A. and Simmons, J.Q. (1977) "Bedtime soliloquies and linguistic competence in Autism." *Journal of Speech and Hearing Disorders 42*, 376–93.

7. Delacato, C.H. (1974) *The Ultimate Stranger*. Novato, CA: Academic Therapy Publications.

8. Ornitz, E.M. and Ritvo, E.R. (1968) "Perceptual inconstancy in early infantile autism." *Archives of General Psychiatry 18*, 76–98.

9. Lovaas, O.I., Schriebman, L., Koegel, R. and Rehm, R. (1971) "Selective responding by autistic children to multiple sensory input." *Journal of Abnormal Psychology 77*, 211–22.

10. Sacks, O. (1995) *An Anthropologist on Mars*. New York: Alfred A. Knopf. (pp.179–232).

11. Brown, W.A. *et al.* (2003) "Autism-related language, personality, and cognition in people with absolute pitch: Results of a preliminary study." *Journal of Autism and Developmental Disorders 33*, 2, 163–7.

12. Hewetson, A. (2002) *The Stolen Child: Aspects of Autism and Asperger Syndrome*. Westport, CT: Greenwood Press (pp.46–47).

13. Sinclair, J. (1992) "Bridging the gaps: An inside-out view of autism." In *High-Functioning Individuals with Autism*, edited by E. Schopler and G.B. Mesibov. New York: Plenum Press (pp.294–302).

14. Andron, L. (2001) *Our Journey Through High Functioning Autism and Asperger Syndrome: A Roadmap*. London: Jessica Kingsley Publishers (p.73).

15. Feingold, B.F. (1975) *Why Your Child is Hyperactive*. New York: Random House (pp.1–21).

16. Ornitz, E.M. and Ritvo, E.R. (1976) "The syndrome of autism: A critical review." *American Journal of Psychiatry 133*, 6, 609–21.

17. Rutter, M. (1999) "The Emanuel Miller Memorial Lecture 1998: Autism: Two-way interplay between research and clinical work." *Journal of Child Psychology and Psychiatry 40*, 2, 169–88.

18. Frith, U. (1989) *Autism: Explaining the Enigma*. Oxford: Blackwell Publishers (pp.1–15).

19. Asperger, H. (1991) "Autistic psychopathy in childhood." In *Autism and Asperger Syndrome*, edited and translated by U. Frith. Cambridge: Cambridge University Press (pp.37–92).

20. Kemper, T.L. and Bauman, M.L. (1993) "The contribution of neuropathologic studies to the understanding of autism." *Behavioral Neurology 11*, 1, 175–87.

21. Soper, H.V. *et al.* (1986) "Handedness patterns in autism suggest subtypes." *Journal of Autism and Developmental Disorders 16*, 2, 155–68.

22. Escalante-Mead, P.R., Minshew, N.J. and Sweeney, J.A. (2003) "Abnormal brain lateralisation in high-functioning autism." *Journal of Autism and Developmental Disorders 33*, 5, 539–43.

23. Sacks, O. (1973) *Awakenings.* London: Gerald Duckworth (pp.294–6).

24. Nordoff, P. and Robbins, C. (1971) *Therapy in Music for Handicapped Children.* London: Victor Gollancz (pp.104–6).

25. Hermelin, B. (2001) *Bright Splinters of the Mind.* London: Jessica Kingsley Publishers.

26. Kobayashi, R. (1996) "Brief report: Physiognomic perception in autism." *Journal of Autism and Developmental Disorders 26*, 6, 661–7.

27. Hobson, R.P. (1992) "Social perception in high level autism." In *High-Functioning Individuals with Autism*, edited by E. Schopler and G.B. Mesibov. New York: Plenum Press (pp.157–84).

28. Kracke, I. (1994) "Developmental prosopagnosia in Asperger syndrome: Presentation and discussion of an individual case." *Developmental Medicine and Child Neurology 36*, 873–86.

29. Filipek, P.A. *et al.* (1999) "The screening and diagnosis of autistic spectrum disorders." *Journal of Autism and Developmental Disorders 29*, 6, 439–84.

30. Gillberg, C. and Coleman, M. (1992) *The Biology of the Autistic Syndromes.* Second edition. London: MacKeith Press (pp.43–51).

31. Peeters, T. and Gillberg, C. (2000) *Autism: Medical and Educational Aspects.* Second edition. London: Whurr.

32. US Department of Health and Human Services (1999) *Mental Health: A Report of the Surgeon General.* Rockville, MD: US Department of Health and Human Services, Substance Abuse and Mental Health Services Administration, Center for Mental Health Services, National Institutes of Health, National Institute of Mental Health (pp.31–116).

33. Folstein, S.E. and Santangelo, S.L. (2000) "Does Asperger syndrome aggregate in families?" In *Asperger Syndrome*, edited by A. Klin, F.R. Volkmar and S.S. Sparrow. New York: The Guilford Press (pp.159–71).

34. Martin, A., Patzer, D.K. and Volkmar, F.R. (2000) "Psychopharmacological treatment of higher-functioning pervasive developmental disorders." In *Asperger Syndrome*, edited by A. Klin, F.R.Volkmar and S.S. Sparrow. New York: The Guilford Press (pp.211–28).

35. Szatmari, P. (1991) "Asperger's syndrome: Diagnosis, treatment, and outcome." *Psychiatric Clinics of North America 14*, 1, 81–93.

36.   Tantam, D. (2000) "Psychological disorder in adolescents and adults with Asperger syndrome." *Autism 4*, 1, 47–61.

37.   Volkmar, F.R. and Klin, A. (1998) "Asperger syndrome and nonverbal learning disability." In *Asperger Syndrome or High-Functioning Autism?* edited by E. Schopler, G.B. Mesibov and L. Kunce. New York: Plenum Press (pp.107–21).

38.   Warren, R.P., Foster, A., Margaretten, N.C. and Pace, N.C. (1986) "Immune abnormalities in patients with autism." *Journal of Autism and Developmental Disorders 16*, 2, 189–97.

39.   Warren, R.P., Foster, A. and Margaretten, N.C. (1987) "Reduced natural killer cell activity in autism." *Journal of the American Academy of Child and Adolescent Psychiatry 26*, 333–5.

40.   Warren, R.P. *et al.* (1997) "Brief report: Immunoglobulin A deficiency in a subset of autistic subjects." *Journal of Autism and Developmental Disorders 27*, 2, 187–92.

41.   Comi, A.M. *et al.* (1999) "Familial clustering of autoimmune disorders and evaluation of medical risk factors in autism." *Journal of Child Neurology 14*, 388–94.

42.   Krause, I., Xiao-Song He, M., Gershwin, E. and Shoenfeld, Y. (2002) "Brief report: Immune factors in autism: A critical review." *Journal of Autism and Developmental Disorders 32*, 4, 337–45.

43.   Gupta, S., Aggarwal, S. and Heads, C. (1996) "Brief report: Dysregulated immune system in children with autism: Beneficial effects of intravenous immune globulin on autistic characteristics." *Journal of Autism and Developmental Disorders 26*, 4, 439–52.

44.   DelGiudice-Asch, G. *et al.* (1999) "Brief report: A pilot open clinical trial of intravenous immunoglobulin in childhood autism." *Journal of Autism and Developmental Disorders 29*, 2, 157–60.

45.   Plioplys, A.V. (2000) "Intravenous immunoglobulin treatment in autism." *Journal of Autism and Developmental Disorders 30*, 1, 73.

46.   Howlin, P. (2000) "Outcome in adult life for more able individuals with autism or Asperger syndrome." *Autism 4*, 1, 63–83.

47.   Konstantareas, M.M. and Hewitt, T. (2001) "Autistic disorder and schizophrenia: Diagnostic overlaps." *Journal of Autism and Developmental Disorders 31*, 1, 19–28.

48.   Volkmar, F.R. and Cohen, D.J. (1991) "Comorbid association of autism and schizophrenia." *American Journal of Psychiatry 148*, 1705–7.

49.   Gillberg, C. and Coleman, M. (2000) *The Biology of the Autistic Syndromes.* Third edition. London: MacKeith Press.

50.   Steingard, R. and Biederman, J. (1987) "Lithium responsive manic-like symptoms in two individuals with autism and mental retardation." *Journal of the American Academy of Child and Adolescent Psychiatry 26*, 6, 923–35.

51.   Casanova, M.F., Buxhoeveden, D.P. and Brown, C. (2002) "Clinical and macroscopic correlates of minicolumnar pathology in autism." *Child Neurology 17*, 692–5.

52.   Minshew, N. (2002) "Ask the editor." *Journal of Autism and Developmental Disorders 32*, 6, 615–16.

53.   Minshew, N. (2001) "Ask the editor." *Journal of Autism and Developmental Disorders 31*, 5, 517.

54.   Courchesne, E. and Pierce, K. (2000) "An inside look at the neurobiology, ethiology, and future research of autism." *Advocate 33*, 4, 21–2.

55.   Schultz, R.T. *et al.* (2000) "Abnormal ventral temporal cortical activity during face discrimination among individuals with autism and Asperger syndrome." *Archives of General Psychiatry 57*, April, 331–40.

56.   Rogers, S.J. (1996) "Brief Report: Early intervention in autism." *Journal of Autism and Developmental Disorders 26*, 2, 243–6.

57.   Charman, T. and Howlin, P. (2001) "Research into early intervention for children with autism and related disorders: Methodological and design issues." *Autism 7*, 2, 217–25.

58.   Wakefield, A.J. *et al.* (1998) "Ileal-lymphoid-nodular hyperplasia, non-specific colitis, and pervasive developmental disorder in children." *Lancet*, 351, 637–41.

59.   Lee, J.W. *et al.* (1998) "Autism, inflammatory bowel disease, and MMR vaccine." *Lancet 351*, 905.

60.   Taylor, B. *et al.* (1999) "Autism and measles, mumps, and rubella vaccine: No epidemiological evidence for a causal association." *Lancet 353*, 2026–9.

61.   Patja, A. *et al.* (2000) "Serious adverse events after measles-mumps-rubella vaccination during a fourteen-year prospective follow-up." *Pediatric Infectious Disease Journal 19*, 12, 1127–34.

62.   The Irish Health Boards Executive (2002) *Measles, Mumps, Rubella (MMR) Vaccine Discussion Pack: An Information Guide for Health Professionals and Parents.* Department of Public Health, Southern Health Board, Ireland (pp.31–32).

63.   Nelson, N.W. (1994) "Clinical research, the placebo effect, responsibility to families, and other concerns stimulated by auditory integration training." *American Journal of Speech-Language Pathology*, September, 106–111.

64.   Klin, A., Volkmar, F.R. and Sparrow, S.S. (2000) "Introduction." In *Asperger Syndrome* edited by Klin, A., Volkmar, F.R. and Sparrow, S.S. New York: The Guilford Press (pp.4–5).

65.   Scott, J. (1995) "Psychotherapy for bipolar disorder." *British Journal of Psychiatry 167*, 581–8.

Index